On the Go with Baby

the

with

A Stress-Free
Guide to Getting
across Town or
around the World

Ericka Lutz

SOURCEBOOKS, INC.®
NAPERVILLE, ILLINOIS

This publication is designed to provide accurate and authoritative information in regard to the subject matter covered. It is sold with the understanding that the publisher is not engaged in rendering legal, accounting, or other professional service. If legal advice or other expert assistance is required, the services of a competent professional person should be sought.—*From a Declaration of Principles Jointly Adopted by a Committee of the American Bar Association and a Committee of Publishers and Associations*

Published by Sourcebooks, Inc.
P.O. Box 4410, Naperville, Illinois 60567-4410
(630) 961-3900
FAX: (630) 961-2168
www.sourcebooks.com

Library of Congress Cataloging-in-Publication Data
Lutz, Ericka.
    On the go with baby: a stress-free guide to getting across town or around the world / by Ericka Lutz.
        p. cm.
    ISBN 1-57071-952-7 (alk. paper)
    1. Infants—Care. 2. Travel—Planning. I. Title.

HQ774.L88 2002
649'.122—dc21
2001057621

Printed and bound in the United States of America
BG 10 9 8 7 6 5 4 3 2 1

Dedication

This book is for Annie, World Traveler,
and for the parents of the world, *all* the world.

Acknowledgments

Gratitude to Jennifer Fusco and Sourcebooks, Inc. for helping this baby really go places, and to Andree Abecassis and the Ann Elmo Literary Agency for ever believing in this book—and in me. Parents parent best when parented well, and for this, and for endless, ongoing and active support, I thank my parents, Arthur Lutz and Karla Lutz.

I can never do my work without my friends and community, especially Tilly, Ami, Milo, Saill, Ailsa, Annie (Big) plus Baby Tessa, Susan plus Baby Jai, Ralph, the Wild Plums, Johanina Wikoff, and my writing cabal (featuring Chris, Elizabeth, and Monica). Gracias to the many others who made the first go-round of this project spin so spinningly and to my gorgeous, hardworking sister. Thanks to Anaya for her patience and stories and love. And, especially and always, thanks to my husband/lover/friend, the inimitable Bill Sonnenschein, fellow traveler.

Table of Contents

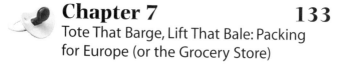

INTRODUCTION

On the Go?

I should like to rise and go
Where the golden apples grow;—
…Where the Great Wall round China goes,
And on one side the desert blows…
—*Robert Louis Stevenson*

Baby Maneuvering

Slowed down by a mere baby? Me? No way, that wasn't going to happen. I was one tough cookie, able to balance a job, a passion for writing, and a full social life—and cook a mean gourmet meal. I'd masterfully handled border-crossing guards in Asia, built trails in the Wyoming wilderness, penned an unpublished novel, married a wonderful man, and lived through morning sickness. I was efficient, I was woman, *hear me roar.*

Then Annie was born. An hour after our new little family returned from the hospital, I stood over the changing table sobbing, "I'm *sorry,* Baby," my hair and hormones askew. I stared at my tiny newborn daughter's day-old naked bottom—the same bottom I had just tried three times to diaper in our new, environmentally correct cloth diapers. If I couldn't pin this scrap of fabric around this teeny tush, what would happen to my plan and my resolutions? How would I prevent this child from keeping me penned in and pinned down?

I looked around the tiny closet packed with crib, bassinet, stroller, car seat, changing table, diaper pail. How would we maneuver with all this *gear*? How would we gallivant around the world together when I couldn't even open the stroller? And what would I do when I was alone in the house with this little bitty baby and I absolutely, no doubt about it, had to wash my hair?

Ericka's Problem, and the Sociological Reason for It

Here's the situation: in the past, people rarely relocated far from family. New parents relied on Mom or Aunt Martha for tips on the simple logistics of caring for small kids—basic things like how to cook dinner with a colicky baby, or how to survive a cheerful jaunt across the continent. Babies were part of the daily scenery, and wise relatives were easily accessible—often right next door, maybe even right upstairs! In recent years, however, the "Death of the American Family" has meant that many new parents have never even *held* an infant until their own comes squalling into the world. How are we supposed to know what to do?

At the same time, we're a more mobile culture. Mothers travel for business, and traveling dads bring their kids along, too. The mom-and-pop grocery store has made way for the super warehouse store—but (arghhh!) the super warehouse store is a fifteen-minute drive away. The beaches in Thailand are cheaper and more exotic than the beaches in Florida, if you can survive the twenty-hour plane ride. Economics are tight for most new families. Most of us have to earn a living. How do you fax with one hand, phone with the other, and nurse a baby at the same time? Sometimes the idea of going anywhere or doing anything with your little tax deduction is enough to make a capable grown-up break into tears. We need help, guidance, tips, suggestions, reassurance. We need to know how to maneuver.

The Story Continues

I rallied. I learned to diaper, and I fell head first and life-long into the absorbing, exhausting, and joyful world of parenthood. And three mornings later, Bill and I took Annie to her first restaurant, ordered eggs, and spent the entire meal mesmerized by her tiny sleeping form in its car seat, terrified that somebody would breathe on her. "Well, that was pretty easy," I thought, loading her (still sleeping) back into the car. I renewed my resolve. I was not going to be trapped in the house (except for the daily, tension-filled trip to the grocery store and the annual, agonizing schlep to a neighboring state) until the kids were in college. Babies *could* gallivant, and even short of gallivanting, babies could and should participate in daily life.

I still believe this. By the age of four, Annie was a veteran traveler, at home and abroad. And though restaurants aren't quite so simple when the kid is awake, we've patronized a gazillion of them, and with *rare* exceptions, we're always welcomed back.

This Book Is for You

I'm not alone in my struggles. The current baby boomlet has created a new breed of parents—brave, resourceful, and resolved to fully incorporate their children into their daily lives. These parents are determined that having kids won't mean the end of their own adventures, near *or* far— but they *may* be overwhelmed by all the logistics of maneuvering with a small child. This book is for us.

This book provides resources, factual information, reassurance, and perhaps some inspiration about the logistics of toting and traveling, anywhere and every-where, with very young children—from babies through pre-school. It's a tool kit that blends general "how-to" principals with essential tips for baby and child care at home and on the road: How do you diaper a baby on a bus? How do you wash your hair while the little screamer is, well, screaming? How do you change a

sloppy diaper at a fancy restaurant? What's the best pack for trekking just north of Kathmandu?

This book is for those who have not yet traveled with kids, and for those who have and want their future outings to be easier and less stressful. This book will relieve the minds of new parents, vacationers-to-be seeking specific tips, parents dreaming of adventure, and people contemplating reproduction and wondering if they can ever "have a life" again. It's for those who wonder how two people can get three sleeping children from the car to the apartment when the only parking place is two blocks away.

Packed within these pages is a double-diaper bag's worth of factual information and encouragement, as well as anecdotes straight from the experts—parents who have done it themselves.

How It's Organized

The book is divided into three sections: Crawling with Baby, Walking with Baby, and On the Go with Baby.

Crawling with Baby

No baby begins life as an Olympic runner, and no parent happily gallivants without basic child-care skills. Crawling with Baby, chapters 1, 2, and 3, covers fundamentals that translate to anywhere on the globe. We'll deal with fears about the safety and hassles of traveling with babies, and try to put those fears to bed.

Then you'll learn:

- How to put baby to bed
- How to change a diaper...and change a diaper *on the road*
- All about babyproofing
- How to entertain a toddler on a rainy day
- How to be the parent the other kids love because you always carry great snacks
- How to picnic with a preschooler
- What to do when your baby needs to nurse in Venice and the hotel is three canals away

Walking with Baby

In chapters 4 through 9, we'll hit the road...slowly. You'll learn how to choose appropriate travel destinations for your family ("No, honey, let's *not* go to Sri Lanka this year; I think the civil war might be a little too *intense* for Lukey."). We'll go over transportation—the ins-and-outs of lugging the little rug rats around town and around the world—and how to shop, hang out, and choose a baby-friendly cafe. There are sections on how and what to pack for the zoo, for the woods, or for a plane ride; how to navigate an airport with both child and wits intact; and where to stay once you get to your destination.

On the Go with Baby

Yow! It's the big time, baby! In chapters 10 though 13, we get serious (though not glum). Here's the scoop on removing beach sand from a toddler's tender bottom, "roughing it" in the woods, traveling as a single parent, and doing business with a baby in tow. We'll talk about long-term travel, and the joys of taking the kids on the traveler circuit to developing nations.

At the end, you'll find chapter 14, Troubleshooting A to Z, which includes first-aid information, tips on dealing with large animals, tantrums, illness, and what happens once you go home. The Appendix lists recommended readings, and travel and parenting resources.

Little Babies, Big Travels

Little children didn't used to *go* anywhere. Neither did their parents, except on rare occasions when they parked the papoose with the grandparents and, depending upon their style and circumstances, spent their vacation either wracked with guilt and worry (phoning home every other hour from the beach house or casino floor), or wild with irresponsible abandon (whipping off cheery postcards once a month from the jungles of Malaysia). But mostly everybody stayed home.

Times have changed, and parenting has changed with the times. Many parents want their kids with them when they travel—for work and for pleasure. During the multi-tasking nightmare we live in, otherwise known as the New Millennium, what better way can you spend both quality and quantity time with your kids?

I should know. My now-school-aged daughter Annie has covered more ground than many adults. She's flown coast to coast four times, up and down the West Coast six times, and to Mexico, Guatemala, Europe, Eastern Europe, Hawaii, and Canada. She's camped in the wilderness and dined in fine restaurants, been transported by trains, cars, planes, buses, and boats, and all of us have lived to tell the tale.

Do we have boundless energy? No. Are we rich? Hardly. Crazy? I don't think so. Abusive? Absolutely not. Is all this really good for her...and fun for us? Yes! Can *you* do it too? Of course! (Thought you'd never ask.)

The First Time

Some people notch their bedpost for lovers slept with; I spent my twenties notching my passport for countries slept in. My husband Bill also has strong tendencies towards the footloose and fancy free. But with three kids between us (his two big ones and our one little one) we've had to learn to balance our wild desires with hardcore pragmatic reality.

When Bill's kids were teenagers, we all spent time together in Mexico and Southeast Asia. But babies are a different matter—aren't they? For the first few months after Annie was born, we spent every night at home. But having a kid doesn't completely alter your personality. Bill and I got restless. When Annie turned seven months old, we began our adventures with a month-long, modified European Grand Tour.

Our friends with babies were dismayed: "You're so brave!" "What will you do about diapers?" "Can you nurse in a restaurant in Italy?" We had images of quiet walks along Venetian canals, romantic Parisian dinners. But with a baby in tow? Could it be done? Could we *enjoy* ourselves doing it?

Off we went in search of answers, strewing Europe with tiny socks, diapers, and lost sun hats. Yes, we had brief moments of exhaustion when we regretted our impulses, but overall, we had a fantastic time.

That first adventure with Annie allowed us to transcend the role of Tourist. The often too-formal French and Dutch approached us with smiles and questions, and the Italians stumbled over themselves in an attempt to get close. Traveling with Annie enabled us to see a side of European culture that had eluded us before—a world of well-dressed children and doting grandparents, where babies hold the central role of attention, and a row of newly washed stuffed animals hangs, pinned in order of size, from a Venetian clothesline over a silent, blue-green canal.

A Baby Has No Language Barrier

Little children are natural explorers. They're curious, interested, easily engaged, and open to new experiences. Maneuvering them around may seem daunting, but please don't keep them cooped up in their house or neighborhood. My friend Mary, a psychologist, tells me that flexibility is the key to a well-adjusted personality, and the more positive experiences children have, the more comfortable they will be in the world. The key is your confidence in caring for them wherever you are— if you're relaxed and having fun, they will be too.

Little children also have a healthier sense of pacing than most of us busy people do—they can teach us a thing or two. With a child, you're forced to slow down, to look around, to see the world through their eyes. Everything is new, everything is exciting (even the fifteenth hour-long stroll around the block). As companions, children can refresh the tired eyes of the most jaded adult.

The Joy of Family Travels

Family travel can and should be more than a dreaded occasional necessity. At its best, it's a liberating, exciting experience. Avenues and adventures you never expected await you. From their earliest childhood, your children will gain flexibility, a sense of adventure, and a healthy perspective about the world. Traveling together, sharing experiences and time, brings a family closer. (Little children are delighted, in this busy decade, to get the in-depth parental attention that a family trip brings.)

Everybody loves a child, and traveling with a child breaks down barriers. Little Anthony smiles and the world smiles back—no longer are you "the other," "the foreigner," "the alien," or "the ugly tourist." Countless times I've witnessed the way babies and little children open the arms and hearts of adults. I've become convinced that traveling with little children, while requiring extra planning and flexibility, provides a gift to the entire family. I don't plan on stopping.

I love watching my little girl learn, grow, and experience the world. I love the looks of warmth she elicits wherever we are. I love, too, that my life has not been impeded, that I am a parent *and* a person. You too can make it work. Join me. Have a baby, see the world.

PART ONE
Crawling with Baby

CHAPTER 1

Crawl Before You Walk

Meet it, accept it, and let it go.

—*San Francisco self-actualization slogan, circa 1975*

A Child Is Born

Let's begin at the beginning. Your baby has come to live with you in one of the ways that babies do. He's arrived with a lot of gear, and with an agenda and schedule all his own. You want to travel, but just getting into the car with him takes forty minutes, what with the gear, the loading, the diaper change, the other diaper change, and now baby is hungry, and, "Did I pack that little teeny sweater—where is that little sweater anyway? Oops, I'd better start a laundry so we have clean clothes to come home to, and...oh no, better do another diaper change. Oh. Shame to take him out when he's sleeping so nicely."

Europe, Florida, Hawaii, the neighbor's house...they all seem a million light-years away in distance and time. That was a different lifetime when you fantasized about Berlin nightclubs and romantic Alpine hikes. That was a different you. Besides, it's too tiring. Forget Paris—let's take a nap.

Whoa—hang on, Sloopy. It's becoming evident that— like the child squirming in front of you—before you walk, you gotta learn to crawl. This chapter provides a brief

overview of basic and not-so-basic child-care skills that will translate to anywhere in the world.

Crawling

Travel and parenting require the same three skills—flexibility, good humor, and a sense that life itself is an adventure. These skills take time to learn. Have you watched a baby learn to crawl? She's on her knees rocking, one minute sobbing in frustration, the next, giggling with joy. Developmental movement experts Peter Brown and Vicki Gunter of Oakland, California, stress the importance of allowing an infant to go at her own developmental pace, and not be pushed into sitting, standing, or walking before she can do these things by herself: "An infant who is crawling on the floor is organizing and programming her nervous system. She is laying the foundation for walking, running, reading, math, and creative thinking."

The same is true for parenting, and for travel. The keys to your successful future travels are found here at home. As a new parent, you don't know how to crawl yet. Don't push it. If you take the time to learn to "crawl" effectively, the next thing you know, you'll have the skills to run around the rest of your life.

Your first jaunts with your infant will rarely be more ambitious than walking to the video store a few blocks away and stopping in at Farmer Joe's Market to buy a few organic nectarines and a box of cereal. That's cool, they shouldn't be. Adjusting to new parenthood requires time. If you've given birth, your body needs time to heal from its ordeal. If you haven't given birth, you're still adjusting to a completely new life. Give yourself time.

Reprogramming
Your Nervous System

Before your sweet bambino came to live with you, you organized your life one way. Now everything has changed. If you're going to travel with your baby, you need to reorganize—you need to reprogram your *own* nervous system.

The first months of parenting, you'll be deeply involved in the new emotional and physical aspects of being a parent and getting to know your new baby. Many of us spend hours poring over parenting books written by experts, looking for clues. Good parenting is about combining common sense with love. Read the experts (I've included my favorites in the Recommended Readings Appendix), and remember that none of them are right all the time—they don't know you, and they don't know your baby. The most valuable piece of advice I received from any expert is on the first page of the baby-care classic, *Dr. Spock's Baby and Child Care*: "Trust Yourself."

Though you'll probably stay close to home for the first few months, this time with your baby is the time to build the tools that later on will let you feel comfortable journeying anywhere together.

Traveling with a Newborn

No matter how you slice it, gallivanting for pleasure with a *teeny* infant is not the best idea. Give her a chance to master a small part of the world, and give yourself a chance to rest. If you *need* to travel during the first three months, relax and go with the flow. (I know a woman who hitchhiked from Alaska to Philadelphia with a ten-day-old baby. Of course, it *was* the '60s....) For gentle travel, it's *your* comfort that's largely at stake. Remember, for your newborn, home equals you. Cuddle her close.

If you plan on taking your newborn or infant to a medically "risky" locale, make sure you talk seriously with your pediatrician before you go. Babies are not fully inoculated until at least eighteen months. Maintain breastfeeding if at all possible—it is the best way to boost your baby's immune system.

Safety, Fear, and Exhaustion

Let's get serious for a moment. Sometimes the whole *idea* of planning, packing, and going somewhere strange feels overwhelming—even wrong. The main objections most parents have to traveling with children can be divided into two areas: safety issues, and concerns about the hassles and exhaustion of being on the road.

I understand. As soon as I got pregnant, my sense of what I was willing to risk changed profoundly. The world suddenly had sharp corners—I was no longer Wild Ericka, jaunting around the world, flinging myself into danger and experience. No, I was nervous crossing the street. I felt conflicted—overjoyed to have new life inside me, deeply aware that I was responsible for a life other than my own, and terrified about the restrictions a baby might put on my life.

The Voices of Fear and Despair

The Voice of Fear hisses in our ears as we admire the tropical beach posters in the local travel agency window. It begins its relentless squawk as we sit in a pile of clean laundry, toys, and suitcases that must be organized, packed, and stowed in the car some time in the next six minutes. Here it comes...listen for it...does it sound familiar?

"Don't go! There are serial killers out there! Besides, Malcolm hates new places, Eliza eats nothing but buttered noodles, and Baby Barbara is terrified by men with beards. Think about your delicately balanced routine! And what about all those strange diseases—malaria, Montezuma's Revenge, Ebola?!"

The Voice of Fear is often accompanied by its ugly sidekick, the Voice of Despair: *"Life as you know it is over. No more itsy-bitsy overnight bags for a week on the Riviera—now you have to hire a U-haul for a weekend at the beach. Here's your new scenario: dragging bags o' stuff, desperately seeking places to feed the baby, chasing the hyperactive little toddler around a strange city. A vacation? Ha! Try again in eighteen years when the little squirmer goes to college."*

Minimizing the Hassles

To defeat the Voices of Fear and Despair, you have to prepare. The more you prepare, the fewer hassles you'll have. True, maneuvering a baby or young child through life can be an exhausting, awful hassle. *But it doesn't have to be!* And while wandering with the teeny ones is not without its complications, once you understand what to expect and how to pace yourself, once you rid yourself of the fear of the unknown, you can change a dreaded experience into a great time. Read on—this book is designed to help you minimize the hassles and free yourself for the joy.

Ericka's #1 Law of Baby Travel
The slower you go, the less exhausted you'll be.

Keeping Your Children Safe

Your approach to the world helps determine how your child will live—seizing adventure and opportunity carefully but with enthusiasm; or hiding, timid, from its dangers. Yes, the world has real dangers in it. You keep your child safe by being realistic about these dangers, taking certain precautions, and fostering autonomy and self-reliance. You can't keep a child safe by locking her away from the world.

Educate them. I believe that you teach small children safety by teaching them not to fear the world, but to be aware of all the world has in it, good and bad. Teach them how much control they *do* have in their lives by educating them about the world.

Involve them. Involve little kids in the world, and involve them in decisions about their bodies. Get them active and doing—if they feel in physical control of their bodies, they'll be clearer about their own boundaries.

Embrace the world. Children are perceptive; if they sense your fear of the world, they will fear it, too. Better to embrace the world, with all its dangers. After all, the

dangers won't disappear just because you close your eyes to them.

Babyproofing—At Home and at Aunt Martha's

Part of getting comfortable with a baby is feeling safe, and feeling safe means taking certain precautions. Right before Annie learned to crawl, I finally got off my fattening duff and babyproofed. You need to do this, too. If it feels too overwhelming, do one or two rooms first—say, the room where baby sleeps and the living room, if you've got one. Wherever you are in the world, you need to relax occasionally, and no parent can be utterly vigilant every minute of every hour of every day. Creating a space where you know your child can exist in safety and peace will be a boon to you and your child. Then you can barricade the rest of the domicile until it, too, is ready.

The first step is educating yourself about what presents a danger to Snookums—beyond the standard finger-in-plug or "tasty" drink of Drano. There are lots of books and resources available to help you with this venture. Some people with disposable income pay consultants to advise them, or to do the job *for* them. This is not strictly necessary (you're saving your bucks for travel, remember?).

When you're on the road, you may not be able to arrange everything exactly as it should be, but you can try. The list below will help you assess and babyproof whatever environment you may find yourself in. (I've put some additional details about babyproofing hotel rooms in chapter 9.)

The Hand-Bone's Connected to the Finger-Bone

A six-month-old baby's fingers still function as one unit. He reaches for an object and scrapes it into the palm of his hand. By the time he is eight months old, he is fully "human"—the opposable thumb opposes, that tiny forefinger works nicely with the thumb to create a pincher, and everything small gets grabbed, examined carefully, and, usually, popped in his mouth.

Whoa. Time to get detail-oriented. Haul out the vacuum cleaner. We want our children to fully taste the world, but we want that tasting to be more figurative than literal. Some things were just not meant for mouths.

The Take-It-With-You Emergency Babyproofing Assessment

Get on the floor at baby-eye level. (Come on, I know you haven't been getting to the gym regularly, but you gotta start somewhere!) What looks inviting? Interesting? Dangerous?

🐣 Where are the cleaning supplies? Check the kitchen cabinets and remove the substances or secure the doors.

🐣 Medicines: Get them way up and out of the way. (This is a good time to mention the importance of carrying Syrup of Ipecac to induce vomiting after ingestion of potential poisons. Call a Poison Control Center or your physician before administering—it's *not* for use in all situations.)

🐣 Windows: Are there gates? If not, how hard is it to get the windows open and how far is it to the ground? Do the blinds have accessible cords? Tuck them away or tie them up. Horrible stories abound about strangulated little ones. I won't repeat them here.

🐣 Check for outlets, electrical cords, and appliances. Carry plastic covers for open outlets—they're cheap, small, and light.

🐣 Remove sharp objects lying around on floors or low surfaces.

🐣 Coins, shiny and delectable, present a risk of choking. Now is the time to find all that couch change you were saving for a rainy day. Use it on a trip to the hardware store—to buy childproofing safety devices!

🐣 Turn down the water heater to a maximum of 120 Fahrenheit.

🐞 Staircases are a hazard for the crawling child and the new toddler. Get gates—they come in a variety of designs for all needs.

🐞 Bookcases: Your child might suddenly start channeling the ghost of Sir Edmund Hilary and decide to scale the peaks. Is the bookcase attached to the wall? Pull out all the books and reorganize, either putting the largest and heaviest, or the ones you don't mind having strewn about, on the bottom shelf.

🐞 Is the bureau stable? Check for lamps and other unstable furniture that might not stand up to standing up.

🐞 Corners of tables, bookshelves, etc.: Move 'em or pad 'em.

🐞 Many house plants are poisonous. Move all plants out of your child's reach.

🐞 Fabergé eggs and other fragile knick-knacks need to be moved up and away.

🐞 Floor heaters? Ducts? Vents? The burner knobs on the stove? Does that oven, freezer, or refrigerator door open too easily? You may need to create temporary barriers to keep danger areas off-limits.

🐞 Kitchen knives? Firearms? Make *sure* these are not remotely accessible.

🐞 Open toilets (there are a variety of childproof and not *too* adultproof toilet locks on the market).

🐞 The fireplace: Glass doors get very hot, fireplace tools are heavy and ill-balanced. If you have a wire screen, you might want to wire it shut for the duration (not usually more than a year or three).

🐞 Can Baby escape through the front or back door?

Once you get used to the routine, it will take you only a few minutes to create a relatively child-safe space. When traveling, babyproofing is a good way to accustom yourself to a new environment. We tend to plunge from activity to activity without taking those few moments of emotional adjustment that both children and grown-ups need, especially when we're excited and "on-the-road." Assessing your

surroundings for danger provides an extra moment to *breathe*.

> At four, I was a very resourceful, if sometimes stupid, child. One of my earliest childhood memories is of the time I wanted something on my mother's clothes bureau. (I don't remember what I sought—secrets, magic spoils, money?) I carefully opened each drawer to fashion a stairway, and began climbing. The next thing I knew, CRASH! I was on the floor, the bureau slammed down on top of me. My screams were followed by the crazed, pounding footsteps of my parents coming to rescue me. Their terrified expressions scared me far more than the light wood bureau hurt.

Sleep—How To

Whole library shelves are devoted to the subject of baby and child sleep patterns. Through my own copious anecdotal research (i.e., the whining of friends), I've come to the following conclusion: this is child-rearing. Welcome. Get used to the following fact: one way or another, your child will get enough sleep, but you may not.

Author Penelope Leach divides parents into two rough divisions: those who take the Happy-Go-Lucky-Approach, and those who go for the Regular Routine approach. Both have their advantages and drawbacks. And, you might not have a lot of choice in the matter. Your baby's individual temperament will help determine which approach you will take.

Happy-Go-Lucky Approach

Pros:
- Take your baby with you anywhere, anytime.
- Don't restrict your life just because you have a kid.

Cons:
- Baby will stay up until whenever he's tired—which may be *well* after you become exhausted.
- Not a lot of evening privacy.

Regular Routine Approach

Pros:
- Peace and privacy in the evenings.
- A predictable schedule.
- A break from the baby during the day.

Cons:
- Only works if you are absolutely consistent.
- Must arrange your life, your evenings, and your travels around baby's routine.
- Some babies determine their own schedules no matter *what* the parents do.

Sleep Patterns

At the beginnings of their lives, some glorious babies sleep around fifteen hours a day. I think of this as nature's way of allowing parents to catch up on life—the problem is that these fifteen hours are not sequential; they are spread randomly throughout the day and night as she drifts in and out of slumber. Many active newborns sleep as little as ten hours in forty-minute segments (sigh). With all this up-and-down, it is very difficult to do as the doctor orders: "Sleep when the baby sleeps."

By the time a baby is twelve weeks old, she is awake for longer periods of time and more alert. The good news is that she cries less. The bad news is that her sleeping is still irregular and unpredictable. An older baby sleeps somewhere between nine and eighteen hours a day (thirteen hours is about average) depending upon her own rhythms and needs.

Once a baby reaches nine months or so, she is able to keep herself awake. This is when a vacation can wreak havoc on the Regular-Routiners—even after you get back home. For toddlers and preschoolers, sleep patterns and problems may vary with each child. What the hell, take the vacation. If sleep isn't easy at home, why should it be any easier on the road?

Sleep deprivation is *not* a foregone conclusion. Many babies go down easily and sleep through the night. Many

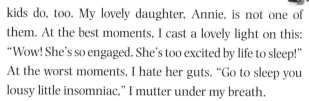

kids do, too. My lovely daughter, Annie, is not one of them. At the best moments, I cast a lovely light on this: "Wow! She's so engaged. She's too excited by life to sleep!" At the worst moments, I hate her guts. "Go to sleep you lousy little insomniac," I mutter under my breath.

It doesn't help that she's probably genetically wired to be a terrible sleeper—Bill and I are up and down all night—trips to the bathroom, jaunts to the office to jot down that pressing thought, journeys to the kitchen for hot milk and buttered toast to soothe the worried mind. So, it's probably no wonder we ended up with a family bed...without it, we'd probably have just added another destination to our nighttime rambles: "Gee, I wonder if the baby is still alive. I'd better check!"

They Just Come Out That Way

Annie's best friend Alonza has always operated in two modes, "On" and "Off." Her "On," beginning slightly before 7 A.M. (including weekends and holidays), is ON!! Her "Off," occurring somewhere around 7:30 to 8:00 P.M., is OFF!! as she transforms instantly from busy bee to little log.

"Come On Baby, Let's Go for a Drive!"

There seems to be a strong relationship between movement and sleep. For this reason, thousands of parents daily resort to the car in order to get the baby down. No, it is not ecological. Hey, you have to pick your battles.

When you're traveling, there's a tendency to double-up on naps and travel time. If your baby will nap in a bed, build in some time for a solid mid-day snooze—not in the car, stroller, or backpack—every few days.

For a while, Annie napped only in the car or in her stroller. In desperation on a rainy day when she was maybe six months old, I popped her in the stroller and began pushing her rapidly through the house, around and around the living room, through the kitchen, back through the living room, into the master bedroom until...the stroller was silent. After about ten minutes, I thought, "She's down!" and allowed myself to peek. There was Annie, grinning up at me ear to ear, with sparkling, energetic eyes—not even close to sleeping, and obviously wildly amused by the whole adventure.

Happy-Go-Lucky or Regular-Routiner—Rituals on the Road

You may get everything arranged just as you like it and go on your trip, only to find that the sleeping schedule goes south and you spend your vacation in a drowsy fog. You may also find that your little insomniac takes to travel like a duck to water and is solidly dreaming moments after you put him down. Travel and excitement do funny things.

Young children like familiarity, and one way to keep your child calm is to establish a bedtime routine at home and perform it every night. When you take the show on the road, take the ritual materials—the toothbrush, Mr. Washcloth, her favorite bedtime books, your songs, even his night-light. Try to recreate the same serene mood as at home—it will help the little one get to sleep even in a completely foreign place.

Networking (Parent Support/Child Care)

New parents can use some support—their lives have changed dramatically, and hanging out with a baby all the time can feel very isolating. Creating a network is key to survival for the many parents who have no family around, who have moved, or who have given up jobs. Luckily, having children automatically gives you something major in common with every other new parent. Early parenthood can be a wonderful time to build new friendships—a baby breaks down barriers at home as well as abroad. Go to the playground and chat with other parents—babies are an instant ice-breaker. Strike up conversations in children's clothing stores and libraries (I met my pal Ailsa over a rack of miniature rain jackets, and my friend Anna at Pajama Time at the

library). You'll meet people you never would have otherwise talked to (it's sort of like school in that way). I've
joined an extensive email list based in my community
where parents post child-rearing advice, recommendations for everything from contractors to vacation spots,
child-care resources, and garage and block sale
announcements.

Parenting Groups

Parenting groups—female, male, and mixed—often
develop out of childbirth-preparation classes. If you are
interested in joining or beginning a parenting support
group or parent/child play group, you can also try reading the local parenting periodicals. In addition to their
articles (some of which are excellent), most of them
have extensive listings for parenting resources and
schools. Many will run a personal ad for free. Also look
for listings on bulletin boards around town. Work the
playground "grapevine." Ask your pediatrician for
suggestions. Join one of the many on-line parenting
communities (but remember that a virtual friend can't
come watch the little squirt while you run out for a well-
needed jug of milk...or something stronger).

More and more fathers are becoming actively
involved in parenting, and more and more are joining
fathering support groups. Don't worry—these are not
just for the sensitive, New Age, "Let's go drumming in
the woods" set. Parenting is hard, and fathers have
traditionally had few support networks. It's about time
things changed. To find a fathering group in your area,
see the suggestions above.

Our Play Group

For over a year, our play group—two boys and two
girls—met twice a week for an hour and a half each
time. We four moms began with the idea of occasionally
excusing some of us and turning it into more of a child-
care exchange, but we enjoyed each other's company so
much, and the support felt *so* important—we were all

new mothers in our thirties and forties—that we ended up chatting and watching the babies play.

Like all groups, our play group had a natural life span. Happily so, it ended not with a bang but with a whimper as we all eventually went on to other things. As for Bill and me, we've found true, lifelong friends with one of the families. We celebrate holidays together, share child care, take short overnights together, and, now that our kids are a little older, we often schedule play dates where we *do* exchange child care.

Sharing Child Care

Nothing brings families closer than sharing a child-care provider. Especially for "relocated" families, sharing child care can provide a sense of extended family. The kids get close, and the parents get to enjoy an "alternate child." As my friend Susan said, "No one ever told me how important my kids' friends would become to me." (I've got more information about hiring a child-care provider in chapter 13. Also check out "Child-Care Resources" in the Resources Appendix.)

Joint Vacations

Yes, this chapter is about "crawling," but sometime soon you're going to hit the road. Why not consider doing it with another family? (In chapter 5 we'll look at this option a little closer.)

Still Life with Baby

Part of realigning your life and reorganizing your nervous system means learning to feel comfortable with having kids in your house. Kids are messy. Imagine this: the house is filthy, you're alone with the baby, your cleaning solvents are poisonous and the fumes are dangerous, and you've got company coming over for dinner. Ideally, you would be able to hire help, even a cleaning service once a week, or once a month; however, life is not always ideal, and besides, you're saving your money for next summer's dream vacation.

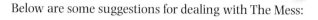

Below are some suggestions for dealing with The Mess:

Lower Your Standards

When company arrives, shrug it off, and try not to apologize too much. Those with children will (or should) understand that little ones create enormous messes as a by-product of simply being alive. For guests without children, or whose children are long grown (like your in-laws), if they get huffy or sneer at your housekeeping, try to be compassionate. They don't understand, and they may not ever understand. Their houses may be clean, but they aren't experiencing the daily joy of a child.

"Bin" Things

Babies and small children seem to accumulate detritus—little bits of this and that, small toys, and what about all those photos of the li'l darlin' collecting dust? The solution: "bin" them. Get some inexpensive, brightly colored plastic bins for toys. Get some inexpensive, classy-and-subtle-looking boxes for your pictures. Label the backs, and throw 'em in. You'll get around to putting them in albums in time to show your grandchildren.

Hide It

Company coming? Shove the mess in the closet. One mom confesses to hiding dirty dishes in the oven when friends come over. You can clean later—and feel comfortable *now*.

Use Environment-Friendly, Non-Toxic Cleaning Products

More and more, people are cleaning "green." Environmentally friendly products aren't just better for the plants and insect-life around you, they're better for your family, too. A variety of non-toxic cleaning products are available in your local health-food store.

Washing Your Hair

So you're alone with the babe, you're supposed to be at an appointment in twenty minutes, your hair is disgusting, and the little screamer is...screaming. Face it, you're going to be late. Nobody *else* is on time all the time, so just give it up. Time to get Zen about it, darlin'. Here are your choices:

- ♣ Go with dirty hair.
- ♣ Beg a friend to come over to watch your kids for half an hour.
- ♣ Wait until the little Poopsker is less annoyed, stick her in her car seat, and put the seat in the bathroom. (In an emergency, *don't* wait until she is calm. Do it while she wails. Let the cries spur you on.)
- ♣ If Buddy Boy can sit up, spread a towel on the bathroom floor and scatter some toys. Then prepare to *move*, because you'll have a window of exactly three minutes before he starts howling for you again. Before you try this, make sure that the bathroom is completely baby-safe and that the toilet is closed and locked.
- ♣ Wash your hair in the kitchen sink. Put baby in her car seat at your feet, or strap her in her high chair next to you where she can watch the soapy action.
- ♣ If you have a little more time, bring her in the shower with you. Babies usually love the warm misty feel of the water, and the delicious feel of your body against them. You may not be able to actually *wash* your hair, but at least you'll have a good rinse. You can sit a bigger baby on the shower floor while you shampoo. Watch where that soap flies, though. And make sure there aren't any loose "safety" razors around.
- ♣ Bathe with baby. I once heard author Isabelle Allende say that one of the most sensual experiences in her life was bathing with her grandkids. I can relate.

Indoor Water Adventures— Keeping Your Kids and Yourself from Insanity

Get enough days cooped up by rain or snow, and everybody goes nuts. If you're having fun, though, "cooped up" becomes "cozy." Even on the road, there are rainy

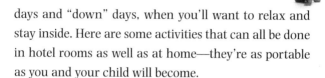

days and "down" days, when you'll want to relax and stay inside. Here are some activities that can all be done in hotel rooms as well as at home—they're as portable as you and your child will become.

Water Play

Bathrooms and kitchens are potentially dangerous places. Water play must be supervised, but you'll get a lot less wet when you supervise than when you participate. Water play also is engaging enough for your kids that you can usually do something else! (Ah, what did we do before multi-tasking was invented?) Plan to do your "something else" in the same room until the child is old enough and sensible enough that you aren't risking damage to her, or to any possessions.

- Sit the naked child in the empty bathtub with old yogurt containers and other plastic vessels, all filled with lukewarm or warm water and watch her go. You can sit on the closed toilet and read a book, occasionally refilling the containers.

- Stand the child on a chair (with the back of the chair against the sink so it won't tip backwards) in front of a sink with running cold water, and a couple of plastic vessels. In a hotel room, try empty shampoo bottles, or ask for containers at the desk. While she stands, sit on a chair next to her, catching up on your long-neglected baby shower thank-you notes.

Some little kids are scared of the bathtub—are they afraid of swirling with the water down the drain? Letting your baby hang out with wet toys in an empty tub can help allay those fears and teach her to love one of life's great pleasures.

The Aquatic Baby-sitter

There is nothing like warm water to soothe a wild child. Once your child is old enough to sit by herself in the tub, you can pop her in the tub with bath toys and maybe a washcloth or two. Sit on the floor and do your bills or balance your checkbook while she plays (just stay out of splashing range). Out of town? There are lots of light-weight bath games, like finger-paint and crayon soaps, that may feel too pricey for everyday use but are good for a vacation splurge. While she's playing, read your travel guides to plan tomorrow's itinerary.

Shaving with Daddy

Shaving with Daddy is a fine old tradition with a razor-edged line of danger. My cousin Rebekah, now very grown up, still bears a scar on her chin from where she tried to "shave like Daddy" when Daddy wasn't super-vising—of course, that was way back in the olden days of the '60s, when people used real razor blades instead of safety razors.

In our house, when Annie shaved with Daddy, her "razor" was an old cosmetic brush of mine. The brush part made a fine lather, and the handle made a great (and safe) scraper. Our real razors are stored up high, where she won't be able to reach until she's twelve.

CHAPTER 2

Bodily Functions

Perfect little body,
without fault or stain on thee,
with promise of strength
and manhood full and fair!
—*Robert Bridges*

The Down and Dirty Details

No sir, there is nothing ethereal about caring for a child. Yes ma'am, many elements are downright primal. Since babies and little kids spend much of their time ingesting and evacuating, and since *you* are the one who is going to have to deal with it, this chapter presents the hard-core realities of—and solutions to—many of the bodily function situations you may encounter at home and on the road.

> **Disclaimer:**
> **This chapter is rated NS: Not for the Squeamish.**
> Proceed at your own peril. On the other hand, once you become a parent, even picking your own child's nose won't gross you out. (Ericka, that's disgusting!)

Breast-feeding

Nursing your baby is healthy, natural, and creates an incredible bond of joy between mother and baby. It's healthy. It's the easiest way to feed your baby when you are traveling. Yet, despite what you might see in diaper commercials, nursing is not just a soft-focus, pink and glowing, bonding experience. It is, at times, very...leveling. Hang on to your sense of humor. Here are some tips for making your public breast-feeding experiences positive ones. (See the Resources Appendix for breast-feeding resources.)

Tips for Subtly Nursing in Public

Our society has a double standard when it comes to male and female torsos, and whether they should be allowed to be exposed in public. I'm very pro-breast-feeding, but even I get a little uncomfortable with the women who yank their shirts completely up to nurse their babies. Here are a few tips for keeping the public discomfort level down...

Wear Appropriate Clothes Wear biggish shirts that you can pull up. Avoid blouses that button down the front unless you can pull them up from the bottom. By all means do *not* wear a leotard or a body suit where you need to pull your breast up and over.

The Old Magician's Trick While most of the time nursing is important for interacting with your baby, sometimes you want to be subtle. If you don't want people to notice what you are doing, misdirect them with your eyes. Don't look down at your baby. People will follow your eye patterns. If you are looking around, casually chatting, or paying attention to something else, people will assume (if they notice at all) that your baby is asleep. (This technique works best with very young babies. A baby over three months won't put up with your attention going elsewhere for very long at *all*.)

Toss a Blanky Over Baby Here's another use for receiving blankets—throw one over your shoulder and baby's head, and hide his activities completely.

Readjust Casually When Done Little draws attention in this society more than a woman playing with her breasts. Wear stretch bras rather than nursing bras and simply pull the material down and out of the way. When

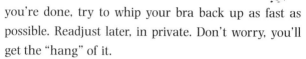

you're done, try to whip your bra back up as fast as possible. Readjust later, in private. Don't worry, you'll get the "hang" of it.

Practice, Practice, Practice Practice in front of a mirror. Have a friend watch you do it. Are you really as hidden as you think, or are you exposing yourself inadvertently?

Breast-feeding and U.S. Law

Life is better than it used to be for breast-feeding mothers. For a few years there, my outrage and imagination worked overtime. A case would hit the media: WOMAN ARRESTED FOR INDECENCY—BREAST-FEEDING IN PUBLIC and I'd suffer nightmare images of a poor mother in leg irons, separated from her sobbing infant, merely because the child was hungry and the mother was feeding her in the most healthy and natural way.

But breast-feeding in public is *not* illegal, and it's *not* indecent, and in order to stress these points, a number of states have instituted laws protecting the right to breast-feed anywhere you happen to be. Even if you live in—or visit—a state without a law specifically protecting your right to breastfeed in public, you're pretty much OK. The federal courts have generally established that breast-feeding mothers have a right to feed their babies. Wherever. Whenever.

Which Breast?

The advice books and videos say to start each time with the breast you last nursed on. Some people suggest that you keep track by pinning a tiny safety pin to your nursing bra on the last side that baby imbibed from.

I could never keep track. Either I'd forget to change the pin, or forget whether the pin went on the last or next side, or forget if I'd already changed the pin, or change the pin twice. (Breast-feeding mothers are notorious for their short-term memory loss, and that dazed, blissful look. Those hormones are powerful stuff—bottle it and the world would be a kinder, if spacier, place.) I finally solved the "which side to nurse on first" dilemma by hefting each breast to determine which was heavier, and thus needed to be suckled first. Not a good idea in public—people may understand, but you'll get some strange looks.

Nursing on the Road

Don't try to wean your baby or child right before, or during, a trip. It's easier to deal with a nursing baby—the breast is always with you, and formula is more complicated, what with bottles and sterilizing and measuring and mixing and warming.

Leaving the breast also presents a big emotional and developmental change in the life of a baby. It is far better to move through that change when you are in a familiar, safe environment and can weather the possible emotional storms.

It's also a big change in the life of the mother—this is true whether or not nursing has been easy and pleasant, or a challenge. Do not underestimate the power of hormones—every time a woman nurses her baby, her brain releases a shot of the hormone *prolactin*, which brings a feeling of balance and well-being. When you wean your child, along with the physical discomfort some women feel (full, tender breasts), you may experience intense, hormone-based feelings. When you stop nursing, your body experiences a prolactin drop. Many women feel like they're in mourning...not a great way to enjoy your vacation.

Hey, You with the Big Ones, Slow Down!

Though the vast majority of breast-feeding mothers have great success nursing on the road, be aware that stress, exhaustion, and changes in diet and time zones all may affect milk flow. Take your own stamina into consideration when planning a trip with a breast-feeding infant. Allow the baby to nurse when he wants to rather than sticking to a strict schedule. And remember to drink lots of fluids—they are crucial for nursing mothers, and it's easy to get dehydrated on the road.

Sometimes the excitement of traveling will make a child "forget" to nurse. This happened to Brenda and her son, Zev. Since Brenda was ready to wean him anyway, she decided to just continue the process.

Breast-feeding in Other Countries

Just as people in other countries are generally more tolerant of children than are people in the United States, most other cultures are also more tolerant of public breast-feeding. When it comes to the boob, however, subtlety is still the way to go. In some instances it may not be OK to breast-feed in public, no matter how furtive you are. Watch how residents behave, and follow suit. If you never see a baby nursed—and you're really looking—then do as in Rome and save it for the hotel room.

On our last trip to Europe, I spent twenty-three days not seeing babies nursed. I have to admit I wasn't really looking, though. I was concentrating on castles, caves, and cassoulet with confit. Babies were being fed (babies are always being fed). It goes to show the power of furtive nursing—and how unobservant most people really are.

In Maureen Wheeler's travel guide, *Travel with Children*, (a must-read for anybody planning to travel off-the-beaten-track or to exotic locations with kids), María Massolo notes that in Argentina, breast-feeding is closely tied with ethnicity and class. In the poorer, more rural areas of the country she observed many women breast-feeding their babies in the markets; in more middle-class Buenos Aires, she never saw a breast-feeding mother.

Dealing with It

As culturally sensitive as you strive to be, sometimes the only solace you can provide a hysterical child is to sit down, wherever you are, and nurse. What do you do when your baby needs to nurse in Venice and the hotel is three canals away? (What do you think they made cafés for?) No, really, I understand that cafés and restaurants are not always an option. Try parks, hotel lobbies, steps, the car (well, not the car in Venice, obviously!). In Venice, where you spend all your time on foot, I ended up occasionally sitting in doorways. This is another reason for keeping that daypack well stocked with things like receiving blankets (see my daypack suggestions in chapter 7). Toss one over baby, and you're set.

Some people recommend nursing in public bathrooms. Yuck. OK, many fancy hotels have bathroom lobbies with chairs and mirrors but otherwise, how awful! I don't want to eat where people eliminate. Why should my baby?

Pumping, Pumping, Pumping...

At times you may need to pump and refrigerate or freeze your breast milk (particularly if you're going out of town and baby is not.) Breast pumps come in two basic styles: manual and mechanized, with permutations of both types (one-handed, two-handed, etc.). Many hospitals and some baby supply stores will rent the big, heavy-duty machines for short or long-term. Keep in mind that pumping milk from your breasts is a skill, and like all skills requires a bit of practice. Don't borrow your buddy's pump two days before you leave town for the weekend and expect to fill the refrigerator with Mama Juice. Most good baby-care manuals have details on pumping equipment and techniques (see the Resource Appendix at the end of the book for suggestions).

Traffic School

A few months into motherhood, after a particularly sleepless night, I stopped in a bad neighborhood at a red light in the left lane and rapidly turned right, barely avoiding a cop car. The blaring siren woke *me* up. My first traffic violation. My humiliating tears merely made the ticketing officer more condescending. He wasn't even charmed by the beautiful baby sleeping in her car seat. How could anybody look at her and give me, her mother, a ticket? Fine, I thought, I'll do traffic school. But we were bonded, Annie and I. I'd never been away from her for eight hours before and she was the kind of baby that nursed a lot. *A lot.*

Our first exercise was to stand up in turn and intone, "My name is Ericka and I am an offender." By the time we broke for our afternoon break, my breasts were hard and nodular, and I was ready to begin mooing. I stepped into the toilet cubicle to express the extra. I'd used a breast pump at home, carefully saving the milk for the rare evening out, but I'd never expressed by hand before. I'd imagined myself like a farmer, deftly milking myself like a cow, with a thin, hissing stream hitting the toilet water. But no, expressing milk by hand takes a little practice, and it wouldn't aim.

So there I was, spraying milk wildly around the cubicle. Spots appeared on the walls, toilet, my clothing. The restroom was full of traffic offenders, waiting for the stall. The break was almost over. "No more running red lights," I swore grimly, soaking up yards of toilet paper. "Never, ever again."

Formula in Foreign Lands

Let's face it, while breast-feeding provides lots of opportunities for embarrassment, traveling with a formula-fed baby is rougher than traveling with a breast-fed baby, what with the sterilizing and the mixing and the equipment and all. If you're attempting it, here are a few things to keep in mind that will make your life and your travels far easier.

Which Formula?

You will likely decide which formula to feed your baby in collaboration with your pediatrician. Formula comes in a number of types, including organic (available at your local yupscale health food store) and "easy to digest" for babies with delicate systems. But not only do you need to choose the particular blend, you need to choose the form that blend comes in: powdered, concentrate, or pre-mixed. For short trips where weight and space is not an issue (like zipping on the plane from New York to Chicago), you might want to buy ready-to-drink formula in pre-sterilized, disposable bottles. This option is more expensive than bringing powdered or concentrate, but may be worth it in terms of convenience.

For longer trips, or if money or weight really is an issue, you'll need to rely on powdered formula. Make sure the water you use is safe (more on this in W for Water Safety in Troubleshooting A to Z).

Quick Tip

For half-day trips, mix formula in advance and keep cool in a thermos bottle.

Formula in Developing Nations

Most major American formula companies distribute their products overseas, though often it's only available in a powdered version. If you are traveling in developing nations, be aware that the formula may have a different recipe and may not have been stored under ideal conditions. Check for tampering and for the pull date—often "expired" products are still on the shelves.

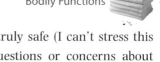

Make sure your water is truly safe (I can't stress this enough!). If you have questions or concerns about obtaining safe formula, call the American consulate for suggestions.

Boil Away Your Troubles

To kill the little nasty bacteria and viruses that swarm and feast on baby bottles and nipples, boil all equipment in a big pot for twenty minutes (that is, twenty minutes at a rolling boil, not twenty minutes from the time you put the equipment in the water).

Mixing it Up

The deal with formula is that everything that goes in the baby's mouth or that touches the formula itself needs to be sterilized. That means nipples, the inside of the bottle, or the inside of the little plastic baggie that sits inside the bottle and actually holds the formula. Mixed formula must be made in a sterile container with bottled, boiled, or purified water.

Sterilizing the equipment is best done with a steam sterilizer (either electric or microwave) or the good old traditional way—boiling. Some dishwashers will steril-ize, but most residential dishwashers don't get hot enough to kill all viruses and bacteria.

When you're traveling with a baby, you doubtless don't want to lug along a sterilizer on top of all the *other* baby gear, so you'll probably do it the old-fashioned way—in the pot. Making sure everything is sterile when you're away from a stove top can be difficult, but don't skimp on this step.

Hints to minimize your bottle-feeding hassles on the road:

- Use sterile formula powder and keep the package tightly closed.
- Carry a roll of disposable bottles and holders.
- If you're using bottles, strongly consider dispos-able plastic bottle liners (good for home, too, and

cheap) and plastic nipple covers that keep nipples sterile for up to twenty-four hours (not so very expensive).

🦴 Pre-measure your formula powder into plastic bottles or disposable plastic bags and seal until needed. Or you can buy special bottle systems that keep the water and powdered formula separate until you're ready to feed your baby—twist this and turn that and shake and you're set.

🦴 Buy bottled water—it's available in virtually every country in the world.

🦴 Ask your hotel to sterilize your equipment for you. (Ask nicely, now!) You may decide to limit your hotels to the ones that have kitchens. Ask about the possibility of getting your equipment boiled when you make your reservation.

🦴 Properly made formula can be kept refrigerated in prefilled bottles for a *maximum* of forty-eight hours, so it is best to make it up as you need it.

Quick Tip

Ellyn Satter's book *Child of Mine* has an excellent section on formula feeding and sanitation.

Warm and Creamy!?!

Babies, who are designed to nurse from a 98.6° mama, tend to like their bottles warm. For maximum flexibility, get your baby used to room-temperature formula before you go. There are at least two other options, though both require technology.

If you're doing a lot of car travel, consider keeping a bottle warmer device in your glove compartment. Plug it into the cigarette lighter hole and you're set.

If you'll be near a microwave, you can heat gel packs and tuck them around a bottle for a few moments. Don't heat bottles in a microwave!

Quick Tip

It's *vital* that you pay close attention and properly prepare your child's nourishment. *If and only if* you follow the manufacturers instructions exactly—don't add more powder or concentrate or more water—you can treat the formula as if it were breast milk and let the baby feed on demand.

Diaper Changing 101

We were on our way to see my sister in Vermont. The second leg of the trip was in a crowded puddle-jumper flying from Newark to Burlington with not a free seat in the house. In our row, all three seats were occupied by parents with babies. Something happened—an air-traffic jam—and the forty-five-minute flight stretched on and on as we circled and circled waiting for permission to land.

Two hours into our nightmare, the mother next to me suddenly exclaimed "Oh no!" Her baby's bottom turned brown. The air grew thick and unpleasant. The plane wheeled and wheeled. No way to change that baby. As I commiserated with the unfortunate mother, I thought, "At least the humiliation isn't mine. This time."

For the virgins among us, here's all you need to know about diapers. Diapers come in two basic styles: cotton cloth and disposable plastic. Disposable diapers are self-closing. Cotton diapers are held together by pins, a three-pronged clip, or with a Velcro-closing diaper cover. The fancy ones are all-in-one; cotton with a plastic cover and Velcro. If you use regular cotton diapers with pins or a clip, you also need to put the child in plastic pants. To change a diaper:

🧳 You can use the floor, a bed, the couch, a changing table, or your lap. *Never* leave the baby alone on a changing table. Put down a cloth or towel to cover the surface.

🧳 Gather everything you'll need in one place— diaper, diaper wipes or damp wash cloth, diaper cover or pins. A toy is usually a good idea, too.

🧳 Talk or sing to the baby. Tell her what a good child she is. Don't rush it. The slower you go and the more you talk to her, the less she'll struggle and object.

🧳 Take off the dirty diaper and set aside.

🧳 If the baby is a boy, casually toss a fresh cloth diaper or other soft cloth over the crucial region. The feeling of fresh air on their bottoms often causes babies to pee and, when we're talking about boy babies, we're talking straight up.

🧳 Clean the baby's bottom carefully and place the wipe near or on the dirty diaper.

🧳 Put on the new diaper. Make sure any diaper pins are well closed.

🧳 Take baby off changing table and dispose of dirty diaper.

🧳 Wash your hands. Every time. With soapy hot water. Feces are more than yucky, they are a chief cause of the spread of many horrible diseases. Don't take any short-cuts here.

Parking in Paris

In Paris, to satisfy Annie's need for rest and exercise, we took to finding parks in the middle of the day so that she could sit on the grass and practice her creeping. In the beautiful Jardin de Luxembourg, treading on the well-groomed lawns is forbidden except for one lawn reserved for children under six and their parents. We spent a blissful afternoon watching the French bébés in their $80 navy-and-white outfits playing with their chic mothers. Annie, while less stylish, had a blast. After

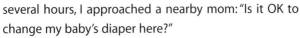

several hours, I approached a nearby mom: "Is it OK to change my baby's diaper here?"

"Yes, of course, eet ees OK."

"Thanks, I just wasn't sure," I stammered, "I didn't see anybody else changing their baby here."

"Oh, zat ees because French babies only make ze poopy in ze morning."

Cloth Diapers vs. Disposables— The Great Debate

Paper or plastic bags at the grocery store, breast or bottle feeding, to circumcise or not to circumcise, cloth vs. disposable—these are the issues that try people's souls and test friendships. In the interests of world peace, I'll present the pros and cons of diapering with cloth and disposables and leave the lectures to the Pundits of Poop.

Cotton Diapers

The Environmental Case

OK, a few reasons to consider cloth diapers from the environmental perspective:

- Using cloth diapers can save you around $500 over the cost of disposable diapers during an average diapering period. That's because babies potty-train faster in cloth; and the larger size diapers (and pull-ups) are expensive.
- It takes twenty trees to diaper one baby in disposable diapers for two years.
- Walk down the grocery store aisles and look at how much shelf space diapers take up. The rest of the shelves hold consumable food and beverages, and the containers are often recyclable. Diapers, the most voluminous consumer item in the store, are 100 percent garbage.
- One baby uses six thousand to ten thousand disposable diapers over a diapering period.

Eighteen million disposable diapers were land-filled in the U.S. last year, generating 3.6 million tons of untreated human waste and solid waste.

> Fecal contamination in child-care centers results from poor hygienic practices, not type of diaper used.

Diaper Services

Hoorah for the times we live in! In most cases, you won't have to buy and wash your own cotton diapers. Diaper services are reasonably priced and convenient—they bring the diapers every week and pick up the soiled ones. Check your phone directory, and phone around for the best deal and service for you.

Quick Tip
Safety-Pinning Tips

If you're having trouble shoving a pin through layers of folded cotton, try:

1. Sticking the pin into a bar of dry soap—the soap will lubricate and enable you to slide it right through.
2. Running the pin through your hair (no, silly, the side of the pin, not the tip!) The oils from your scalp will make the pin slippery. Yes, even if your hair is clean!

A Diaper Is Not a Diaper Is Not a Diaper

If you're going to be buying your own set of cotton diapers, spend some time researching the product. All cotton diapers are not the same—spend the time and money to get the thickest ones.

> My brother-in-law Jim was in his mid-forties when first-time parenting hit him with a bang. My niece Emma was born five months after Annie. Five months is a long time in the life of an infant, so, as the familial experts, Bill and I were consulted on all matters. Shortly before Emma's

birth, Jim called for another informational briefing.

"How do you sterilize the butt?" Jim asked.

"What?"

"My mom told me everything had to be sterilized."

I had a sudden, horrific image of poor Jim, swabbing down his new infant's rear and delicate privates with boiling water or stinging alcohol. "No, no, no," I protested. "Do you sterilize your own butt? Wait, no, Jim. Don't answer that."

The Traveling Diaper Show

If you're planning on parking yourself in one locale for two or more weeks, say, at a relative's house or a rental condominium, you might want to set up a short-term diaper service. Most diaper services have a minimum order—two to four weeks plus a small set-up charge. Some of this may be negotiable; my local diaper source, for instance, says they waive the minimum for traveling families. Call (or have somebody call) in advance and you'll arrive to the familiar stacks of clean, white, fluffy cotton.

Quick Tip
The Duffle Bag Shuffle

A small drawstring nylon duffle bag makes a great day-trip diaper bag. Hang it from the stroller handle to use for dirties, then empty and wash in the evening. A large duffle makes a great dirty diaper hamper for a longer trip. Zip it well, check it with your luggage at the airport, and give the drug-sniffing dogs a special treat.

Maneuvering the Manure—Cloth Diapers on the Road

If you bring cloth diapers on the road, you need plastic bags for the dirties, too—small ones for day trips, strong, big ones for general storage. Or use duffle bags.

Some diaper services provide clients with "vacation" cloth diapers. These are older diapers that have been retired from normal service because of wear and tear. Should you lose one or two (easy to do on the road), the replacement cost is less than it would be for a new diaper. Of course, if you're gone longer than a few days, you'll still need to wash these yourself.

Washing Diapers on the Road

In an ideal world, you'll never have to spend a vacation morning washing diapers. At times though, the world is not ideal. Here are a few tips for washing diapers (at home *or* on the road):

- Never use detergents to wash diapers. Carry a plastic bag of real laundry soap (such as White King) and water conditioner (water softener affects absorbency).

- Dump as much solid waste as you can into the toilet and flush. Presoak the diaper in cool water to get out most of the soil (throw it in, let the waste leach out), then pop it in a plastic bag and carry to the laundromat or machine. If you do the presoak in the toilet, make sure that there are no chemicals in the tank—bluing, bleach, self-cleaning substances, and so on.

- Wash diapers in the hottest water available. If you're at a friend's house, crank up the water heater as high as it will go (*don't* forget to turn it down again after the wash cycle ends). Horrible diseases live in feces.

- Never use bleach or chemicals of any kind. Even a thorough washing can't remove all traces, and baby skin is hypersensitive to chemicals. In case of diaper rash, add ½ cup vinegar to the last rinse.

- Be prepared for dingy diapers. Babies don't care. If you hang the diapers in sunshine, the sun will bleach them white again (don't do this in the city where the fumes of industry or auto exhaust might settle).

In Defense of the Disposable

On the other hand, there's a lot to be said for convenience, especially when you're traveling with a child in diapers. There's also a lot to be said for hygiene. A day's worth of soiled diapers in a plastic bag on a warm summer day is a health hazard. Disposable diapers were originally designed for travel. It makes sense. They are easy to use, and easy to dispose of.

Every Family Finds Their Comfort Zone

Some parents stick with cloth diapers all the way through to toilet training, some use a combination, some use cotton for the first year or so and then switch, some use disposable diapers from day one. In our somewhat-schizophrenic case, we used only cotton until our first trip to Europe when Annie was seven months old. We used disposables on the road, and much as I believe in cloth diapers, man, it was hard to go back to cloth. Go back to cloth we did until Annie was a year old, and then we gave in to the powers of the modern world.

Disposables Round the World

Many of the major U.S. diaper companies sell diapers internationally. Be aware that it's a bit of a crap shoot (groan). Sometimes the product name is different than what you're used to but the diaper is the same, and sometimes the product name is the same, but the diaper is made to different specifications—thicker, thinner, or made with different materials. Some companies sell an "economy" (cheaper and bulkier) diaper in developing countries.

Diaper costs also vary from country to country—some are pricier, some are less expensive. If you're on an extended trip, you will have little choice but to sample the local merchandise. Let your baby's rear have a cultural experience.

Health Concerns

Most disposable diaper manufacturers add super-absorbent materials, such as acrylic acid polymer salts (polyacrylate), to their diapers. This chemical forms into gel beads when wet. Many parents (me among them) have found this gel on their babies' bodies or in genital crevices, raising issues of safety. In 1985, the first year chemical super-absorbent "gels" were used in disposable diapers, fifty thousand babies went to emergency rooms with diapering problems. Parents using disposable diapers also need to be concerned about avoiding tears in the outside plastic covering. Ingesting the gel-filled fluff might cause choking. Yucko.

There are now gel-free diapers on the market, disposable diapers filled with cotton and wood-pulp fluff for absorbency. Gel-free diapers are a bit pricier than standard disposable diapers but they're definitely a better health—if not environmental—choice. Some cotton-diaper services are even selling them to their clients (there's a listing for "Tushies Diapers" in the Resources Appendix under "Equipment").

Diapering Accessories

Cloth, disposable, or a combination, you'll need a few other "accessories."

The Joy of Diaper Wipes

I love diaper wipes. Even once Annie left her diaper days behind except for the nighttime pull-up, I bought them by the boxful. I still do, although we don't plow through them in the same wild and unabashed fashion (In Chapter 7, there's a partial list of the multitude of things wipes can be used for). Get the unscented kind. Many children are sensitive to scents, and, at least for me, the delicious smell of clean, milk-fed baby is endlessly better than the chemically tinged odor of artificial flowers or baby powder.

Do-Your-Own Diaper Wipes

Even the unscented commercial wipes contain some chemicals that aid drying, and these chemicals can occasionally cause reactions. Here's a recipe for hand-made diaper wipes:

Paper towels (thick paper towels folded in thirds, or use baby wash cloths instead of paper towels, and half again more liquid)

1 cup of water

1 teaspoon of mineral oil

1 teaspoon of soft soap

Place towels in waterproof container (Tupperware would work). Mix liquids and pour over towels to dampen.

The Problem with Powders

If you're going to powder your darling's derriere, verify that the product you choose does not contain talcum powder. Talc, a mineral, can cause respiratory problems.

Ointments—Not Always OK

Rashes are usually caused by long exposure to urine. Be careful choosing a diaper rash ointment. Many contain fish oil, and fish oil has been shown to promote bacterial growth—exactly what that wee rashy rear does not need. Any ointment containing calendula is good—and then there's the good old "open-air" method. Leave baby without a diaper as much of the day as you can manage.

Rashes are more common during travel. Make sure to change your baby frequently. If a rash persists for more than two days, stop using wipes and switch to warm water and mild soap, apply anti-yeast cream mixed with 1 percent hydrocortisone ointment, and put barrier cream on top of the mixture (petroleum jelly would work). If you're having trouble cleaning the area with all those creams, remove the creams with unscented mineral oil, swab the little rear down, and then reapply more goop.

Too Much Time on Her Hands

I know a mom who traveled with a thermos bottle of warm water and soft squares of cotton flannel. Her son had the privilege of never having a cold wipe touch his butt. As my old therapist used to say, people have many ways of living. If you are tremendously concerned about the shock of wet and cold each time you clean your baby, you can buy a diaper-wipe warmer (plugs in near the changing table and maintains the wipes at a steady temperature of 98.6 degrees) but come on, enough is enough! Crumple a wipe in your hand for a moment. It will warm up.

Potty Training and Traveling

We have friends who are planning to go to Europe once their kids are out of diapers. They don't need to wait—in some ways, it is easier to deal with diapers than it is to deal with the half-trained or newly potty-trained child.

Alternatives to Strange Bathrooms

Some kids are nervous in strange bathrooms and unwilling to go; especially common is the child who won't move his bowels other than at home. Some kids get so excited being in a new place that they simply forget. For a child who has some trepidation, or whose patterns are unpredictable even to herself ("I have to go potty, Mommy, and I have to go now! Oops."), you might want to revert to diapers or disposable pull-ups for the duration of the trip. Here are some other solutions:

- For car trips around town, keep a potty seat in the trunk of the car.
- There's always ye olde jar-in-car trick for boys. For girls, use a bigger jar, and have them practice in the bathtub or shower first.
- Plan around poop. Some kids have a bowel movement at a regular time each day—try to maintain that schedule. For example, if she always poops after a hot liquid in the morning, arrange to be close to comfortable plumbing then.

🦿 Inexpensive portable fold-up seats/toilet seat adapters are available through baby catalogs and stores. These help with the hygiene issue.

🦿 Carry a small travel-sized plastic bottle of anti-bacterial gel to clean hands afterwards.

Maneuvering around Public Toilets

In many places, public bathrooms are well kept. In other places in the world (or in many U.S. gas-station bathrooms), hygiene is of less concern. What I'm really saying is sometimes public toilets are just plain disgusting.

🚽 Ask to use public restrooms in hotel lobbies, or "better" restaurants and stores. Most places in the world will allow leeway for small, uncomfortable-looking children, even if they have signs posted "For Customers Only."

🚽 If the bathroom is unsanitary and your child cannot wait, hold him above the toilet.

🚽 *Always* carry toilet paper or facial tissue—many facilities are not supplied.

🚽 Travel with disposable toilet-seat covers, but be aware that many places in the world don't have seats. (Squat toilets can be more hygienic anyway. For more information, see chapter 13.)

🚽 Be aware that in many places, it is OK for a woman to take a small boy into a woman's room, while it is socially unacceptable for the opposite to happen—a man taking a little girl into the men's room. (Dads: In a case like this, you may need to rely on the kindness of strangers. If you do, make the best snap judgment about the quality of the woman you are relying on, and stand right by the door the entire time.)

Travails of the Newly Potty-Trained

Tiny children are blissfully unashamed of their bodily functions, as they should be. This lovely innocence can lead to embarrassment for the adults—like the time when his grandparents took three-year-old Sascha to a fancy, formal function at the Plaza Hotel, and in the middle of the lowered voices and canapés he suddenly screamed, "Mommy, I have to go potty!" Our pal Joannie (at two, a little less articulate than Sascha) has the bad habit of announcing at the top of her lungs, "Poop! Poop! Poop!" And then there's two-and-a-half-year-old Mickey, who in the middle of his mother's wedding ceremony shouted, "Momma, the pee is coming out! Hurry!"

Dealing With Dirt

Kids get dirty, and they should. It's part of your job to, at least occasionally, freshen them up.

Dirty Bodies

Bathing is not always a possibility on the road, and you'll need to occasionally excavate their tiny faces from the layers of grime, and de-stickify their hands and feet before they climb into bed. Here's where your ever-useful diaper wipes come in handy again.

Dirty Clothes on the Road

Much as I've traveled, the dirty clothes thang remains a problem. If you were alone, you could do as my dad did in Europe in the '50s—travel for months wearing a single white shirt. This legendary shirt was made from Dacron, it was thin and gauzy, and it dried in two hours. Each night he washed out his shirt in the sink. In the morning it was dry and he put it on again. With a white T-shirt underneath, and the sleeves rolled up (these were the James Dean years), nobody could tell it wasn't freshly pressed cotton. Now *that's* traveling light.

As a parent, you don't have that option, though you'll still probably find yourself bending over hotel room sinks.

I'm ambivalent about doing laundry, even at home, and when I'm on the road I prefer to pay somebody else to do most of it. Whether you're willing to pay for clean

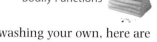

clothes or are hell-bent on washing your own, here are tips for laundering overseas:

- Do laundry as you go, don't try to bring enough clothing for the whole trip (a seven-day supply should be more than sufficient).

- Bring clothes that can survive mixed loads of whites, darks, and brights.

- Strongly consider paying for wash-and-fold services. In Barcelona, we recently paid a mere extra two dollars to have the laundromat actually *do* the job for us, leaving us more time to ramble on La Rambla and check our email at the world's largest Internet café.

- If you're having a laundry service wash cloth diapers, let them know. It's only polite.

- Bring liquid castile soap for hand-washing underwear and socks in your hotel-room sink. Consider bringing a small piece of rope to use as a clothesline. A couple of clothes pins might be a good idea, too. Hotels charge an arm and a leg to do your wash for you, and you won't want to waste precious museum time watching boxers and panties spin in a Parisian laundromat.

- Thin cotton clothing or cotton/polyester blends dry fastest. Don't try to wash your own "sweats," they'll stay damp for years.

- To find a laundromat, ask at your hotel, or look it up in an on-the-cheap guidebook.

- If you're renting an apartment advertised as having laundry facilities in Europe (check out the section on house, apartment and castle rentals in chapter 9), be aware that home washing machines are often much smaller than the one you might be used to, and that homes rarely have dryers.

- Damp baby clothes can be dried on the back seat of the rental car as you cruise through the Carpathians or across the Russian Steppes. Your own underpants and socks can be too, if you don't mind hearing snickers from the local constables who may stop you at the occasional road block.

Take a Lesson from Us

In Florence, we splurged for a couple of nights at a famous pensionne. When the concierge offered to do some baby laundry, we jumped at the chance. She returned twelve beautifully pressed tiny garments to us the next day (they were practically tied with a ribbon) and presented us with a bill equivalent to fourteen dollars. Ouch.

Laundering Clothes in Developing Asia and in India

Hired personal services are usually very inexpensive in South East Asia and the subcontinent. In Bali, the local washerwoman scrubbed a hole in my new jeans, trying to remove a coffee stain. In India, the laundry wallahs take your clothes down to the river and pound the bleep out of them before lying them on a rock to dry in the sun. Your clothes will come back stiff and faded…but definitely clean.

CHAPTER 3

Eating with Baby

It's a very odd thing
As odd as can be—
That whatever Miss T. eats
Turns into Miss T.
—Old Nursery Rhyme

Chomping the Chow with Children

Every parent spends hours each day thinking about food, preparing food, helping the children eat—and hopefully getting to eat, too. This chapter provides food for thought on eating, everywhere, with babies and small children. Once again, we'll start with the basics—eating at home. By the time you're done, you and baby will be eating everywhere!

Food—It Feeds More Than the Body

Remember those quiet weekend breakfasts, she with the Sports section, you with the comics? The coffee was hot, the kitchen was quiet save for the rustle of newspaper, the occasional snort of humor or outrage, or the occasional murmur, "Honey, could you pass me the

Datebook section?" Remember, too, your romantic candlelight dinners served by the fabulous waiter who anticipated your every desire? (A glass of wine, a single rose.) Remember it well, file it deep in your brain. As you'll learn once you have a child, eating will never be so simple again.

While *all* serenity is not completely in the past (that's what they invented baby-sitters for!), it will no longer be the norm. Eating with a baby, eating with a toddler, eating with a small child—these tend to be noisy, boisterous adventures, sometimes fraught with *issues*. Yet food is far more than fuel for fighting, and eating is one of the sensual pleasures of life, one that you can, and should, share with your kids.

Eating In

In too many families, meals are hastily snatched affairs—little more than stuffing sessions. Three hundred and thirty-odd years ago, Samuel Pepys wrote, "Strange to see how a good dinner and feasting reconciles everybody." I don't think it's strange—while the shared dinner hour may have gone the way of the rotary phone in many households, eating together is one of our favorite and most valuable family practices. "Training" kids to appreciate eating *en famille*—whether the family numbers two or twenty—may take some time, but it's well worth it. At least once a day, you get to share time, attention, and pleasure as a family.

There's a Baby in the House

Start at day one. Baby is part of the family, she's involved in dinnertime, too. That said, don't count on her sleeping through the dinner hour, or even being quiet. For many babies, the evening hour is the time for wailing, not for "reconciling." She's not having any of the Chicken ala King, so why should she be happy? How then, can you eat while the baby is screaming?

The Rocker. Take that great infant car seat—the kind that rocks (you'll find out about it in chapter 5)—

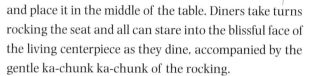

and place it in the middle of the table. Diners take turns rocking the seat and all can stare into the blissful face of the living centerpiece as they dine, accompanied by the gentle ka-chunk ka-chunk of the rocking.

The Nurser. Of course, only a breast-feeding mother can do this part. A baby with his mouth full of warm milk is likely to be a happy and quiet baby. For a right-handed mom, nursing on the left breast and eating at the same time is a challenge, but doable (same goes for a lefty nursing on the right). What happens when it's time to switch sides? Maybe mom's dining partner can insert select morsels into her mouth. He or she can, at the least, cut up her food.

The Swinger. This must be the reason they invented those awful battery-operated swings: The Neglect-O-Matic, for the Exhausted, Fed-Up, New Parent—"Wind it up and let it go, we'll escape to Mexico!"

In all seriousness, it isn't good to swing the baby. Many child development people think these are terrible for kids. I'd say that for *very* selective uses (like both parents sitting at the dinner table at the same time once in a blue moon) the swing can be a lifesaver.

The Wolfers. If life is too problematic (and sometimes it just turns out that way), you can always just feed yourselves on-the-fly, standing over the kitchen sink, pacing with baby, taking turns, and swearing to try again or at *least* hire a baby-sitter for two hours so you can sit down and eat a meal together. Wolfing should be a last resort.

Too Tired to Cook?

Especially with a new baby, there will be many times when you have no energy to cook, and no energy to go out. Check out food delivery services (there are more details in chapter 9). How luscious! Go on a vacation without leaving the privacy of your home! While restaurant delivery goes against my general anti-cocooning sentiment, when you're having "one of those nights," there's no beating it.

The Kindness of Friends

Set up a network of friends to share or trade shopping trips and cooking responsibilities. It's almost as easy to cook for six or eight as it is for three or four, and that way you have to do it less often. Can't cook? Exchange a night of baby-sitting for a meal.

Dinner with a Colicky Baby

If your baby is colicky, you're having a hard enough time without trying to be a gourmet chef, too! If there was ever a time to simplify your existence, this is it. Don't try to juggle a bawling baby and cook hot food at the same time. What did they make microwaves, fast food, and marital partners for? Or, cook dinner early in the day before the "colic hours" set in. Don't skip dinner—you need the fuel to get through the nerve-jangling hours of Howling Howie—but don't make it anything special. Just get yourself fed. This, too, shall pass.

Home Catering

Check your local phone book under "catering." Some catering companies specialize in small dinner parties, or will even bring you dinners for just your family—if you order on a regular basis.

Grocery Delivery Services

Sometimes the mere idea of going shopping is exhausting. Pack up the kid. Get the kid in the car. Strap the kid in. Get in the car yourself. Drive. Park. Get out. Get the kid out. Go into the store. Put the kid in the cart. Shop. Wait in line. Leave the store. Get the kid in the car. Strap the kid in. Get in the car yourself. Drive. Park. Get out. Get the kid out. Go into the house. Put the kid down. Leave the kid alone. Unload the car. Put the groceries away.

Pre-dot com bomb, while Internet companies abounded, life was easier for parents who could order groceries (and prepared meals for that matter) on-line. A few companies still exist, a boon for parents who can jiggle a baby with one hand while pointing and clicking with the other. And while it's not as common as it used to be, some grocery stores will still allow you to order your groceries over the phone, and then deliver them to your door. Try the remaining Mom 'n Pops. Of course, you *might* have to pay a delivery fee, you *will* have to come up with a tip, and you *won't* be able to squeeze your own tomatoes. Then again, you won't have to pack up the kid, get the kid in the car, strap the kid in...

And for the Organic Among Us...

Quite a few small organic farms nationwide participate in Community Sustainable Agriculture (CSA) where community members pay a fee to receive a weekly share of the harvest. Yes, you too can have organic veggies delivered to your door! Check the Resources Appendix for more information on CSAs.

Food and the Older Baby

Baby is getting older, and all of a sudden, "Egads! It *eats*!" A whole new world of culinary adventure awaits you and your little muncher.

At Home with the Older Baby

Kids start clicking in to the joys of food at different ages— for Annie, though she was introduced to solids at six months, she really didn't *get* food until she was close to a year old. (Food interested her for its texture—we did a point'n'shoot photo series of her little head bathed in stewed prunes, in banana, in cereal...). Other kids love the tastes of food from the time they are four months old.

Viva Italia!

At nine months, Annie was far below average on the weight charts. Our pediatrician, Dr. Mangravite, wasn't too concerned—she was healthy, she was alert, energetic, charming, intelligent. "Make her a little spaghetti carbonara—bacon fat, cream, eggs—make the noodles soft enough for her to gum," he told us, his eyes growing ever so slightly misty at the thought of what may be for him a childhood comfort food.

The dutiful new mother, I went home, looked up Spaghetti con Carbonara in my Italian cookbook, and discovered a whole new world of sin. Bill and I enjoyed dinner immensely. Annie looked at the long, coated noodles as though they were a very interesting piece of furniture, nibbled one or two, then patted my breasts emphatically, wanting to nurse.

Traveling with That Mushy Stuff

If you're traveling with a mush-eating little moochie, check out the natural and organic baby foods available in most supermarkets. (Most of the standard commercial baby food doesn't taste very good, or is loaded with sugar and fillers—read the labels!)

You can create wonderful, tasty meals for your baby with the aid of a food grinder. Much of what you eat is OK for an older baby. A portable, battery-operated food grinder is good for sharing restaurant food. (A bit noisy, though.)

Escargot, Baby?

Bottled baby food is heavy, but when you're traveling across time zones, make sure to leave some room in your luggage for an emergency supply. That first day, (or night) after you arrive, your baby's body (and your own) will still be living in another time zone and he may get hungry at 2:30 A.M. On our first trip to Europe, poor seven-month-old Annie had to make do with a stale rice cracker and tap water—all we could find on a furtive midnight kitchen raid in our friends' house.

The next day you can hit a supermarket, but be prepared for some strange discoveries. The Dutch begin feeding their kids bottled food at three months—try a puree of cabbage, tomato, green beans, and non-iron fortified rice cereal. The French baby food is delicious but filled with sugar and salt. Here's where your newly minted flexibility begins: take a breath and practice saying, "Ah, what the hell, it's a vacation."

Toddlers at the Table

Man, life was eeeaasy back when your kid only drank breast milk or formula. Even that mushy stuff was OK, though messy. Now your kid is almost, or truly, a *kid*, and if your family is like many families, you've already donned your boxing clothes:

"Ladies and gentlemen! In this corner, wearing the anxious smiles of the desperate-to-feed, that fabulous duo, the PARENTS! And in this corner, presenting the not-so-fresh-from-the-womb, the ever-hungry-for-junk-food, the food tortuous, TODDLER!"

Typically, when Baby is a baby, she grows at a tremendous rate, inhaling victuals like air. Then, suddenly Baby is a toddler with seemingly no appetite at all, and you, her parent, are freaking out. As our beloved Dr. Mangravite asked me, "Does she have enough energy to play? If so, she's probably getting enough to eat." Trust your child, provide healthy choices, enjoy your own food, and watch her follow your example to the extent that her appetite will let her. Try to provide a balanced diet, but think in terms of the course of the day or week, rather than trying to strictly balance each meal.

Engage His Imagination

Food is fun, and involving a kid's imagination doesn't qualify as the dreaded "playing with food." Eating a banana "like a baby monkey" (half peeled, peel draping on small fist) is endlessly more delicious than eating peeled, boring, banana pieces. Pancake "monsters" taste better than pancakes— everybody knows that. If your child wants strawberries and all you have is blueberries, tell them that these are magic fairy berries: tiny, blue, and round. It's not a lie— it's pretend.

Eating Out with the Family

Eating "out," whether in a restaurant, fast-food joint, hotel room, campground, or picnic spot, brings its own agonies—I mean, *challenges*. But as with most things in life, there are trade-offs, and many times eating "out" is just what the doctor ordered to break the monotony or add a little adventure to your lives.

Cuisine as a Cultural Experience

We're a relatively food-oriented family—oh, who am I kidding, eating is our *life*—so for us, a big part of the joy of travel is the thrill of eating. Much of human culture is based around food, and a vital part of experiencing any culture is savoring, and understanding, the local cuisine. From the beginning, introduce your kids to many different kinds of foods. Your own encouragement and enthusiasm will pay off. Your travel experiences will become easier and more rewarding if you show them that food is fun, that adventure is fun, and that new food is an adventure.

- Think long-term. If you're excited about new food and consider it an adventure, Junior will learn to be excited, too.

- Be flexible. Kids love familiar foods, so allow them the occasional lapse into pizza or burgers, even—especially—in exotic locales.

- Have compassion. During travel, food can look and taste different, schedules are askew, even the plates and spoons are unfamiliar.

- Use desserts as an entree into new cuisines. ("I don't *like* Indian food." "Try this sweet coconut pudding, Honey." "Yum. I *love* Indian food, Mommy!")

- Tolerate a little whining ("This looks yucky!") and keep trying. Young children are very conservative about food. I like to think of this as a survival mechanism from the hunter/gatherer days, if the little ones were popping everything edible-looking into their mouths, the human race might not have survived to this illustrious day.

🐾 Try not to be irritated when even the youngest toddler begins to pine and sigh within days for his usual food—the food he is *not* eating this vacation.

> We don't drink milk in Mexico. For Bill's kids, the cravings would begin immediately, as soon as the border guard welcomed us with, "Bienvenido a Mexico." Once back in the U.S., we'd head for the closest supermarket, where Aaron and Rachel would each down a quart as though it had been a year, not ten days, since they'd last drunk from the cow.

Restaurant (cough!) Etiquette

Restaurant rules and etiquette are the same across town or across the world. Some restaurants are clearly appropriate for little kids, others are clearly inappropriate, and still others are borderline—depending upon your kids, and how you deal with them. The way to teach your little ones how to act in a restaurant is to *take* them to restaurants. If you want to travel with your kids, begin by taking them to local joints, and branch out from there. Here are some restaurant tips:

🍴 Sit near the door. If baby cries, take her outside *immediately*! (And don't be upset at her—she's just a baby. Crying is the only way she has to communicate.)

🍴 Order your food and then go for a walk while one of you waits for the food to be served.

🍴 Bring toys, food, or coloring books to keep him happy.

🍴 If necessary, you can use cloth napkins to strap your child to the high chair.

🍴 Make a strict rule: toddler can toddle next to the table but no further. No bugging "that nice, smiling lady over there."

🍴 If your baby is very messy, get a table near the wall and surreptitiously lay a small plastic cloth under the baby's chair. When the meal is over, quietly fold up the cloth and take it with you. Do not shake it out until well away from the restaurant.

🗂 When the meal is over, offer to clean up under the high chair. They'll refuse (they can't have other customers see you cleaning up) but they'll appreciate your offer.

🗂 Leave a big tip. You may have been extra work, and you want to be welcomed back.

Restaurants Where Little Kids Are Always Welcome

You know 'em, you love 'em, you shouldn't be limited to 'em: franchise fast food joints, taquerias, pizzerias, and coffee shops. The pace is fast and furious, there are tons of hyped up little kids and babies, and the food is edible but not (even at a stretch) fancy. Other than the fact that most babies can't handle this much stimuli, there is little wrong with these establishments. The problems occur when you feel you are doomed to eat here, and nowhere but here, until Junior is over five feet tall.

Restaurants Where Little Kids Are *Usually* Welcome

I've seen some parents peek through restaurant windows and, if they see tablecloths and candles, back away and head for the nearest fast-food joint. "Oh no, my baby would just disturb everybody else!" they exclaim in horror and disappointment.

It doesn't have to be this way. Contrary to your fears, most people don't mind children in restaurants, as long as they aren't too disruptive. Informal but excellent restaurants abound if you behave with courtesy (no, don't whip your kid into shape). You'll be welcomed again and again. These include:

🐜 Moderately priced ethnic restaurants

🐜 Trendy hangouts

🐜 Casual but elegant dining of all kinds

🐜 European restaurants

Can you take your infant to a fine Parisian restaurant? Well, we did. Suddenly, the formal waiter we remembered from three years before, the one with the scornful upper lip, melted into cries of "Coo Coo! Coo Coo!" as he presented our smiling child with spoons, bread, and a tiny plate of her own. Annie spent many an hour sitting under restaurant tables in five countries, and was greeted with, for the most part, joy and pleasure by the restaurant staffs and patrons. Europeans tend to be more tolerant of babies. After all, many of the other tables have small dogs sitting politely under them.

Restaurants Usually Inappropriate for Little Kids

Note the word "usually" in the title of this section. As usual, I suggest you use your own judgment. A sleeping baby poses no problem anywhere. A three-year-old awed by the idea of a "fancy restaurant" may behave just fine. But in general, avoid:

- Anyplace with a formal dress code.
- Anyplace where an entree costs more than your monthly phone bill.
- Anyplace where the music or smoke makes it hard to talk without shouting and hard to breathe without coughing.
- Anyplace where the question "Do you have a high chair?" is greeted with intense hostility (some places aren't prepared for a baby, but are willing to accommodate). If the maitre 'd stares at you for a long, time-stopping moment and then asks, "Did the nanny take ill?" it's probably time to leave.
- Anyplace where the baby is the youngest in the room by forty years or more (with the exception of visiting Great Uncle Joe in the nursing home. See chapter 6 for more).

How Do You Change a Sloppy Diaper at a Restaurant?

Don't ever, *ever* change a baby or toddler at the dinner table. There are many areas in life where you can push the limits of social acceptability. This is not one of them.

🧰 Are you sure it can't wait? Sometimes it cannot.

🧰 Scope out the bathroom. Is there a changing table? A make-up counter? How wide is the sink? How dirty is the floor? Lay down a lot of paper towels and do the dirty deed. If the floor is that disgusting, do you want to be eating at that restaurant, anyway?

🧰 How close is the car? Is it worth another few bucks to get the valet attendant to bring it around?

🧰 Is there an unused room (perhaps a banquet facility) in the restaurant? How about a staff office? A storage room? (Politely turn down use of the walk-in refrigerator.) Ask! Believe me, it is in the restaurant staff's best interest to help you get this small situation resolved.

Borderline Restaurant Behavior (…and you'll see a lot of it)

The I'm-Too-Big-for-a-Booster Phase. At four, Annie thought of herself as extremely sophisticated and mature. She was also only three feet tall, a fact that began to cause her problems at restaurants where she was too cool to want to be seen in a booster seat or (heaven forbid) a high chair. Her nose, however, often barely cleared the table. We spent many meals seeing little more than the top of her head and her two busy hands. For other meals she relented, and, seated on a booster seat, joined us in her lovely, regal way.

The Make-a-Concoction-from-Condiments Stage. Kids love mud pies, kids love ooze, kids love to mix and combine. I personally think it's gross when I see a child making such a concoction (mustard, sugar, salt, pepper, A-1 sauce), but as long as he makes it on a plate and not directly on the table (which I've seen more than once), I have no real complaint. A concocting kid is a quiet kid. (Note: If you allow this behavior, be considerate! Glance at a waiter or two—if you see disgust or disapproval, end the project. Take the child for a walk.)

That said, I gotta confess, it's not just toddlers who make concoctions. I remember sitting with my friends for hours at Salmagundi's soup and salad bar on Geary Street in San Francisco—age fifteen and still mixing it up on the table with the salt, sugar, mustard, and ketchup.

Utterly Unacceptable Restaurant Behavior

Yelling and screaming. "Hey, c'mon, pal, shut that kid up! We're tryin' ta have a romantic dinner heah!"

Throwing food. As far as I'm concerned, lack of coordination is acceptable, deliberate rudeness or food throwing is not. Some kids bend towards eating sensibly and neatly, and use a fork at eighteen months. My mom, a woman of incredible patience, taught my sister and me to eat with utensils at twelve months, taking a long time at meals and praising us profusely when we managed to get the food into our own mouths. "Children like to please," she says. Then again, some kids still, at the age of four, require a warm, wet washcloth after a meal for (in this order) hands, face, legs, torso, table, and floor.

Dancing on the High Chair. If your kid is in an energetic mood (or is one of those babies that has two speeds: High and Asleep), you may be treated to a little song-and-dance on top of the high chair. Stop this behavior: 1) It is dangerous, and 2) It draws a lot of attention.

The Littlest Stripper in the West

When little Sarah was two and one-half she treated, to their horror, her parents Suzanne and Tom to her debut as a table dancer. They were in a nice restaurant (not too fancy, but definitely a place you wouldn't be ashamed to take a first date) when they realized that Sarah had escaped while they were enjoying their fresh sand dabs, and was somehow four tables away, standing on an empty table, removing her diaper with a great flourish! A trail of tiny garments led to the aspiring entertainer.

> The crowd's response was somewhat mixed, and
> Suzanne and Tom still cross the street when they shop in
> that neighborhood.

Fun Food to Order

Scope out the "side order" section on the menu, and try
a few selections. In general, little kids often like
"discrete" food—food that comes in tiny, natural packages, such as noodles, beans, peas, blueberries,
Cheerios, Goldfish crackers, cheese squares, tangerine
segments. Many don't like their different foods to touch.
And don't limit your kid to the classics (pasta, pancakes,
grilled cheese, burgers), give her tastes of your dish and
don't be surprised when she likes it.

Maintaining Meal Patterns on the Road

It's not what meals, but when. Kids adjust rapidly to
time changes, and it doesn't matter if you're eating eggs
at "dinnertime" or a burrito for "breakfast." Problems
arise when the excitement of the trip interferes with
eating at regular intervals. Generally for little ones, the
chow should come every two and one-half hours or so.
If you keep the intervals between meals similar to the
schedule at home, you'll reduce grumpiness. Less
grumpiness is a good thing.

Finding Fabulous Food
without Forking Over a Fortune

When you're on the road, you don't have to spend a lot
of money on food, even if you don't do your own cooking. Breakfast and lunch can be catch-as-catch can. If
you're on a driving trip, bring a cooler—you can keep
milk on ice for a couple of days. Remember that even in
the most highfalutin tourist locale, the locals have to
eat, too. Ask a friendly salesperson for a good place to get
a bite, "Not fancy, I mean where *you* eat lunch." Follow
the off-duty taxi driver to the best alley cafe in Cairo. At
LAX (Los Angeles International Airport), we were

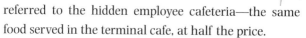

referred to the hidden employee cafeteria—the same food served in the terminal cafe, at half the price.

The island of Maui in Hawaii is known for its expensive food, yet we ate very well, and quite cheaply. A fish-and-chips stand offered fresh-from-the-water, delicious-broiled-or-fried Hawaiian fishes—ono, mahi-mahi, or ahi tuna—plus fries for $5.95. Twice for lunch we sat at a stone picnic table in front of a Bento restaurant in a local shopping center where, to Annie's delight, noisy little birds hopped by to steal scraps of food. Here, for $3.40, we had a lunch plate consisting of a pile of rice, a hamburger patty, and sides of green peas, potato salad, and Japanese pickle.

Picnics, Teddy Bear and Otherwise

Eating outside is an excellent way to save money on the road. Unless the weather absolutely forbids it, we try to combine our travel experiences with picnicking wherever we are in the world—what could beat the taste of pears and brie on the pier in Vancouver as the seagulls call and the tiny ferry boats dance on the bay? Tote it with you, or buy it at the nearest market. Restaurants can be confining and expensive—eat like the locals, let the baby relax, and enjoy the sights.

Summer Dinner Picnics

Picnics also are a great way to break the hometown monotony of three meals a day plus snacks, day in, day out. Even in the most urban settings there are usually parks and playgrounds, a patch of fresh green grass, and some swings, a slide, and a sand box. In the summer or fall after a long hot day, it's worth a little extra effort to get out for a dinner picnic. Exchange your stuffy apartment and chilly air-conditioned office for the clean smell of fresh grass and the sound of birds calling and kids playing. Your little picnics will feel like vacations, even if they aren't.

It doesn't have to be fancy. A few sandwiches, some cold salad picked up at the deli on the way over, juice boxes and a bottle of spring water, some cut-up fruit. The idea is simplicity. Call another family and ask them to join you. Spread a blanket, plop down, and watch the baby crawl and the preschoolers run and swing. The sky gradually turns pink, and in the cool evening air, the grown-ups take turns resolving conflicts, pushing the kids in the baby swings, and leisurely eating their food. The kids check in for an occasional bite, and because there is no table, the stress on manners is relieved. The children go home flushed and happy—for a special treat, stop for frozen yogurt on the way home. Everybody will sleep better that night.

Snacks and Snacking

The world is divided into two types of parents: those like my playgroup pal Bonnie, who traveled at all times with a lunch box full of snacks for her kid and other hungry tots; and parents like me. Unless I'm careful, I'll daily knock myself on the head at noon with the realization, "Oh! Lunch!" and then scrounge around the kitchen for something to feed Annie and myself. This wouldn't be so bad except that Bill tends to be that way, too. "Oh! Dinner!" And then we scrounge around again. For people like us, planning ahead is essential—it helps to carry non-perishable snacks at all times, buried in baggies deep in the diaper bag and in the glove compartment of the car.

Snacks have gotten a bad name, when in reality, they're just food. Yes, the world is full of junk-food snacks that can fatten the little calf and make her refuse her dinner, but most little kids need to eat between meals, and healthy foods eaten at "off-hours" are no less nutritious than healthy foods eaten at dinnertime.

Try to select from the basic food groups, and try to offer a mixture.

    🐜 Any food that you carry with you should be non-perishable or kept on ice. (You'll find more details under F for Food Safety, in chapter 14, Trouble-shooting A to Z.)

🍼 Car snacks need a little extra care—avoid cut-up apples, carrots, celery, and other crunchy veggies and fruits—choking danger! Also avoid ice cream—way too messy—and anything with powdered sugar—ditto! Plus, you don't want them bouncing off the car walls, now do you?

🍼 Grapes are great, but make sure you cut them in half for kids under fourteen months.

🍼 Cheese squares or string cheese (be careful of spoilage).

🍼 Dried fruit, dry cereal (individual boxes), cereal "Os" necklaces on dental floss, bananas (but be aware that you might have a major mess on your hands and face, and clothes, and so on), bagels, bread, pretzels (without salt), Goldfish crackers!

🍼 Peel an orange or tangerine. If you're in the car, pass back a few segments at a time. Tastes great and fills the car with a wonderful odor. (For babies, cut them into pieces so they don't have trouble with the membrane.)

Food and Dietary Issues

It's easy to get into food battles—our society is obsessed with food and weight, and few of us are free from these concerns. Very early on, your child will internalize your opinions about food, and about his or her body. I've heard two and one-half-year-olds ask, "Is this food healthy?" or "Will this make me fat?" I once overheard a couple of three-year-olds bantering: "I'm very heavy." "Well, I'm very skinny." (Annie used to announce regularly, "I'm small for my size.")

It's a challenge for most of us to relax, to present healthy food, and let the children regulate their own intake. As Ellyn Satter, author of *Child of Mine* writes, "You are responsible for *what* your child is offered to eat, *where* and *when* it is presented. She is responsible for *how much* of it she eats."

Finding Your Balance

Try to balance what you serve not only between the food groups, but with the fats, salts, sugars, chemicals. If you establish a basically healthy eating and meal pattern, then it's OK to break it a bit while traveling. We eat organic fruits and vegetables at home as much as possible and I'm a regular at my local macrobiotic restaurant (not just because these foods are healthier, they tend to taste better, too), but we're not too rigid about food—the occasional slab of barbecued pork ribs, french fries, gooey chocolate cake, or bright pink cotton candy *does* pass our lips. As I've heard it said, "Everything in moderation, including moderation." By not making these less-healthy foods "off-limits," we manage to eat a balanced diet without feeling as though we're missing something deeply desirable in life.

The Candy Monster

Let me introduce you to a family tradition:

"Hey Annie, the Candy Monster is coming to our house tonight! The Candy Monster *loooves* candy, and that's all he eats. The Candy Monster eats candy for breakfast, candy for lunch, and candy for dinner. And then, do you know what the Candy Monster eats for dessert?"

"What?"

"Salad!"

(Wild giggles) "But he's a nice monster, isn't he, Mommy?"

"Oh, very sweet."

"What does the Candy Monster look like?"

"I don't know, I've never been awake."

"Well, I'll be awake."

"Nope, the Candy Monster is very shy of people, especially kids, and won't come until we're all fast asleep."

The Candy Monster visits three days after Halloween or *any* holiday involving vast quantities of sweets. Our dentist says it takes three days of candy eating for damaging quantities of bacteria to build up in a child's mouth, so rather than fight it, we allow Annie to eat her fill of candy (after meals!) for three days.

On the third evening we decorate a bag ("Write, 'To the Candy Monster from Annie,' Mommy"), put the remaining candy inside, and with great ceremony, place the bag on the porch before going to sleep. The next morning, Voila! The bag is gone! The Candy Monster has been fed, Annie is delighted, the "poison" has been disposed of, and everybody has had fun.

While this may work for three- and four-year-olds, it may not work for older children. When the protests begin, the Candy Monster can take a lesson from its cousin, the Tooth Fairy, and modify its M.O., leaving behind a little toy in trade. Hey, I believe in bribery. More so, I believe in fun.

Dealing with Treats on the Road

Many kids reach an age where the only seemingly acceptable food is buttered noodles. But watch him. What is he really eating? Studies have shown that babies and small children allowed to select their own food from a variety of healthy choices will unconsciously balance the nutrients they receive. Too much sugar in the diet can, however, throw this natural system off.

- Avoid sugary juice or soft drinks—kids should drink mostly water and milk.
- Allow some sweets so they don't become a major power issue.
- Decide on a stance and then stick to it—this will help reduce childhood whining. ("No treats until after dinner," for example, or, "One sugar a day.")
- When you're on vacation, relax your home rules.

Lila and the Lucky Charms

Three-year-old Lila, much to her parents' dismay, is a sugar hound. A few months before they went to Hawaii,

Lila started bugging her parents for Lucky Charms. Anna and Armand began avoiding the cereal aisle, at least while Lila was along for the ride. Anna told Lila, "Lucky Charms are not the kind of food we have for everyday eating, it's vacation food."

Lila is a smart child. Lila has a memory. A few months later, the family went to Hawaii and as soon as the plane hit the runway, Lila asked for Lucky Charms. True to their word, Anna and Armand's first stop after the car rental agency was a supermarket. Lila had Lucky Charms for breakfast every day of the vacation, enjoyed herself immensely, and on the last morning happily dropped the three-fourths empty box into the trash can. "You can have Lucky Charms again on our next vacation," Anna promised.

Fast Food—Overcoming the Golden Arches

We, personally, use fast food only as a last resort. Part of this is because of health concerns—fast food tends to be fatty, salty, and chemically processed. Part of this is aesthetics—I only enjoy fast food if I eat it less than once every three months. But fast food has its place, especially when you're far from home, longing for the familiar, or *starving*. Almost anywhere you go, you'll be able to find those familiar foods. And even Groovy Ericka often finds herself beating down the door of the nearest American-style burger joint after a couple of months overseas.

The advantages to fast food are that it is: fast, familiar, inexpensive, and standardized. Yes, fast food is a boon for the parent on the road, but don't fool yourself—it is not good food. Food is part of the poetry of existence, and part of our responsibility as parents is to educate and cherish our children's palates. Fast food doesn't do that.

If your family struggles with McDonalditus or BurgerKingus:

🍱 Substitute other fun activities for that trip to the fast food joint, like dinner at home and then an evening jaunt to the playground.

🍱 Ethnic restaurants offer a wide variety of good quality, healthy, and inexpensive fast food. You can feast like royalty on burritos, Asian noodles, or good-quality pizza.

🍱 Remember that kids like to eat what the big folks eat. If you keep a watchful eye for sugar and salt content, offer lots of healthy choices, and don't make a fuss about it, your kids will end up eating healthy!

🍱 And yes, if you serve salad at dinnertime for years on end it will, eventually, "take." Just ask Annie.

Well, it was one of those days. Annie and I had sinned and hit McDonald's for lunch. As we were getting out of the car in front of our house, Happy Meal toy clutched in one of Annie's hands, cup of Coke clutched in one of mine, an acquaintance, we'll call her Organic Olga, and her son Olaf happened to walk by. Olaf, at the age of three, had never so much as tasted white sugar or played with a plastic toy. Olga cast one horrified look at Annie and me and our booty, grabbed Olaf, and strode away from us. She's never spoken to me again.

Defeating the Picky Eater

♟ Serve your child very small portions; don't overwhelm her with large amounts. If she wants more, she'll let you know.

♟ Let him serve himself as soon as he can get food from the serving plate to his own.

♟ Encourage her to try everything, but don't force the issue. It's her body—respect it.

♟ Realize that it takes a long time to learn to differentiate between not liking something, liking but not being in the mood for it, and being tired of something. I've watched children gleefully wolf down most of a plateful of something, and then, full to the brim, push the plate away saying, "It's yucky!"

♟ Avoid commenting on how much or how little he is eating. I know, it's hard. You got the food on the

table, now your job is over. Enjoy your own meal. Bite your tongue. Little kids have little power in their lives except over what they ingest. If he understands how concerned you are, he may choose to make food into a power play. He'll eat when he's hungry.

PART TWO
Walking with Baby

CHAPTER 4

Getting Out of Town

Where shall we adventure, today that we're afloat,
Wary of the weather and steering by a star?
Shall it be to Africa, a-steering of the boat,
To Providence, to Babylon, or off to Malabar?
—*Robert Louis Stevenson*

Geography Is Destiny

Okay, let's get to the meat of the matter. You've got the basics down, now you're ready for the big stuff. Getting on a plane, maybe, or spending some nights away from home. Here's the $40,000 question: Where are you going?

Choosing a destination is vital to ensuring that you and your little ones will have a good time. In the Hugh Lofting *Dr. Doolittle* books I read fervently as a young child, the good doctor-who-talked-with-the-animals and his pals Dab Dab the Duck, Gub Gub the Pig, and the two-headed Pushmepullyou chose their next adventure's destination by gathering around the map of the world, throwing a dart, and going wherever it landed.

(One time the dart landed in the middle of an ocean—
and off they sailed!) Though romantic and adventurous,
this is not a recommended approach for traveling with
babies and small kids.

Whether you're traveling overseas or domestically,
you face the same decision-making process.

Step 1: What *TYPE* of trip?

The world is a huge place, full of different types of destinations. Are you in the mood for excitement and adventure?
For relaxation? Do you want to hang out with other
people, or are you sick, sick, *sick* of the teeming masses?
Does your small one vomit on windy roads? Do you *really*
need to shower every day? The short descriptions below
should help you get the destination discussion started.

Urban. In any city, there are activities for children,
and often they are low-cost or free (see chapter 6). If you
need relaxation, look somewhere else; a busy city's pace
can be infectious and stimulating. Might be just what
the doctor ordered to cure your baby blahs.

Rural. Especially for city toddlers, a rural setting can
be more exotic than a trip to Sao Paulo or Cairo.
Toddlers who've only known cats, dogs, and pigeons will
love watching cows being milked and eggs being gath-
ered—and learn important lessons. Digging potatoes,
harvesting cherries or pumpkins—all those activities
that are chores to kids who live in the country are
adventures to city kids and their parents. Enjoy a slower
pace of life. Stand under a night sky in all its starry
glory. A trip to the country also can require a great deal
of adult energy—farms are not childproofed, ponds
don't always have fences, horses kick—be prepared to
watch your child like a cat watches a birdbath.

The road trip. With the right preparation and
mental attitude, a few days in a car can be a fun family
adventure. Watch out—too much driving and grown-
ups get crabby, kids get restless, and siblings fight. But all
that time together is a great way for a family to create or

renew bonds. And who knows what you might discover around the next bend in the road?

Beaches—oceans and lakes. The classic family vacation—the little kids spend their days running and digging in the sand, the adults relax and contemplate the idea of wallowing in a trashy novel. Kick back, soak up the rays, but be prepared! The sun can easily burn your baby's delicate skin, and the water is deep and strong. However, at the end of a busy, wet, sandy day, your toddler will sleep like a log.

Imagine Maui…

Smooth white sand stretches in either direction; children cavort, chase each other, tumble, and fall giggling into the frothy waves. Beaming adults read novels. The green surf purrs. Leave your baby with your partner and float over glowing coral reefs and deep canyons, waving seaweeds, colorful fish, sea turtles, eels, the warm sun on your back. Or, stand waist deep in the blue green waves holding your frightened two-year-old. Look down—a small school of colorful fish is visible through the clear water, swimming through your legs, nibbling gently at your knees. A little foot slides down, and your daughter slowly relaxes her lower body into the ocean. Delighted, she looks at you. "It's warm and cold at the same time!"

Organized fun. Family resorts, theme parks, cruises—while most tours are not appropriate for children, family travel is big business these days, and many areas have travel agents who specialize in family vacations (check out the Resources Appendix). Some cities and universities sponsor inexpensive family camps where *they* do the cooking and *you* do the relaxing. There are real benefits to the organized approach: you'll meet lots of other families, the activities are geared towards kids, you know kids are appreciated, and somebody else does all the planning for you!

Outdoor adventure. Backpacking, skiing, or camping with your children is a wonderful way to incorporate them into your interests. Logistics can be rough—no amenities. But exposing your child to nature early can lead to a lifetime of love and respect for nature (you'll find many more details in Chapter 11).

Foreign. Visiting other countries can provide educational and stimulating adventures. Unless the foreign country is very near, make sure you have enough time to balance out the hassles of long flights, jet lag, and culture shock. Some developing nations provide great value for the dollar—once you get there. Read chapter 13 and strongly consider climate and medical factors. Then go—and have a great time!

The family reunion. For little kids, spending time with extended family provides a sense of their personal history as well as an opportunity to just hang out with relatives they may rarely see. For you, it may provide an opportunity to pass the baby to your aunties-with-the-hungry-arms. (And it may be a nightmare of well-meaning but inappropriate advice.) Family reunions can be a great choice when traveling with more than one child. Siblings tend to do their best at family reunions since there are lots of adults to connect with and often cousins their own ages. The kids disappear to play, checking in only occasionally, and, for a moment or so, you remember what it's like to be an adult!

Going Home Again

Visiting the homestead? Even if you own a palapa in Yalapa or are off to visit lonesome family in Laredo, there's probably lots you *don't* know about the old hometown. Now that you are a parent, you're returning to old haunts with new eyes. ("I've been to this park sixty times; I never realized there was a playground here!" or: "Our zoo has the finest collection of wombats in the world? Amazing!")

The joint family vacation. Joint family vacations can be wonderful, or they can ruin friendships—so think carefully about who to travel with, and make sure that...

- You discuss your plans and expectations about the trip, including food issues and how much time you want to spend together.
- You are operating on a similar budget.
- Your travel "styles" are compatible (some people are early risers, some are lazy-bones; some like to "hang," some need to see everything; some buy everything in sight, some are thrifty, etc.).
- If your styles aren't compatible, you all know it and are comfortable with that fact.

Step 2—Consider Your Children's Development and Temperament

As you consider each type of trip, consider your child's developmental stage and general temperament.

Each age has its complications and its joys. Now might be a good time to pull out those books on child development and review. Step into Jenny or Joey's teeny-tiny shoes and think, "Would I want to spend four days strapped into a car seat as my parents drive across country?" "Would I like the ocean?"

Infants and Small Babies

Babies can enjoy a trip to any venue as long as their needs for food, shelter, comfort, and love are met. In some ways, the best time to travel with a baby is before the squirmer is mobile. For nursing mothers, travel can be a breeze (as you learned in Chapter 2.) Many people recommend very short trips with an infant. Always consider your fatigue factor and don't push it. If your infant is colicky and you are delirious with exhaustion, you might want to wait a few months. On the other hand, car travel is an age-old remedy for soothing colicky babies. Babies sleep a lot—especially in planes, trains, and cars. This can be a bonus!

The Older Baby

Traveling with older babies can be fantastic. In the second half of their first year, babies are often at the peak of their baby cuteness—little ambassadors who provide great entertainment for you and other baby-friendly adults. They'll love having Mommy and/or Daddy with them at all times. Rarely are they so mobile that they can get away from you—but be cautious! The baby that walks early has physical abilities without common sense. Take extra safety precautions. And babies can be overwhelmed by too much stimulation. Build in a lot of "down" time.

Toddlers

Toddlers are entranced by the world, and what fascinates them may surprise you. Travel with a toddler and you'll see the world through refreshed eyes; the twist of an ornate fence, the puppy in the window of a shop. Toddlers are self-centered. They work hard on internalizing their own veto power—a fancy way of saying they love to say "No!" As they become more aware of the world and their place in it, stranger-anxiety becomes common.

Toddlers like to walk *sometimes*. Luckily, they're not too big to pick up, and they're sturdy enough to put down. (Though when you try to, they have a bad habit of retracting their legs into their body, thus straining your back irrevocably.) Plan to go slow. Build in "down" time, and provide opportunities for daily physical play.

Preschoolers

Three- and four-year-olds can be great travel companions—old enough to enjoy learning about new places, and fun to talk to about them. Many of them are past the stormy two-year-old tantrum stage, but be prepared for nagging and whining. The famous quote, "Are we there yet?" was invented by a three-year-old. Like toddlers, kids this age need plenty of exercise every day. Sleeping in strange places can be scary for preschoolers—maintain as many bedtime rituals as you can and provide lots of reassurance.

Consider Mobility

Richard Langer in his classic book, *The Joy of Camping*, divides children into three distinct categories: Carry-alongs, Anchors, and Catch-Me-If-You-Cans. Carry-along babies are the easiest to lug—they fall asleep in backpacks and can follow their own rhythms most naturally.

Anchors (otherwise known as the Toddler and Preschooler set), are too little to walk all the time and too big and restless to be constantly carried. This is a good period for base travel—choose a lovely spot, get there, and venture out briefly.

Once your child is seven or so, she'll become a Catch-Me-If-You-Can—you'll be eating her dust up the mountain trail.

More Than One

It's a challenge to travel with kids in different stages of development. Gear the pace of travel to the youngest, but make sure activities will be available for all the kids. Travel is definitely different with two or more, and it's best to be prepared. Read the sibling material in *Becoming the Parent You Want to Be* by Laura Davis and Janis Keyser (this book is listed in the Recommend Readings Appendix), and talk with other parents with two or more kids. And then go!

Sibling Stress

Travel can be stressful. Over the course of any trip, make sure to take some focused time alone with your kids every day. Try an outdoor activity. How about the local playground? Be prepared for fur to fly—they may very well take their added stress out on each other.

Sometimes the stress is displaced. Say Emma's feeling a little jealous—at the family reunion, Cousin Annie got the biggest cookie at dessert, and Grandma Karla whispered a secret in Annie's ear! Rather than take it out on Annie, Emma might bonk her little sister Alexandra for no reason at all when they are alone at the playground.

Remember: Your kids will feel most comfortable with each other. They'll "clear" their emotions with each other. Doesn't mean you have to put up with it, just understand that it might occur.

Know Thyself, Know Thy Child

Understanding your child's temperament, and your own, is a big part of the secret to making good decisions about what *type* of trip to take, where *to*, and for *how long*.

Modify all advice you receive from guidebooks, friends, or me with self-knowledge (and improve your self-knowledge by checking out Temperament under T in chapter 14, Troubleshooting A to Z). Don't expect yourself, or your child, to become a different person once you're on the road. If heat makes you grumpy, try to avoid heat. If your kid has a hard time with strangers, either modify the trip or expect the behavior that too many strangers elicits in your child. You cannot force a boisterous child to be silent in a quiet setting. You can't force your child to enjoy Disneyland if she flips out in large crowds.

What if your child is firmly set in her routines and howls if something new is introduced? Go slow, but go. Take as many routines with you as you possibly can—the "Morning song", the "Bedtime story," the "This-is-the-way-we-wash-our-face poem". These rituals are the bedrock of your child's existence. With a few key rituals that she can rely on, your child will learn to be flexible. Flexibility is one of life's great coping mechanisms. Better to teach your child to be flexible now than to watch her suffer later because she is unable to cope with a swiftly changing world.

Quick Tip

ID bracelets or dog tags are a good idea for all children, especially mobile ones. If you're staying at a hotel, tuck a hotel business card into a child's hard-to-access pocket. As soon as they are able, teach kids their full name and phone number. Leave an emergency number on your answering machine or service at home—that way, if your kid is found, you can be located.

Be kind to your less-stalwart child; show patience and compassion, but get them into the world. You become their home, their security, their routine. Pack extra loveys and plan to spend a lot of quiet time in hotel rooms or quiet country pastures with little stimulation. Calm their fears. Love them enough to show them the world.

Children with Special Needs

Kids with medical problems or mental or physical disabilities can travel, too. Plan to modify your activities to fit your kid's needs. Consult your pediatrician for any special advice, and choose a destination where those needs can be easily met. (Many resources exist for travelers with disabilities, I've listed a few in the Resources Appendix under Disability Resources.)

When to Go Where

Not all vacations, or "travels" are age-appropriate with small children. Think long-term (maybe not the Himalayas this year; wait until Angela likes to hike). You have many years of parenting and travel ahead of you.

Step 3: Establish Your Travel and Budget Style

Reality can be painful—how much money do you have, and how much time? There are many ways to have a fabulous time with a limited amount of both money and time. Sometimes money is short, sometimes time, often both.

Independent Travel On-the-Cheap

When you're broke, just getting out of your own environment can do a world of good for your mental state. Visit friends or family in a nearby city for a weekend. Inexpensive "street" food (hot dogs and pizza slices in this country, you name it in others) can be as delicious and more fun (though not always as sanitary) as dinner at the Ritz.

Or throw in the towel, put the furniture in storage, grab your kid, and head for Laos. It is possible to travel the world on pennies and take your kids along, too; we've met people shoe-stringing with young kids and babies all over Asia (see those inspirational stories in chapter 13). Not ready for something that extreme? Camping is cheaper than hotels, and often more fun for little ones, too. Even nearby state parks can provide cheap camping facilities (more on the joy of outdoors in chapter 10.)

Pros: More bang for your buck. On-the-cheap travel makes adventure affordable for just about anybody.

Cons: Less comfort and more potential travel hassles than a more organized, structured family vacation.

Caution: Don't ever be thrifty when it comes to safety and medical care.

Tips for Saving Money (Or Making It Affordable)

Ask. Ask for discounts (AAA, family discounts, discounts because you're a nice person, AARP discounts). Ask at hotels, car rental agencies, cruise offices...ask!

Check the "bucket shops"—**discount travel agents**—for cheap air tickets. Make sure they don't mess up your booking (always check it with the airlines, too). Bucket shops often advertise in Sunday newspaper travel sections.

Be flexible about travel dates. Off-season rates are *significantly* lower for both hotels and airfare than high-season rates.

Call hotels directly when looking for inexpensive rooms. Don't use the 800 number (the cost of the phone call may be well worth the savings). We were once quoted $300 for a room in Bangkok on the 800 line—and $55 directly at the hotel.

Package deals really are deals (usually). Sometimes the car is virtually thrown in free!

Go for the **cheap room in the expensive hotel** (do you really care about the view?).

Once you get there, ask the hotel if they have **discount coupons** for local restaurants or services. They often do.

When going to a resort area, book a hotel a **short distance from the beach** instead of right on it.

Keep an eye on the exchange rate and choose destinations where you can take advantage of the strong dollar. You'll aid the local economy and aid your own personal economy, too.

Going the Extra Dollar

When Bill and I traveled in India, the difference between a dump and a decent bed, between rancid, inedible food and a delicacy, was often little more than a single dollar. An ounce more comfort—and a little more money—can often make a tremendous difference to a young child. We're still budget travelers, but we've learned our lessons well. And a trip with a little kid is no time to fool around. We watch our budget, but spend more than we used to. We buy little, and opt for comfort.

Pros: Makes travel affordable without too much stress.

Cons: Often takes more time to seek out the good deals.

Quick tip

Follow the business traveler. From our travels in Mexico and India we've learned to stay in business traveler hotels where the amenities and costs fall between tourist hotels and dumps.

The Classic Middle Class Vacation

You'll probably spend too much, but you'll have a great time. You'll come home relaxed, having let somebody else do much of the planning. You'll have memories, souvenirs, and probably too many slides to torture the neighbors with. Since you probably only take a trip like this once a year, what the hay!

Pros: Somebody else is doing a lot of the work. You're free to enjoy.

Cons: So, you come home broke! So what?

The Total Treat

What a life! Bring along a baby-sitter, schedule massages and daily facials, enjoy breakfast in bed as you lie in your penthouse suite overlooking the warm ocean. Be pampered. Have it all done for you.

Pros: Everything.

Cons: Unless you are very wealthy, vacations like this will, by financial necessity, be very short and rare.

Step 4: Gather Information and Decide

Talk to friends, visit the travel section in your local library and bookstore, contact chambers of commerce, call a travel agent. For every destination, consider what there is to do, for you and your kids. Ask lots of questions. Take it all with a grain of salt. Relax, breathe deep, don't stress...

Working with a Travel Agent

Many travel agents specialize in family travel and will understand—maybe even anticipate—your special needs. Many travel agents charge a small commission for every ticket they sell you (around $13 per ticket) and it's probably worth it for the information and the service. When you approach a travel agent, it's helpful to have a general sense of the type of experience you'd like for your trip *before* you make that first call. Don't feel apologetic for asking questions and making certain you get exactly what you need. Travel agenting is a service industry—they are there to help you. (It is not nice, however, to spend hours getting information from one agency and then buy the tickets from another agency, or from the airlines themselves.)

A good travel agent should have more than good rates on tickets, he or she should be accredited as a Certified Travel Consultant, and should be a member of ASTA.

Late Night Internet Browsing

After the baby is finally (or at least for the moment) *down*, hit the Internet and do more research on your own, not only on tickets (yes, you can *definitely* get some great deals) but also on potential destinations. Because web pages tend to be visual, you can virtually see the cabins on that Costa Rican coast or the size of the rooms in that Casablanca hotel. More hotels—even the tiny ones—have websites than you think. Plus every city in the world's chamber of commerce seems to be in on the act, too. The Resource Appendix lists a few travel sites to start with for information and for booking.

The Right Place

Once you decide on the type of trip you'll take, get a general sense of your travel style, analyze your family's needs, and do your destination research, all you need to do is decide. Choose a destination that will delight all of you, *including* the adults. Don't skimp on yourself—you have to have a good time, too. Enjoyment is infectious and so is tension. If you're relaxed and having fun, your kids will have a good time, too.

Buyer's Regret

Some people (it seems to be a matter of temperament) will always have buyers regret; that ticket to France means *not* going to China, that ticket to Shanghai means missing the Eiffel Tower. Bill's like that.

Yes, indeed, the world is a big place, and there will always be the road not taken… "Next year, Honey."

Planning Ahead

Whoa, Nellie, there's more work to do! Now that you're really going, you need to make some plans.

Plan your itinerary to minimize fatigue and crankiness. Children need to play. Build in "down time" every day of the trip. You may not cover as much territory, but you will all be much happier.

Try not to drive during rush hour. Plan to leave early, stop early, and enjoy relaxing afternoons.

Ericka's Rule: With a baby or small child, places are farther away than they look on the map. Here's a good guideline: the number of hours it takes to reach a vacation destination should not exceed the number of days you stay there. That means no four-hour car rides to visit friends for a two-day weekend, and don't brave that twenty hour flight to Thailand unless you've got at least three weeks to relax and eat tropical fruit (yum!).

Schedule your days, but build in flexibility. Spontaneity is the spice of travel—don't schedule the trip so tightly that you can't pull over to watch the cows eating, pick up berries at a fruit stand, or spend twenty minutes at a cool bookstore you happen upon next to the restaurant.

When planning your trip, *always* make reservations for *at least* the first night. If you hate the hotel or motel you can make changes in the morning, when you and the baby are fresh.

Build in private time for the adults—alone and together. All-day-every-day togetherness can be oppressive, no matter how much you all love each other. Partners can take turns doing separate activities—one plays, one has private time with the baby. Hotels often provide sitting services (and you'll find out about *that* in chapter 9). Adults traveling alone with kids deserve a break, too.

And try not to expect perfection. Aspects of traveling with little ones can be hard. Your other option is to stay home and not have a life...and that is *not* acceptable.

Reducing Conflict in Advance

On the road, normal routines and rules are often disrupted. Before you leave, discuss with your traveling partner (or, if you are traveling alone with the kids, decide for yourself) what you'll do about special food treats, buying souvenirs, bedtime, TV. Some parents relax their normal rules, others feel it's important to remain consistent on the road. Work towards finding policies that are comfortable for both parents. Knowing where you stand on these tricky issues before you go may help you avoid uncomfortable policy fights.

Three things to help ensure happy travels:

1. A sense of humor
2. No tight timelines
3. Flexibility to (radically) change your plans

If you can't have the last two things (and, as Mick Jagger says, we can't always get what we want), concentrate on the first thing ("it's funny, it's funny, it's funny, it's funny....")

The Last Word

And go *now*. When your children are babies and toddlers you have a certain flexibility that you may not have again for years once school schedules come into play.

CHAPTER 5

Lugging the Little Rug Rat Around

What's the use of worrying?
It never was worthwhile,
So pack up your troubles in your old kit-bag
And smile, smile, smile.
—George Asaf

Hitting the Road, Jack

All right...ready, set, go! Travel is about traveling, not just about the experiences you'll have once you get there. The minute you leave the house, you begin dealing with transportation systems—feet, cars, buses, subways, boats—you name it. This chapter is about managing the moving around part of traveling with babies and little kids. Some sections are broken into "local" and long-distance travel but, as you'll find, the same tips and information often apply both near and far from home. After all, walking with your toddler from home to the post office involves some of the same issues as walking from the *l'hôtel* to the Notre Dame.

And, a crying baby in a car seat won't know whether she's cruising the highway near Cleveland or Rio de Janeiro.

Hoofing It

Wherever in the world you are, you will probably be doing some walking and, at least part of the time, bearing the burden of Baby.

The Long March (Around the Block)

You start small—you leave your house for a walk. Terrific!—a trip around the block is an adventure for a toddler. The very smallest walkers may spend hours getting from point A to point B. Kids with another temperament might take off and be somewhere around point Q while you're still getting off the front stoop.

Obsessions!

At about fourteen months old, our friend Jesse became obsessed with parking meters. He'd point and moan and fuss until his stroller was wheeled over to it and he could pat the cold metal pole. Only then would he be satisfied—until his stroller was wheeled past the next meter. Since meters are usually only a few feet apart, navigating commercial streets became a bit of a challenge.

Annie, on the other hand, was entranced by key holes. I'd never noticed how many small, low key holes there are on any given street—commercial buildings with glass doors locking on the bottom, garage doors handles, and so on. As she toddled along, Annie wanted to, no, *needed* to touch each and every lock with a single, tiny index finger.

"Carry me, Daddy!"—Saving Your Spine

For the next few years you will be bending and lifting a constantly inflating bundle of wriggling flesh—your baby. Remember to bend your knees when picking your baby up, and try to alternate which side you carry baby on. Strollers have saved many a spine. When actually walking with your child, consider a front pack for a small baby, and a backpack for a larger baby (I'll discuss backpacks in a bit). Once your toddler outgrows the backpack, you may still be able to negotiate a stroller. Or you may simply have to negotiate: "Honey, you are big enough to walk now. I'll hold your hand."

> Sadie doesn't walk. She operates in two modes: Running and Carried.

Herding Behavior of the Human Young

Remember the sheepdogs in the movie *Babe*, how they raced 'round and 'round the sheep, underfoot, nipping at their heels, until the sheep went the way the dogs wanted them to, baa-ing all the way? Toddlers often act like sheepdogs. They'll run in front of your feet and stop, refuse to move, and start yapping, "Pick me up, pick me up, pick me up, pick me up!" At two and one-half, Annie began her sheep-dog behavior. At four and one-half, the end was not in sight.

"Don't Pick Me Up!"

And if your kid refuses to be carried? Recite today's mantra: "His agenda is different from my agenda. His agenda is different from my agenda." Then either put up with his behavior, or put up with the evil looks of strangers who think you're killing your child as you forcibly pick him up and haul him away.

Solving the Great Leash Controversy

If you've got an active kid and not enough speed or hands or either but don't want to use a child leash, try this solution: sometimes people with very active children use wrist bands—two rubber wrist bands with a stretchy cord between attaching parent to child and child to parent. You may get a few glares from strangers, but your child won't get a sore back from walking with his arm in the air, and the alternative (a child in traffic or a lost child) is far worse.

Choosing Your Tote-Mode: Backpacks, Slings, and Strollers

Until they are well into their preschool years, children will often need to be toted. Luckily, many options are available to save your back and free your hands.

Front Carrier or Sling?

For infants, front carriers provide a good way to keep your little baby close to your body—since that is where she wants to be—and enable you to move around and actually do stuff.

Slings—swaths of wide fabric that strap over one shoulder and down your side—are also very popular. Wait until baby is born to buy a carrier or sling, then borrow a friend's to try it out. Many babies like to be carried in a particular way and you won't know that way until you have your particular baby. (Do you have a vertical baby or a horizontal baby? Belly baby or back baby? You'll know.) Make sure to alternate sides when you're using the sling. With some brands, it is even possible to nurse your baby while on the go. Talk about subtle!

Backpacks

Once your baby gains the strength to hold her head up (usually around four months), you can carry her around the neighborhood or around the world in a baby backpack. Babies and toddlers usually love being so high, and you'll enjoy the freedom of movement. If the backpack is the proper fit, your child will be able to look over your shoulder to encounter the world, yet have the warmth of your body in front of her for emotional support, and the back of the pack for physical support. Many babies prefer to nap while in the backpack. Go ahead, take a hike! Get in shape while baby sleeps! Stroll around the neighborhood. If you poop out, take a bus home.

Baby backpacks can usually carry up to forty pounds (when your baby is approximately four years old), though some top-of-the-line models can carry up to sixty pounds. (Do you really want to carry sixty pounds of child on your back?) In addition, most baby backpacks come with rear pouches for carrying diapers, wipes, clothing, and other supplies. Some also come with sun, rain, or wind screens. Accessorize!

There are many types of backpacks available, depending upon your needs. A good children's store or camping supply house should have a broad selection. Ask for help—the fit matters!

> **Warning:** Never carry your wallet in the back pouch of a baby backpack. It's an easy target.

Baby backpacks have somewhat wobbly retractable stands for loading and unloading your child, leaving him asleep in a restaurant (braced by the wall), or putting him down (with your support) for a short break where he can see the world. Ideally, loading Baby into the pack involves two adults, and, indeed, the manufacturers tell you not to load the backpack alone. If you must, practice getting the backpack off and on before you go for a jaunt alone with the baby. There are at least two techniques:

Try putting Baby in with the stand extended. Then lift the pack 'n baby onto a higher surface, and back into it.

Put Baby in, cross your arms, grasp the straps, and swing the backpack (with baby) around onto your back.

No matter how you get the pack on, make sure to always attach all the straps to yourself—both belt and chest restraints. This will help save that back of yours. You only get one.

Packing It through Europe

In Europe we opted for a lightweight backpack. Annie was able to view the world from her perch and we took turns toting the well-balanced load. In Italy, our pack was looked at longingly by many Venetian mothers who spend their days pulling strollers up and down the four hundred bridges of Venice (many people don't know that the famed Venetian bridges are all steps).

Umbrella Strollers

There are strollers and there are *strollers*, and they range in price from $20 to over $300 for the schmancy ones. For travel, the most useful stroller is usually the collapsible "umbrella" stroller. They are small, light, and inexpensive. They can easily live in the trunk of your car or be checked through at the airport. Umbrella strollers are more suitable for the "older" baby through small preschooler, as they don't provide enough head or body support for infants.

If you have a large clunky stroller and are going on a short trip, consider renting or borrowing a light-weight one. Many children's stores rent them.

Packs and strollers are not welcome in all European locales. In both the Rodin museum in Paris and in the Van Gogh in Amsterdam we were requested to check the backpack. Be prepared to argue your case (we won in Amsterdam) and be prepared to lose (we lost in Paris).

Combo Stroller/Car Seats and Stroller/Backpacks

When you hit the baby supply stores (whether in person or over the Internet) you'll find a variety of combination stroller/car seats and stroller/backpacks. They cost a bit more than one (stroller, carseat, or backpack) but not quite as much as two. I've yet to see a three-way combination— but maybe I'm not looking hard enough. Combination carriers are not for every family, though many travelers swear by them. You can, for instance, stroll your baby down the road to the trailhead then, presto change-o, pop her on your back and hike up the mountain. Better yet are the stroller carseats. If you do a lot of moving around with your baby (yay!), consider checking out these options.

And Let That Baby Crawl!

No matter which tote method you decide on for your little one, be careful that you don't rely on it too much of the time. A child must move her body—she needs lots of time on the floor learning to crawl, and, once she can walk, she needs lots of time to run and walk unrestrained. It's important not only for her emotional well-being, but for her physical and neurological development as well.

In the Car—Short Trips and Long Travels

If you're an average American, you're gonna spend a lot of time in the car. Most children learn to like, or at least tolerate, the car from a very early age. Many won't nap during the day anywhere else. Riding in the car is soothing and entertaining—as long as the ride isn't too long. The information below is applicable to short, local trips as well as trips abroad.

Infant, Toddler, and Booster Safety Seats

Child restraint seats come in three types: infant, toddler, and booster. There are good reasons that safety seats for infants and toddlers are now a requirement in every state—they save lives. Look for booster seats (for kids over four years and forty pounds) to be increasingly required. Child restraint seats are designed to keep the baby or child from being thrown forward during a crash. They also distribute the crash force over the child's body so that no single area takes the full brunt.

Here's the problem: little kids *must* be strapped in for safety, and little kids *need* to move their bodies. Neither is optional. Here's the solution: keep the car trip short, and/or keep the breaks frequent.

Infant Seats

Infant seats are the law—you won't be allowed to take your new baby home from the hospital until a nurse verifies that you have an infant seat installed in your car. Infant seats face backwards in a reclining position. They attach with the usual, car-equipped seat belt or with the built-in anchoring systems in cars built beginning in 2002.

Most infant seats can double as baby carriers for the first couple of months, until your kid gets too heavy and your arm feels like it's about to break off. Just undo the seatbelt or latch holding the infant seat in place, and *voila!* No need to wake up Baby. There are infant seats with and without bases, seats that turn into strollers (see above), and seats that are round at the bottom and rock.

We had great success with the model we used for Annie as an infant—the rounded bottom enabled us to get through dinner for the first three months.

Buying Car Seats

Used car seats can be risky—are you sure it's never been in a crash? Are the instructions included? Are all the straps in place? Don't accept a seat unless you are sure it meets all codes. If you can, before you buy a particular brand, ask friends with babies who have the same model how they like it. Here's a bit of scary not-so-trivia: not all car seats fit all cars! The car company who made your car should have a list of what fits what.

Toddler Seats

Once your child grows to twenty pounds and is a year old, he can go into a toddler car seat. Toddler seats face forwards so the child can see out of the windows. They, like infant seats, are safest when installed in the middle of the back seat. Make sure to periodically check the car seat's adjustments to accommodate for your child's growth. Also remember to adjust the straps for different climates. A strap that is snug and reassuring on a sunny autumn day may be tight and binding in winter, with all those extra layers.

Children heavier than twenty pounds and younger than one-year-old still need the physical support of riding backwards. It's a developmental thing. If your baby is a bruiser, try a convertible infant/toddler seat—you can use it facing the rear up to thirty-five pounds.

Booster Seats

Boosters look enough like a regular seat to satisfy most children that they are a "big kid," yet the best ones retain their five-point harnesses for kids between thirty and forty-five pounds, and provide an over-the-collar belt for kids from forty-five pounds up.

Do you need to "boost" your child? It depends. Booster seat legislation is changing rapidly. It used to be that at four years old and forty pounds your children could technically leave all that behind, and take their risks like the grown-ups in a regular seat belt. Legally, in most states, that's still true (though legislation is changing constantly). In some states, child restraints are now required up to six years and sixty pounds—and that means a booster. But even if your state (and the states you'll be traveling through) don't yet require boosters, for safety and sensibility, plan to seat your child in a booster seat while she's between forty and eighty pounds—that's the National Highway Safety Transportation Agency's recommendation.

Children and Air Bags and Safety, Oh My!

Never put your child in a seat with an airbag; babies, children, and airbags don't mix. The force at which an airbag is released in an accident can severely injure or kill a small child. Do *not* seat your toddler or child in the front passenger seat of a car with an airbag (not only is this dangerous, it may be illegal in your state). Kids under twelve are safest riding in the back seat of the car, anyway. Rear-facing infant seats are not designed for use with passenger-side airbags. The NHTSA hotline and website (listed in the Resources Appendix) have hot tips on which vehicles have manual on/off switches for airbags. If you're buying a new car, make sure to check with them first.

Emergency/First-Aid Kit for the Car

Fill a cardboard or metal box with the following items: a list of emergency phone numbers, some coins, a flashlight, a couple of flares, two diapers, a baggy of diaper wipes, Band-Aids, antiseptic, safety pins, tweezers, children's Tylenol, a thermometer, sunscreen, gauze pads, scissors, washcloth, a small bottle of water. Keep it in the trunk or the back of the car. Forget about it. You'll remember it someday when you need it, and you'll be happy it's there. Bonus: transfer this emergency kit into a travel bag for quick getaways!

Sleep and Run

So how *do* you carry three sleeping children into the apartment when there are only two of you and the only parking place is two blocks away? In theory, it goes like this: the strongest adult gets dropped at the door, and totes the two smallest sleeping kids up the stairs. The other adult finds the parking spot, and totes the remaining snoring child. In reality, unless you have the brawn of Arnold Schwarzenegger, or progeny who sleep like Rip Van Winkle, somebody is going to wake up—usually in a cranky mood—and that one will wake up the others. Oh well, sleep is overrated anyway.

Eating in the Car

Warning: You're gonna get good at the back-hand back-seat pass maneuver.

True meals in the car are not a great idea—you need mealtime to stretch the body. However, it's a good idea to have snacks with you during car travel (go back and review the car snack suggestions in chapter 3), and it's a must to carry water—in sippy cups, baby bottles, or, for the over-three crowd, in small plastic bottles or cups with straws. Avoid juice in the car—it's sticky when it spills (and it *will* spill), and the sugar will get your child wired (you don't want *that* in a confined space) and may even get them thirstier. If you're determined to do juice, try juice boxes. (Check the sugar content—there is a great juice scam going in this country, and sometimes "juice" contains very little juice at all.)

Be aware of the dangers of choking. Avoid small hard foods, ice, and anything that could possibly plug a weeny-teeny windpipe. If possible, have an adult sit in the back with the child during munch sessions.

The Case of the Missing Hamburger

It was one of those days—too many errands and I'd forgotten to budget time for lunch. On the horizon loomed the Golden Arches and so, with pangs of P.C. guilt and regret, I pulled into the drive-thru line, ordered a Happy Meal for Annie (Burger, Apple Juice, Toddler Toy) and a Filet O' Fish for me. No sooner had I unwrapped her burger, placed it in her hungry fist, wolfed my own morsel, and gotten back on the freeway towards home when three-year-old Annie let loose a mighty wail:

"Mommy, I lost my hamburger!"

With my right hand I felt behind me onto her lap, careening for a moment on the freeway. No burger. I cast a quick glance at the floor. No. The windows had been, and still were, closed.

Annie howled, "I'm hungry! I want my burger!" Finally, I pulled off at the next exit, stopped, and tore the car seat and car apart. Annie's burger was nowhere to be found. Though she denies it to this day, I came to the only conclusion possible: she'd eaten it. Or…was it hamburger-eating fairies protecting her from the evils of fast food? We'll never know for sure.

Soothing the Screaming Little Baby…

Depending on how adept you are, you can even learn to nurse your baby in a moving car while she is still strapped into her car seat—as a passenger, not a driver, of course (I don't even want to try to visualize that picture). If your child is in a rear-facing infant seat, sit in the back seat next to her, and lean forward and over. Try bracing yourself on the front seat. This won't work for long (unless you are a circus contortionist).

…the Screaming Bigger Baby

Talk sweetly, sing, play with him. Offer him a snack. If you need to nurse a child in a forward facing seat, you'll have to be even *more* adept, and some physiques will never be able to accomplish it. Try it a few times when the car isn't moving. Make sure the neighbors can't see—they may think you've gone totally bozo. Believe me, if your family is cruising down the German autobahn at 160 kilometers an hour without an exit in sight with a screaming baby, you'll be glad you figured this trick out, neighbors be damned.

…and the Screaming Toddler

Sometimes you can reason with them ("Breathe, honey, use your words, I can't understand what you want when you are screaming like that") and sometimes you cannot. Try to change the mood by playing a tape, or by offering a treat. Try ear plugs (just kidding). Try a "stretch break." Then try another one. Some folks stop more often for their *dogs* than their kids (no, I'm not talking about you!).

The Booga Booga Method

This is a method developed by my Aunt Kathie in which the whole family gets out of the car, once an hour on the hour, and runs three times around the car, waving their arms high in the air and screaming, *"Booga, booga, booga!"*

This method has the added bonus of amusing drowsy fellow motorists, causing them to perk up, and thus preventing any number of accidents caused by sleeping at the wheel.

Cruise While They Snooze

For driving long distances, try leaving late at night or early in the morning (depending upon your temperament) so you can get in many solid hours of driving while your children blissfully dream of sugar plums, being forced to *share*, or whatever else little ones dream about. When Bill drove from Oakland to Los Angeles alone with four-year-old Annie, he left at 9 P.M. and drove into the night. Annie fell asleep after an excited hour of chatter, and Bill, who usually hits his stride after 10 P.M. anyway, was free to drive and ponder life in glorious silence.

Rental Cars and Car Seats

Most U.S. car-rental companies rent car seats of all three types, infant, toddler, and booster, usually for about five dollars a day. You'll need to reserve the carseat in advance, and you probably will need to return it at the same place you picked it up. Ask if any of their rental cars have built-in car seats.

Here are some reasons why you should bring your own car seat, rather than rent one:

Safety. If your seat is approved by the National Highway Transportation Safety Administration (all the decent ones are—and you'll know by the embossed NHTSA logo), you can use it on the airplane. (More details on this in chapter 8.)

Familiarity. Babies and little kids get very accustomed to their car seats, and very territorial. In a strange place, familiar items help keep them calm.

Fit. You'll know it fits your child. Every brand of car seat has a different "fit." When you rent a seat through a car rental, you don't know what you're getting until you get there, and you may not have the choice of changing.

You'll have the option of a one-way rental.

You'll even save some money. Five buckaroos a day starts to add up.

What Size Car Should You Rent?

Advantages of a Smaller Car

- If you're traveling with just one child, you probably won't need more space.
- You'll save money (rental fees plus gas can add up).
- Parking (in cities) becomes easier.
- Keeps you from packing—and buying—too much stuff.

Advantages of a Bigger Car

- If you have more than one kid (especially more than one in a car seat) you will need the extra room.
- Generally a more comfortable drive.
- Power. You don't want to drive a sewing machine on wheels.
- You can take as much stuff as you like, and fill the trunk with souvenirs for Dear Aunt Martha.

If you don't mind driving a small car (and you don't want to pay for a bigger one), reserve a compact or sub-compact, cross your fingers for luck, and ask for an upgrade when you arrive at the car rental joint. They might be out of the smaller models. It never hurts to ask.

Oh, and make sure you understand *all* the costs connected with renting a car, including that pesky extra insurance. (We're still fighting over that unexpected $15 a day from our most recent European trip—oh, don't get me started.)

Keeping Sun Out of Eyes

Sun in the eyes is one of the chief complaints of little kids in the car (even if they can't verbalize it). And who can blame them? You don't like it either.

There are several suction-cup attached window shades on the market, some that pull down and roll up with the snap of a wrist. Check 'em out.

- 🐜 Bring extra pillows in the car and rearrange them as needed (best done by the non-driving adult). Extra pillows are also useful for solving sibling squabbles. Have them build a soft wall of separation between them.
- 🐜 Sunglasses and sunhats can help.
- 🐜 Keep a couple of old receiving blankets to drape—close the car window over one end and stretch to the appropriate place. Or sew Velcro strips to an old blanket and attach to the car interior.
- 🐜 Sometimes the combination of car direction and sun position is just bad and you may need to combine a couple of solutions.

Unrestful rest stops

Keep in mind that "rest stops" are not always that restful for the parent. If you've stopped near a stream, you won't be able to simply flop down on your back in the grass and shut your eyes as you would if you were alone, or childless. No, you have to make sure that Darling Clementine isn't throwing herself into the foamy brine, or falling down into the dog doo-doo, or eating that strange looking plant over there. Remember, pace yourself! Stop pushing! It's the journey, not the destination.

Boating with Baby

Babies and little kids usually love ferry boats and cruise ships. Perhaps the gentle rocking motion reminds them of the womb...

Fabulous, Fabulous Ferries

Ferry boats are cool. Your kids can stretch their legs, the air is wonderfully fresh, and you don't have to do the driving. Ferry boats provide relaxation for the parents and fun and excitement for the kids. Take the usual safety precautions depending on the ferry boat, its size, its setup, and your kid's climbing proclivities (keep them away from the railing).

The ferry from Swartz Bay on Vancouver Island, B.C., to the mainland is great for kids. We crossed on *The Spirit of Vancouver Island*, a tremendous boat that carries two thousand passengers and 470 vehicles, and offers fancy buffets, a snack bar, and several children's play areas, as well as changing and nursing rooms. Annie and the other kids played wildly all the way across—sliding, climbing—it reminded me again how much children need to play. Through the large windows, we enjoyed the view of leaping dolphins. They seemed to need to play, too.

Cruise Ships

When Annie was sixteen months old, Bill's dad took the whole family on a three-day Carnival cruise from Los Angeles down to Mexico. Annie spent a lot of time staring at the other nautical vehicles through the porthole window, pointing with a crooked index finger and yelling, "Boat! Boat! Boat!" Our cruise was also memorable for two reasons: it was the first time Annie had her own plate of food in a restaurant, and it rained the entire time (and I'd even bought my first post-pregnancy bathing suit for the occasion). Despite the weather, Annie had a great time hanging with her relatives and being entertained by the singing restaurant staff.

Some cruises are definitely not appropriate for babies or little kids—many are marketed primarily to seniors, or have reputations as floating singles bars. Others specialize in families and hire special clowns, magicians, and other child-oriented entertainment. Find out as much as you can about the tone of the cruise before you book passage, or contact a family-oriented travel agent for advice.

If you're thinking about cruisin':

- Book the early seating for meals. Less formality prevails.
- Ask in advance about reserving high chairs, cribs, and refrigeration units (some boats have them available for passengers).

🚢 Cruises are good for toddlers, less good for babies. State rooms are very small—you may be spending the night pacing your restless baby in cramped quarters.

🚢 Some children may experience seasickness. See S in chapter 14, Troubleshooting A to Z for motion-sickness advice; if sickness is a pattern (and you use boats regularly), have your pediatrician prescribe medicine.

Riding the Rail—Local Travel

Chug-a-chug-a-chug-a-chug-a-CHOO-CHOO! Everybody loves trains, especially little kids.

Subways, Undergrounds, Metros, Els

Crowded city trains can be a hassle for parents. Be prepared to move swiftly through those sliding doors, and be prepared to have to stand.

🧸 Make sure you're able to pick up all your belongings and your child at the same time—you won't have the option of loading a little at a time, and you won't have time to practice.

🧸 The loud noise of subways may actually put a small baby to sleep (too much input, and baby tunes out).

🧸 Kids are too little to reach the straps. Have them hold on to you, or to a pole, at all times. Subway cars lurch and come to sudden stops. Your unrestrained child can easily become a flying projectile. This may be hazardous to his and other passengers' health.

🧸 Be extra-careful when moving between train cars. This is where the train hinges together and there are lots of moving, sliding, bending parts where little fingers can get caught and injured. The area between train cars is noisy, too—the booms, clangs, and scraping noises can easily frighten a small child.

🚇 The best place to be in the subway is the front of the first car. Peering through the front door, you have a great, eerie view as the train careens down the tracks. Fascinating for any toddler or preschooler—or grown-up.

Long-Distance Trains

Many people who travel with children consider the "getting there" part to be the worst part of the trip, a nightmare to be gotten through, so they try to minimize the amount of time they spend actually traveling. Train travel is a different approach—part of the joy of the trip is the travel time. Many toddlers become enamored of trains. For them, a trip by train is the dream vacation. Here are some advantages of train travel:

🚂 Train travel is slow-paced and romantic, a wonderful way to truly *see* this, or any other, country.

🚂 Train travel often provides beautiful views and the advantage of being able to relax.

🚂 The kids can stretch their bodies and not be strapped into a seat the entire time.

🚂 Since the adults don't have to focus on the road, they can give more attention to the child.

🚂 There's lots to see, many people to meet, and you can always visit the dining or observation car (again).

In some countries, trains offer another advantage: safety. There are some countries where I'm *not* about to drive those roads, and where I take my life in my hands every time I get on a bus. I'm not willing to risk Annie's life. Trains are often a good, safer, option.

Bring It All

If you're going by train, tote it all with you. In the U.S., snack food is limited to a selection you may or may not like, and you won't be able to pull over to hit the local convenience store for diapers. In other countries, vendors may work the aisles with terrific food (sweet tamales in Mexico, sticky rice and mangoes in

Thailand), but you *still* won't be able to hit the local convenience store for diapers. (The nearest one will be one thousand miles away!)

Pack for Portability

Assistance isn't always available. If your destination is not a major station, you may experience a moment of panic as you try to grab all the luggage and your kids and hop off quickly before the whistle blows and the train moves on down the line.

Smaller pieces of luggage are easier to swing up into the luggage bin or stash under your seat. Practice the counting method: add up the number of people and items ahead of time, and do a rapid count before you embark or disembark. One kid, two suitcases, two adults, a purse, and a diaper bag equals seven—make sure you always reach seven before getting off.

Ask for Seats in the Non-Smoking Car

The reason for this suggestion should be (cough!) self-evident.

Get On Early

Get a good seat, get your stuff in the racks, grab what you need, all before the "All aboard!" rush.

Blankets and Pillows

Once you board the train, ask the porter for pillows and blankets, even if you are traveling during the day. The temperature on trains fluctuates. You can also use blankets and pillows to pad the seats—the "fit" may need to be adjusted for young, small bodies (or older, not-so-small bodies—but we won't go into that).

Food Service

Find out in advance what kind of food service your train will provide. Many trains have snack and/or liquor bars; some have full sit-down dining cars. The cafés are a pretty good bet for junk food—hot dogs, pizza, sandwiches. and so on.

In this country, long gone are the days of dining cars with heavy pewter plates and a single red rose on each table, but dining cars can still be fun, and the food can be quite tasty. Whatever food service is available, remember to bring lots of your own, especially if you're traveling on a budget. Food on trains in the U.S. tends to be very expensive. Food on trains in Europe tends to be very *ludicrously* expensive.

Sleeping Arrangements

Sleeping in a moving train can be one of the most pleasurable experiences in life. The gentle rocking soothes and deepens sleep—you'll wake up refreshed, and at a new, exciting locale. Babies usually sleep well on trains. If you're traveling with a mate, you might even find an opportunity for a little romance.

Sleeping cars and couchettes are expensive (from a price perspective, it's usually far cheaper to fly or drive). In the U.S., Amtrak offers family fares—rates are 50 percent for kids under fifteen (two kids can accompany each adult for this fare), and kids under two travel free, if on your lap. Consider whether you want your eighteen-month-old on your lap for two days. Amtrak also runs seasonal promotions on many routes. Call for info or check their website (you'll find the details in the Resources Appendix).

We've taken trains through Mexico, Thailand, Malaysia, and Java with Bill's kids, and they're usually a great experience—the old-fashioned railway dining, the all-day voyeuristic peek into steamy jungles, drowsing to the coconut vendor's song. The slow, steady pace makes you aware that you are really traversing the earth in a way you cannot experience traveling by air.

European Train Travel

Remember that summer abroad in Europe during college? The ragged Eurail pass; the endless swinging movement from country to country; the overnight train rides to save youth-hostel fees; fog-bathed castles on the hills; the time the train from Italy back to France was so crowded that you spent the entire time in the bathroom to get an inch of breathing space? And the people you met—the peasant family from Cantal who fed you the finest bread and cheese of your life; the cute blond guy from Cambridge who kissed you between train cars; the "ugly Americans" who induced you to hold your face in a Parisian kitten pout and speak only in a thick French accent to hide your embarrassment at being "one of *them*...."

Going back as a parent will be a different experience—the blond guy may not be making eyes at you from Paris to Lyon, but you can still buy passes good for unlimited rides within a certain time period. (If you're over twenty-six, you'll be paying "adult" rates now). Kids under four ride free! That family from Cantal (and the family from Turin, and the family from Breve) will adopt your baby for the duration and still share their meal with you—and the bread and cheese will be even better because the goodwill will be even more sincere.

If you do any overnights on the train, resign yourself to spending more money than you did as a student. Rather than trying to tough it out on a seat, consider reserving a first-class bedroom (sleeps two plus a baby) or a couchette (six bunks in a room—good unless your baby cries all night). You can book through a travel agent on this side, or at the train station on that side. It's cheaper to book there.

Here are some other tips for European train travel:

🐚 Don't try to pack in too much. Limit your destinations, and plan several days in each place between train trips.

🐚 Make reservations whenever possible to assure yourself seats (that two-year-old isn't gonna like hanging out in that toilet cubicle for eight hours).

🍱 As with any train travel, you'll need to accomplish the near impossible—packing everything you need for the trip, and packing lightly.

🍱 Food on the train is expensive and unpredictable. Bring your own bread and cheese (and, this time, share some with the family from Cantal).

🍱 Some European trains have special cars geared to family travel. Ask at the station about the baby or family car or train.

🍱 Ask your travel agent about the pass options: EurailPass, EuroPass, Eurail Selectpass, as well as Eurotickets. Many travel options exist; we once combined a few days' car rental with a pass on the trains. You have to reside outside Europe to get these, and you should get them before you go; they're only somewhat available in Europe and they cost significantly more than they do in the U.S. or U.K.

Bus Travel

Buses are one of the cheapest travel modes—they can also be one of the most challenging.

Local Bus Travel

Negotiating a city bus with a baby, a stroller, and a bag full of groceries requires some patience—from the bus driver and the other passengers. If you have trouble getting all of you aboard, ask for help from a fellow passenger, or tell the driver you need to make a few trips. Holding the baby, leave the groceries and stroller on the sidewalk, board the bus and pay, then, *holding the baby the entire time*, first get the groceries aboard, *then* grab the stroller. This is a chance to practice your "Bleep 'Em All" attitude—take your time, and assert your right to courtesy. And never put the baby down. If somebody says, "I'll hold the baby," politely say, "No thanks, but you could help me by getting this stroller up the stairs."

Another option is the baby backpack, though this probably dooms you to standing the entire time, as swinging a "loaded" baby backpack off your back on a lurching bus might produce tragic results. Better to keep baby on board, brace the shopping bags with your feet, grab a pole, and hang on tight.

Long-Distance Bus Travel

Long distance travel on buses can feel frustrating—you know those dreams where you're running and you feel like you're chest-deep in mud? If the bus makes a lot of stops, it can feel like you're going nowhere fast.

Pack everything you need—you won't have access to your luggage until you reach "the other side." Be prepared to hold your baby on your lap the whole time, unless you've paid for another seat. If there's room, let the baby or child sit next to the window—this keeps them from escaping down the aisle or falling into the aisle and rolling to the front or the back of the bus. (For some hints on bus travel in developing nations, turn to chapter 13.)

Diapering Baby On a Bus?

You may need to change your baby on your lap; just hope for an understanding seat partner. Get your ingredients ready, and do it during a stop, if possible.

Resources for Disabled Parents— Toting and Traveling

In this country, 10.9 percent of all parenting families have one or more parents with a disability. The number of disabled parents in all populations is growing.

Physical disabilities are not limited to wheelchair users—our aging parent population suffers from bad backs, computer related issues, pre-arthritic conditions, and so on, all of which can hamper the ability to tote your baby around. If you have a disability, especially if you use a cane or a wheelchair, the issue of how to tote your baby and small child may loom large. Traveling becomes more logistically sensitive—not only do you have to carry your baby, but many places locally and worldwide present access problems.

There is no single easy solution for parents with physical disabilities. Each disabled person's abilities and limitations are highly specific, and there are no products currently on the market specifically for disabled parents.

If, however, you are permanently or temporarily disabled, contact Through the Looking Glass, the national resource center for families with disabilities (see the listing in the Resources Appendix under Disability Resources). They publish *Adaptive Baby Care Equipment: Guidelines, Prototypes, and Resources*, a book describing and displaying fifty items of equipment and ideas for caring for babies and toddlers. The items listed focus on ways to carry, hold, and keep kids nearby. Many are helpful for traveling.

CHAPTER 6

Day Tripper:

Navigating the Grocery Store— and the City Zoo

To market, to market, to buy a fat pig
Home again, home again, jiggety-jig.
—*Nursery Rhyme*

The world is filled with things to do, see, and explore. And so many of these things are easy, fun, and cheap. The possibilities are endless. Go on a day trip! Just 'cause you have a baby is no reason to stay home—almost everything you did before you had a child, you can still do now, and there are millions of activities you may not have thought of in *years*.

This chapter focuses on small, daily activities and adventures away from the house or hotel, and the adjustments you should make on account of Baby. We start with the most common (and dreaded) form of day trip—the errand. Too much to do and you've got the baby, too? You can successfully lug your little one with you, and have a good time doing it. Then it's on to the café, the zoo, the farm, and beyond!

It's been said that there are no geographical solutions, that problems follow you wherever you go, and that—for better or worse—wherever you go, there you are. I've got news—for a cranky bored child and a cranky bored parent, there may be no geographical solutions, but there *are remissions*. Getting out and going somewhere, just for the day, can entirely change your frame of mind.

The Joy of Running Errands

Kids like running errands, especially if you establish a ritual: "First we go to the bank, then we stop at the bakery and get bread and a few samples. We always stop at the post office and the Flower Lady before we go home." Rituals provide security. But, don't squeeze in too many. Always keep in mind your child's personal errand-to-play ratio: the exact number of errands allowed before complete baby meltdown occurs. Some babies and toddlers have a limit of two, some three, some can go all day. You'll know.

The Supermarket

The supermarket can be fun, or a trip through a chamber of horror. When you and Baby are fresh, there's a lot to see, Baby is sitting up high, near you so she's happy, and you're getting things done. And other times...well, supermarkets are *the* classic place for toddlers to throw tantrums, and for parents to completely lose their cool. (For more details and tips on tantrums, see T in Chapter 14 Troubleshooting A to Z.)

"Safeway's Got Cookies, Billy, If You're a Good Boy."
Oh, Mama, can you bribe your way through a supermarket—the key is to avoid having to do it every time.

Keeping your kid occupied with a snack is not necessarily a bad idea. Avoid the candy and chips by opening a bag of crackers or raisins and allowing your child to munch (saving the wrapper, of course, so you can pay for it).

Figure out how you want to deal with shopkeepers who hand your child goodies or food. Although, in general, you don't want your child to accept food from strangers, store samples are not always a bad thing (I still fondly remember the butcher at my neighborhood market, gruffly handing out slices of bologna to children when I was growing up. He didn't make a fuss, or ask for the things grown-ups usually want in return for a gift—a smile, or a thank you. Because he was undemanding, we loved him.).

World-Wide Markets

As far as I'm concerned, food shopping around the world is one of the finest forms of family entertainment. Who could ever forget the baskets of spiky red rambutan in the Chiang Mai, Thailand, night market? The delicate samples of salmon roe and green tea in the Tokyo basement supermarkets? The pungence and colors of the Mercado Libertad in Guadalajara? The haricot verts that Bill practically cried over for lack of a stove in Paris?

Shopping Cart/Car Seat Compatibility Factors

Infant car seats fit in the top of most shopping carts. Some supermarkets provide carts fitted with vinyl infant seats. Make sure all the straps are there, and use them. It's a long way down to that hard, cold floor. When Baby can sit up, she can ride in the front of the cart, facing you. Carry an old belt in your diaper bag and strap her in. If she's still wobbly, prop her up with sweaters—don't let her droop into the lettuce.

I was in Berkeley Bowl, our local market, watching a patient yet exasperated mother try to shop with her wild two-year-old boy. He was in the back of the basket dancing—no sitting down for this child. Every item she placed in the basket was either chewed or stomped on, so she finally solved the problem by handing Sonny a bagel and putting all the groceries underneath the basket, on the rack usually reserved for laundry detergent and ten-pound sacks of potatoes.

Shopping with a Stroller

Sometimes you'll shop with a stroller. In this case, you'll need to do one of the following:

- 🔸 You may be able to balance a hand basket on top of the hood of a standard stroller, or skip the basket and bring your own string bag to hang from the stroller handle.
- 🔸 Fold the stroller, place it on the bottom rack of the shopping cart, and put Baby in the front basket.
- 🔸 Fill a shopping cart, dragging Baby and stroller behind.

Remember that you have to wheel the stroller while carrying groceries. Have them double-bagged in plastic. (I know, I usually ask for paper, too.) Hang the bags over the handles, and make tracks.

Warning: If you pick up Baby with bags hanging on the handles, the back-heavy stroller will fly dramatically backwards and smash your eggs. If the bags are *too* heavy, the stroller will fly over backwards with Baby inside!

Out of the Supermarket and Into the Car

Always strap the baby into her seat before you unload your groceries from the cart to the car. I don't care if the cart rolls away into the parking lot with the groceries inside. I *do* care if the cart rolls away into the parking lot with the *baby* inside!

Baby at the Gym

Many gyms have on-site child-watch services. Baby plays while you sweat. Please note the semantic difference between child *watch* and child *care*: child watch doesn't change diapers, feed your child, or do much at all besides watch the kids play. If there are altercations between kids, the child-watch person may or may not handle the situation effectively.

When checking out the gym, make sure to find out if the child-watch providers have regular schedules (or if the center is staffed by bored aerobics teachers between classes), and try to meet the "regular" person who will be there at the times you plan to exercise. Always tell the child watcher where in the gym you plan to be in case your child gets distressed. If you're taking a class (usually an hour long), plan to hurry on both sides the first few times—come in your exercise clothes and take a quick shower at home afterwards. Later, once you see how your baby does, you can soak in the Jacuzzi, hang out by the muscle men, or give yourself a facial.

Special Note: A longtime "child watcher" told me that one of the primary risks of gym child-watch services is the potential of infection from sick children—that is, children too ill to be in day care or school, but well enough to be out and about with a bored parent who is tired of being cooped up, and runs in to use the gym for an hour.

Baby at the Doctor (Yours)

Sometimes you just have to drag the li'l darlin' along. Though you'd no doubt like privacy during your doctor visits, the day may come when you don't have child care and you urgently need to be seen. Remember that to your kid, you are Everything, The World, Immortal, and that your being sick or in pain can be a terrifying experience. Besides your attempts to be reassuring, you can do something else—be entertaining. Bring toys, books, coloring supplies (if age-appropriate), and non-messy snacks. With toddlers and preschoolers, you can talk about the doctor's tools. Maybe little Jenny can even *help* Dr. Matthews hold the stethoscope (check this out with Dr. Matthews first).

Baby at the Dentist (Yours)

A mobile baby can be challenging at the dentist. Ask the staff in advance if it is appropriate to bring your baby or toddler with you. Some family dentists suggest bringing the child in even before it's their turn, to familiarize them with the strange and potentially scary equipment. A non-mobile baby or an easily distracted child can sit

or recline with you while you have your teeth cleaned—
if the dentist or hygienist is amenable. If you know none
of this will work for *your* child, beg, borrow, or steal a baby-
sitter and pretend that you are getting a massage or a
special treat. You are, at least, taking care of your body.

Hanging Out

The fine art of hanging out is deeply under-appreciated,
but much of what adults do with babies and small children comes under this category. These years fly swiftly
by. Appreciate the opportunity. You may never get this
chance again!

The Mall

Mall hanging doesn't always require shopping—many
malls are also entertainment centers, good in good
weather or bad. When the playground is soggy or
frozen, the mall may provide a good place to stretch little
legs (but be aware that the floors may be hard and slippery). Some malls even have ice rinks. (Some rinks rent
skates as small as size six, for toddlers. Call to find out
before setting up little expectations.) Food courts
provide food to please all palates, ranging from "junk" to
"healthy." If you're mall-crazy, there is a mall to end all
malls in Edmonton, Canada. There—practically at the
North Pole—you can shop, eat, skate, browse, people-
watch, and if you bring your swimsuit, indulge in the
water slides and gigantic wave pool in the basement.

The Library

The public library is too often underrated or forgotten as
a great place to hang out with kids. Some parents are
nervous about taking their kids to a library because
they're incapable of keeping to a whisper. Don't fret—
most public libraries are set up with separate children's
rooms. While it's *not* all right to act out and scream,
children's librarians understand children, and are
happy to help them learn appropriate library behavior

as well as find wonderful books. Visiting libraries on a regular basis helps introduce kids to the joy of books and reading. It's never too early to do that. (Also see "Story Hour," later in this chapter.)

Café Culture

Paris, Rome, Vienna, New York, San Francisco...hell, nowadays every university town is filled with coffee-houses and cafés. Long before I became a harried, multi-tasking mother, I used to be cool. I was an art student with pink streaks in my hair. I wore black and sat in Parisian cafés sipping espresso and smoking unfiltered cigarettes as I wrote long journal entries about men, love, and angst.

I still love cafés and café culture, though sometimes I think I've forgotten how to truly "hang out"...renting a table by the hour with a cup of bottomless coffee or a slowly sipped latté, staring at cute guys, and dreaming of the future. Now I glare at smokers, I tend towards decaf in the afternoon, and it's hard to fantasize about men with dark, soulful eyes when your right shoulder is covered with white goo—the remains of Baby's burp.

But as I learned early in Annie's life, you *can* have it all! Kids are natural hanger-outers. You, too, can be a café parent, and your child can be the Cappuccino Kid—cool before her time, ready for adventure, ready for the world.

Here are tips on choosing a baby-friendly café:

🧸 Listen to the music: if the atmosphere is too "classical" or the hip-hop is too loud, try somewhere else. My ideal musical choices are jazz, blues, swing, eclectic rock, or eclectic anything else. If it's country, don't bother. It's just my opinion, but country and cappuccino don't mix: "Y'all like whip cream on that Café Biànca?"

🧸 Examine the clientele, and don't rule them out for being too young. Some single women in their twenties are deep in the throes of baby-want, and will entertain your child endlessly, providing impromptu, free baby-sitting. Plus, it's great sport watching the really cute twenty-something men squirm as they watch their girlfriends make goo-goo eyes at your Little Georgie.

🎎 Highchairs or booster seats are bonuses, but not a requirement. Your kid can sit in the stroller, eating a snack. In our area, most cafés serve Madeleine cookies, soft vanilla sticks just the right size for grasping in a toddler's hands. (For the more organic among you, try the oat cakes.) Shake out the stroller before you put it back in the car or house.

🎎 A too-crowded café means you have to get in and get out. Avoid peak hours—people getting their morning caffeine fix or trying to pull out of their afternoon slump. You want to be able to *hang* at that table without being subjected to the vulture-like gazes of tableless customers, clutching hot cups of espresso.

🎎 A too-empty café means boredom for baby. Might as well stay home and stick the tea kettle on the stove. The idea is people-watching. Baby is fascinated by the parade of people and the sound of the espresso machine and milk steamer. Baby is not fascinated by the dull sight of Daddy trying to read a newspaper for once in his life. (Exception: You're on a stroll, and Baby goes down for a nap. Now you can park at a café and catch up on Dear Abby.)

🎎 Avoid square tables. André will automatically want to go round-and-round-the-mulberry-bush, and square or rectangular tables with corners are dangerous. You're here to relax, to *haaaannng* out. Search for round, or at least rounded, tables.

🎎 Look for places to play. Cafés that are truly serious about being kid-friendly provide a small play area or (for the older-than-baby set) kids books near the communal newspapers, or crayons and paper at the counter.

🧸 Check out the lighting. Some cafés have great overhead light fixtures that baby can fixate on while you practice your Poet's Pout.

🧸 The best places (and this might be your funkiest corner café) provide, on request, "baby foam," an inch or two of milk foam free for your child. The correct way to ask for baby foam is to add to your own coffee order the semi-apologetic request, "May we also have just a little bit of foam in a cup for the baby?" Beware the barista who asks, "Will that be a large or a small steamed milk?" You don't want steamed milk—you don't want to pay for it, your kid won't drink it all anyway, and it's a production that often involves too-hot and spilling. You want an inch of foam in a cup. (Unless you do want steamed milk, in which case, order it!) A truly classy establishment will give your two-year-old an inch or two of foam in a demitasse cup and saucer with a tiny demitasse spoon. Watch those eyes grow wide.

🧸 And finally, the café should be smoke-free. Finding one in this country shouldn't be too difficult, but you may run into trouble when traveling abroad. It may not be possible to completely eradicate second-hand smoke from your child's environment, but at the least choose a well-ventilated spot by a window or door.

Urban Activities and Entertainment

Check the local periodicals, there are lots of organized activities and entertaining events for kids.

Concerts and Theater for Kids

One of most thrilling moments of my childhood was being taken backstage at a Pete Seeger concert to meet the great man himself. Annie spent her earliest, pre-Britney Spears years growing up on the music of Gary Lapow, Ruth Pelham, Tim Cain, Julie Olsen Edwards, and other wonderful musicians who play music children enjoy. There are many musicians, puppeteers, clowns, and acting troupes who specialize in entertaining kids. You'll find performances listed in newspapers, baby shops, bulletin boards, and so on. The best children's performers engage the children and get them standing, clapping, and singing. Your toddler or preschooler may want to run around; restrain her gently (even if other parents aren't as attentive) and draw her focus back to the stage—too much activity is impolite to the performer and other audience members.

Sometimes theatrical performances and concerts can overwhelm a little one. That doesn't mean don't go—gentle, short-term exposure to crowds will get her acclimated.

Rock and WHAT DID YOU SAY?

You *can* take your baby to a rock concert, but if you do, be very aware that the high decibel levels can be danger-ous. If you find yourselves too close to the speakers, *move*. My stepkids, Aaron and Rachel, grew up with children of famous rock musicians and have horror stories of how some of those friends have moderate to severe hearing impairments. One guy is deaf in one ear—his mom had him napping right next to the speakers during rehearsals.

Story Hour

Many libraries and some bookstores offer regular story hours for babies, toddlers, and preschoolers. These can be wonderful experiences for both young children and their parents.

Most story hours last less than an hour—attention spans are short.

Some story hours incorporate music, and may end with stickers or pictures to take home and color.

If you go often enough, you'll build a regular rela-tionship with other kids and parents who also value the written and spoken word.

"We're All Here Today"

Every Tuesday evening, from 7:00 to 7:30, you would find us at the Piedmont Branch of the Oakland Public Library for Pajama Story Hour. We began taking Annie at eleven months and only stopped, two years later, when we, her parents, simply couldn't bear to hear another rendition of *We're All Here Today*.

An amazing group of talented parents and gorgeous children regularly came to story hour. I bet Doug, the ex-rock musician from the Velvet Underground, never imagined he would spend his Tuesday evenings listening to a dramatic reading of *If You Give a Mouse a Cookie* and adding the vocal bass line to *Let Everyone Clap Hands Like Me*.

Going to the Movies

We love going to the movies wherever we are. It's inevitably a cultural experience. In Thailand, before the movie, the entire audience stands and sings the national anthem (written by the king) as a movie clip of His Majesty saluting is shown. Going to the movies is not a foolproof adventure—judge your child's development before you decide to worship before the silver screen.

Things to keep in mind:

- Make sure the movie is appropriate for your child. Very few are—even PG-rated films can terrify little kids. Child care staffs see a marked increase in "acting-out" behavior (pun intended) every time a new adventure film hits town.
- Some brave parents take their infants to grown-up movies. Depending upon your particular little baby, this may, or may not be a successful outing. The intense auditory sensory input puts some infants to sleep, and makes others scream.
- Some theaters have nursing rooms. Call in advance to find out about facilities.

"Parking" It

Strolling on the promenade, visiting the arboretum, rowing on the duck pond, feeding carrots to the buffaloes, flipping a Frisbee, visiting the horse stables, zooming through the zoo...parks and outdoor recreation areas everywhere are fun, energizing, and restful for every member of the family.

Playgrounds: A Cultural Opportunity

Playgrounds provide the basics—a place to run, a place to dig, and something to climb or slide on. Babies and small children need the outdoors every day. And for the adults, part of having a child is enjoying the life of a child again—guilt free. Playing in the sand with your two-year-old son, you can simply enjoy the sensations of the sun, son, and sand. There is nowhere else you have to be.

Playgrounds also provide an opportunity to meet people. One of the surprises of becoming a mom was my new ability to meet women my own age. When I traveled alone or with Bill, we'd meet lots of men (many of them in the tourist industry)—but where were the women? As a relatively late-starter (almost thirty-two when Annie was born), I guess they were off with their babies, not accessible to travelers or tourists. (If I'd known then what I know now, I would have gone to the playground and admired babies.) On the cultural level, when you're involved in child-rearing, the child-rearing of other cultures and sub-cultures becomes fascinating. What better place to see such practices than a playground?

In addition, in any playground, home or away from home, you will find people with whom you have something very basic in common—you both have kids. It's easy to strike up conversations, and a good way to beat parental isolation.

Playground Survival Skills

Lots of babies like to eat sand. Our little friend Shoshana had a particular passion for the substance. Is it the texture?

Is it the flavor? (Since I haven't tasted sandbox sand myself in thirty-odd years, I can't explain the appeal.) Stop your baby from indulging. A little clean sand probably won't harm a child—but most sand is not clean, and some sandboxes can be terribly contaminated.

Old kitchen utensils make good, inexpensive sand toys. Consider strainers, ladles, plus the ubiquitous plastic yogurt containers. Bring a few to share; your kid may get to play with other things, too. In most playgrounds, kids are pretty generous.

Balls and other age-appropriate sports equipment are also good things to bring to a playground. Some kids develop the ability to throw and catch balls at an amazingly early age. Others are slower. Much basic sports ability is based on years of exposure, and practice.

Zoos and Natural History Museums

Zoos and Natural History Museums are fun for all, and they have the added bonus of exciting your little ones about science and nature early on.

Memberships

Natural history museums and zoos are designed with families in mind, and often offer yearly memberships. If you like zoos or museums, and think you might go more than three times in a particular year (a year is a long time!), consider a family membership. The initial outlay may be expensive (and may feel hard for parents on a budget), but if the museum or zoo is reasonably local, you may save a lot of money in the long run.

Membership enables you to take it slow, not make it a chore. It's counterproductive to have your kid identify museums with what I call "museum feet," the fatigue that makes your feet feel as swollen as your thighs, and makes you feel liiike yoou aaaare moooooving innnnn ssslowww mmmotion. I get that feeling when the morning hit of caffeine has worn off—or I've been in a museum with hard floors and too much visual stimulation.

Memberships also allow you to be casual about visiting. With entrance fees as high as they are, there is a tendency to try to get your "money's worth." With a membership, go for an hour, go for a single exhibit, go visit the ducks. Then move on. Incorporate it into your life.

Many museums and zoos have reciprocity with other facilities across the nation, so when you travel (as you're gonna do, right?), you'll be able to stop by the local zoo or museum and get in free! (Free is good.)

One of our favorite nature museums in the world is the Biodome in Montreal, Canada. Visitors walk through four "environments," complete with climate, plant, and wildlife changes. We learn best through visceral experience. How better to teach your two-year-old about a tropical rain forest than to walk through the double-glass doors into hot, wet air echoing with the sounds of parrots flying overhead? (I can think of another way—Thailand, Mexico, Maui....)

Zoos and Zoo Etiquette

People feel mixed about zoos. Are they a freak show of strange animals for kids to gawk at, or educational centers? The answer depends largely upon the zoo itself. Good zoos are active players in the environmental movement and active centers of scientific research, stressing respect for their inhabitants. Here are some tips for navigating through the zoo.

  ❧ Stay on the path.

  ❧ Don't touch the animals—they bite, and some carry diseases.

  ❧ Never feed the animals. You'd be surprised how many people ignore signs and throw candy, peanuts, and popcorn to wild animals. It can make them very ill.

  ❧ Have respect. Be considerate of their ears. Yelling and tapping on the cage is cruel—and it sends a bad message to your kids.

🐾 Try the "off" hours—mornings, weekdays. On foggy, slightly rainy days, the animals are active and the people are few. A visit to a quiet zoo when the animals are awake and active is far more gratifying than a visit when thousands of families are crowding around the lion's den.

🐾 Be prepared for changes in weather. Try the layered look, and bring hats for sun and cold. Always tote along the sunscreen. (Get the "dirt" on the sun in Chapter 10.)

🐾 You'll be doing a lot of walking, and toddler legs may give out early (usually in front of the second animal enclosure). Bring a stroller. Even if you don't use it for your kid, you can use it to push the day pack, extra sweaters, and any souvenirs you give in and pony up for. Some zoos rent strollers— call in advance.

Petting Zoos and Children's Zoos

Most zoos have petting zoos, though they also can be found in city parks, at country fairs, and so on. Goats, sheep, rabbits, guinea pigs, chickens, and pigs are often featured. Sometimes animal food is available for a small fee. What charms can also chasten—goats are gentle animals, but their insistence on crunching and gobbling the pellets a little one clutches in her hand can be intimidating. Be prepared to carry your child. The first visit, you might want to observe, rather than feed. Then practice at home, offering food from a *flat* hand. First you offer and baby nibbles, then *he* offers and *you* nibble.

Babies Love Babies

At the Beacon Hill Park petting zoo in Victoria, B.C., baby goats scampered, rabbits hopped, guinea pigs squealed, peacocks paraded, and an eleven-day-old pot-bellied pig nursed from her mommy. Annie spent a lot of time brushing the baby goats.

The Littlest Culture Vulture

We instill values and a sense of "culture" early in our children. Part of your task as a parent is to expose your child to some of life's highlights—remember that just because activities are "cultural" doesn't meant they aren't fun. Taking your kids to museums from the beginning helps incorporate art into everyday life, and ensures that they won't single it out as something separate from normal life.

Art museums can bore small children, so I'm talking moderation here, not a steady diet of Mattisse, Rembrandt, or Picasso. Ethnic art museums can give children a sense of family and world history. Call ahead and see if they have resources for kids, and check their stroller/backpack policy (see Chapter 5). There are even museums that focus specifically on children's art, and often have activities and projects geared for young visitors.

"Hungry, Little Michelangelo?"

Art-going is hungry work. Once the head has been fed, you might want to feed the stomach. Museum cafés often serve inexpensive, excellent food in a "family-friendly" atmosphere. Replenish!

Rural Activities

For many years, my sister Jessica and her family lived in Central Vermont, in a renovated barn up a dirt road seven miles from the center of Plainfield, population 1,301. What a far cry from our urban existence in Oakland, California! Yet, when we'd visit, our days were filled with activity. Here are some suggestions for rural day trips. Adjust for your locale and season.

- Drive around looking for cows. Don't laugh—it's fun! When you find a pasture of cows, pull over and practice mooing over the fence at them. They may even moo back. Be polite—do not refer to the pasture as a steak orchard.

- Call a farm ahead of time and ask if you can visit a small dairy farm in action. Even two-year-olds are fascinated by the sight of cows being milked. Look in the Yellow Pages under "Dairy Farm" or call the town clerk.

🧸 Visit a "Pick-Your-Own" farm—pumpkins at a pumpkin farm, apples from an apple orchard, baskets of juicy ripe raspberries.

🧸 Visit the local waterhole. Is there a wide bend in the river, an old quarry, a pond where the locals swim?

🧸 Even toddlers love to visit rural Farmers Markets (particularly fabulous in European countries). There are usually free samples, delicious baked goods, and sometimes a local entertainer.

🧸 General stores have everything—forget snow boots? Need a hat? A leg of mutton?

🧸 Many farm-centered areas hold harvest festivals: fresh ears of corn slathered in butter in corn country; fresh and foamy cider in apple country...

🧸 And—particular to New England winters—visit the local maple sugaring house for "sugar on snow."

Town Clerks in Small Towns

Want to know the skinny on the small town you're visiting? Call the town clerk's office. In rural America, the local town clerk can often provide regional information—what to do, where to go, historical facts, road conditions, gossip.

The town clerk is often elected by community members and is usually someone who has been in the area forever, often a native, sometimes an older, garrulous person who can trace their own history in the area back for generations. Everything that happens is officially noted here—births, marriages, deaths. It's where people pay their taxes and vote. Often the small office is connected to the post office. Look for "Town Clerk" in the phone book under "Government Offices." The number listed is often a home phone number.

Libraries in Small Towns

Libraries can be lifesavers, especially if you're visiting a small town. Once you've walked Main Street three times, hung out in the café, and imitated bulls in the local china shop, what is there to do? Hit the library. You won't be able to take out books, but you can sit in the kids' section and read to your baby in a quiet voice. No matter how limited the selection, there will be more than enough for one day's entertainment. Libraries provide a good opportunity to slow down.

Sporting Events

Attending baseball, football, basketball, hockey, and other professional sports is an American tradition. Can you take a baby or little kid? Sure! (Will they appreciate it? Maybe.)

- Infants are easy to care for at a ball game, though the noise factor might be a bit much. Imagine sixty thousand people screaming at a high-scoring football game. Imagine your baby there.
- Once a baby can crawl, trapping him (and you) in the small space of a few seats with steps and concrete flooring is not a great idea.
- For football, basketball, and other sports where the seats cost a fortune, take the babe-in-arms but don't throw your money away on a seat for a toddler.
- Three- and four-year-olds have a short attention span, but are usually good for a couple of hours at a baseball game, as long as you keep the goodies coming. Be ready and willing to spend *time* wandering around the stadium, and *money* stuffing the little face.
- You're in luck if your team doesn't draw big crowds—it's easier to wander around with a restless kid if you aren't constantly tripping over and bugging people.
- Some stadiums and coliseums have a "game room" for kids, complete with video games and TV

monitors broadcasting the game on the field below. But as my friend Dave says, "What's the point of spending all the money and hassle of going to the game? We could stay home and watch the show on TV!"

My cousin Karl regularly brings little Mark to San Francisco Giants games. Mark enjoys the game, Karl says, as long as he's fed often enough. They have a rule in the family—Mark has to eat a hot dog before he can have any ice cream. Mark doesn't understand the Rules of Baseball yet, but he sure knows the Rules of Ice Cream.

High-Energy Activities

Life sometimes isn't—and shouldn't always be—like a calm, serene summer day. Sometimes the wind is gonna come and shake things up! The world is filled with high-energy family activities. Be aware, but be there!

Activity Centers

WOW! ZOWIE! CRAASH! BANG! BOOM! Indoor, high-tech activity centers are better for older kids than the toddler set, though many of them have small areas set aside for the little ones. Babies and infants may feel completely overwhelmed. Activity centers are good for bad weather, decent for birthday parties, and usually fairly inexpensive. If you join your child in the shoeless zone, be prepared to feel like a mouse in a maze. Bins of balls to jump in, ropes to swing on, mazes to maneuver in, tubes to tunnel through—yes, the place will exhaust your kid, but be prepared: your child will nap, but so will you.

Amusement Parks—The Pros and Cons

When should you start taking your children to amusement parks? Consider the pros and cons below:

Pros:
  🐾 It's fun designed by pros. Professional fun often has a compelling, frantic pace that will rev up and excite every member of the family. Fun is fun!

Amusement parks, theme parks, and water slides can all be thrilling, engaging, and give a pure sense of escapism.

🜲 All-in-one entertainment: you don't need to leave the facility to find food or a bathroom. The largest amusement parks supply everything from pet kennels to aspirin.

🜲 Great people-watching! The crowds at amusement parks are usually multi-racial, of all ages, and kid-friendly!

🜲 Everybody's happy! There's usually something for every member of the family to enjoy.

Cons:

🜲 They're expensive. Surviving a trip to consumerist America with at least a portion of your wallet intact is sometimes a tricky proposition. If you can pack in your own food and limit the number or cost of souvenirs, you may be able to escape with a few solitary bucks.

🜲 Dazed and confused: though you may be eager to relive your childhood and your love of Mickey Mouse, consider your child's age before flinging yourself into the exhausting proposition of a theme park where nothing and nobody stops, where the noise and crowds and larger-than-life figures and garish colors can overwhelm a sensitive little one.

🜲 Size matters: many rides have height limits; for children small for their age, this proposes a particular problem. If she can't go, you can't go. Solution: bring another adult and alternate turns.

🜲 FEAR. Rides are often geared to be scary—and it's that intersection between fear and fun that grown-ups love, isn't it? Kids don't always understand how to process those emotions. Don't denigrate his fear by saying, "There's nothing to be scared of." If your child is likely to be terrified of the ride (the mechanical aspect) or the special effects, go slow. Test the waters on something tamer. Time will pass.

Try to eat *before* you hit the amusement park. Some parks prohibit bringing in your own food—but they won't search your pockets for the spare apple, package of nuts, or fruit roll-up. Food for sale is usually fun—but full of sugar. Try to balance your child's intake with something reasonably healthy—their energy level, and yours, is less likely to spike and then wane.

Nightlife?

Remember the happy-go-lucky parents in chapter 1? They're the ones who try to incorporate their children into their own lives as much as possible. If these parents go out on the town, they'll often bring their kids along, too. These are the babies you'll see riding on their parents' shoulders at nighttime carnivals, or carried to the movies in slings.

Other parents feel that schedules are more important, and put their babies and toddlers to bed early. If these parents get out, it is only with the services of a baby-sitter. Everybody has different styles.

Since Annie is a "night owl" by nature, she does well when we take her out at night. Since I am a "morning dove"—Annie calls me a "Swallow of the Dawn"—I often do not. Here are some ideas for evening prowls with a baby, at home or abroad:

Bookstores

Bookstores are particularly great on a rainy evening when everybody has been cooped up all day. More and more, bookstores are staying open late to catch the evening crowds. Some incorporate cafés. More sponsor readings or author appearances. We'll sometimes head to a bookstore where I'll attend a reading (not appropriate for a baby or a chatterbox of a kid) while Bill and Annie hang out in the children's book area. Then we'll all indulge in a little sweet something-or-other at a café.

> In St. Sebastian, Spain, we saw little kids still playing in the playground along the promenade at 3:00…in the morning.

The Evening Stroll

Anywhere—near your house after dinner to stretch our legs, downtown, or down near the Bay, getting fresh air in the evening helps to calm that inevitable last burst of energy that spikes up before bath and bedtime.

Like Father, Like Grandfather

From the time Annie was a little baby, my dad took her on early evening strolls down College Avenue in Oakland, our local, trendy, commercial strip featuring cafés, restaurants, bookstores, and charming boutiques. They had their usual route: they stopped at the pizza maker to watch him toss the dough. If was early enough, Mr. John's, the dog groomer, was still open, and they'd go in to watch the furry proceedings. They would read a book or two at DIESEL, a bookstore, or further down at Pendragon Books, which had the added panache of the shop cat, Cookie.

The regularity and ritual of these walks brought back fond memories of being a small child myself, clutching my dad's pinkie or riding on his shoulders down to Cliff's Hardware in San Francisco for penny candy, or burying my face in his hair in intrigued terror at the sight of Laughing Sal, a huge, roaring mannequin at now-decades-gone Playland-by-the-Beach.

Kids in Retirement Communities and Nursing Homes

Babies and children should be incorporated into the rhythms of life, and those rhythms include aging and dying. Given the right approach and locale, babies and toddlers usually get along very well with the elderly, who, in turn, are delighted and moved by the beauty and fun of new life.

Be sensible about it—children should not be exposed to an adult in extreme pain. There are also big differences between retirement communities, where relatively healthy older people live independently, assisted living facilities, and nursing homes, where residents are often ill, in pain, bedridden, or close to dying. And consider the physical layout. Some locales are not appropriate for little ones. A crawling baby in a room with bedpans on the floor is not a good idea.

If you decide that the locale and your older relative's condition are appropriate for a visit, be sensitive to any fears or reactions your child might have—odd smells, wheelchair contraptions, and so forth can be scary. Developmentally, children at around four and five become interested in—and sometimes frightened of—death and dying. Depending upon your responses, a visit with an ailing great-grandparent might terrify them. But don't keep away just because your child might be scared. Listen to, talk with, and hold your child, and allow him to get to know his family.

Some retirement communities have small rooms available for family reunions. It might be worthwhile to reserve one if you're bringing a little one along. Older people can sometimes become agitated by little ones playing with their belongings, and babyproofing could be quite difficult.

The Cult of the New

Before they made the flight from Vermont out to California to see the family, Jessica introduced the subject to Emma. "We're going to meet your Great-Grandma Dolly. It's going to be her ninety-fifth birthday. That means she's a very, very old lady."

Emma, familiar with the concept of "old food" as "spoiled food," looked seriously at her mother. "Do we need to throw her away?"

CHAPTER 7

Tote That Barge, Lift That Bale:
Packing for Europe (or the Grocery Store)

Packing Up All Your Cares and Woes...

When you have a young child, even getting out of the house for the afternoon can feel daunting. So much to remember, so much to carry, so little time. I know parents who refuse to travel just because they don't want to pack! Relax. Once you get organized, packing for the zoo or a longer trip is a snap.

The Perfect Day Pack

Your basic piece of equipment for daily adventuring is the day pack. Do you remember Mary Poppins' magical bag? In the movie, it's a large, ordinary-looking purse that somehow magically contains everything she could possibly need, including a full-length coat rack and a mirror. Can anybody tell me where to get one of those? Short of that, for around town, your day pack can be a large diaper bag or light backpack—filled with the normal motley assortment of gear (see below). For hikes and beaches and trips to the zoo, consider a more heavy-duty pack with bottom straps. We try to keep our day pack partially ready to go, adding last-minute items and food right before we whisk ourselves out the door.

What's in the Day Pack?

What should go in it? Here are some suggestions (modify for your circumstances):

- Essential documents (if in a foreign land, your passport and papers). Documents should include a note card of emergency information and a biographical and medical sketch of your child.
- Money, wallet, disposable camera
- At least one change of clothing per child
- Four to six diapers, if applicable, or an extra pair of underpants
- Portable wipes (commercial or moistened terry cloth—see chapter 2)
- Tissue and/or a roll of toilet paper
- Plastic bags
- Medications as required.
- A first-aid kit
- Sippy cup or drink bottle (For a half-day trip, you can pre-mix baby formula and store in a thermos or use a special bottle system that keeps the water and powdered formula separate until you're ready to feed your baby—more details in chapter 2.)
- Plastic container of rice cakes, crackers, Goldfish, or other non-perishable snacks (see the suggestions in chapter 3)
- Pocket knife
- Spare set of house keys

- Small toys for emergency entertainment (spare keys can double)
- Thin paperback children's book(s)
- Sun hat
- Sunscreen—15 SPF or higher (sunscreen information is in chapter 10)
- Something warm to wear (sweater, jacket)
- Old receiving blanket (for nursing privacy, changing diapers, impromptu picnics, or instant shade)

Crossing Borders?

Yes, even your eeny-beeny infant needs her own passport. Children's passports are good for five years. I agree there is something ludicrous about trying to identify a four-year-old from a photo taken when she was three-months-old. Even sillier is trying to fill out the application, gazing into those cloudy newborn eyes to discern what color they will be. Blue? Green? Brown? (For Annie, we guessed gray—they ended up hazel.) For information on how to get your child (or yourself) a passport, see chapter 13 and the Overseas Travel section in the Resources Appendix.

Luggage for the Longer Trip

Your requirements will vary depending on number of adults, number of children, destination, planned activities, and length of stay. Bill, Annie, and I usually share one big and one medium-sized suitcase. Plus, we carry an assortment of carry-ons—at least one per person (including Annie). Make sure you can lift it all, and the kid, in one swoop. The time may come when you'll have to.

Important tip:

Some airlines only allow one carry-on per person! But, generally, your purse does not count as a carry-on. And who's to say that your diaper bag is not your purse, huh? To be sure, check with *your* airline before you go.

Put 'em to Work Young

Children love to be involved, and involving them in the packing process helps you gain "buy in" for the trip. Toddlers and older children can carry (or load and unload) their own little tote bags. Start your child with the idea a couple of days before you go, and let her (with your gentle suggestions and veto power) choose what to bring.

If you have more than one child, the older one can help pack for the baby. Make sure to review and edit all suggestions.

Sturdy as She Goes

For a trip to the Pacific Northwest, Annie, almost three, spent two days loading and unloading her tiny carry-on suitcase. She selected and discarded a wide variety of items before she settled (with our encouragement) on very sensible choices: a sweater, a small spinning top, two books, a brush, a comb, a tube of sunscreen, a sun hat, an extra diaper, and her stuffed Kitty and Pooh Bear.

The suitcase had a loose clasp with a habit of opening and causing Annie's prized possessions to tumble out. (Get a sturdy one.) Bill and I lived in terror that her two favorite stuffed animals would be lost, so Annie's suitcase became the first thing we grabbed each time we made a move from airplane to car to motel to car.

Annie took her job seriously, enjoyed her responsibility, became distressed whenever she didn't know where her suitcase was, and staggered through the Seattle-Tacoma airport dragging it behind her along the floor, yelling, "It's not too heavy! It's not too heavy!" until we rescued them both and praised her for a job well done.

Ericka's Seven-Step Planning System

Organization is not always my strong point. I tend to be of the grab-and-run school of parenting ("What, you're hungry? Oh. Let's see, are there any cafés around?"), but for a trip, I rely on advance planning to smooth the way. It took me a few trips to develop this comfortable planning-and-packing system.

- The week before departure, I carry around a yellow pad to jot down a list of items "To Bring."

- When making the To Bring list, I consider various possible weather scenarios and social situations.

- As To Bring things get collected or bought and piled amidst the general chaos on the couch and living room floor, I put a check mark next to the item on the To Bring list.

- On the same pad (deeper in), I create a separate To Do list (cancel diaper service, arrange pet and plant sitting, do neglected laundry, notify day-care provider, stop newspaper, change answering machine message, call neighbors, and so on).

- As the things-to-do get done, I cross them off the To Do list. Eventually this list can be thrown away (or saved for a future trip's reference).

- As I pack each item into the suitcases, I put a single fine line through each item on the To Bring list.

- As the suitcases go out the door I review the still-legible To Bring list one more time to ascertain if we've forgotten anything truly vital.

How To Pack Light

Ha! Ha! Ha! Ha! Ha! Ha! O.K., I'm done laughing now.

So...What Should You Bring?

There is no one definitive packing list. The general list below includes all the items I either always take or regret not having, plus some more obscure ideas and suggestions. Use this list as a jumping-off spot. Your own list will reflect your child's proclivities, activities, and developmental level, and your own. Trim down if you'll be lugging everything by hand—load up if you have room in the car.

- ✔ Clothes
- ❑ Toiletries
- ❑ Laundry soap
- ❑ Fluids
- ❑ Snack food
- ❑ First-aid kit
- ❑ Day pack
- ❑ Sunglasses
- ❑ Kleenex
- ❑ Chewing gum
- ❑ Bathing suit
- ❑ Socket protectors and masking or duct tape
- ❑ Sturdy toys
- ❑ Plastic bags
- ❑ Sunscreen
- ❑ Books
- ❑ Camera and film or disposable camera
- ❑ Receiving blankets
- ❑ Diaper wipes
- ❑ Flashlight
- ❑ Baby tote gear
- ❑ Lovey toys
- ❑ Lovey blanket
- ❑ Brightly colored Band-Aids
- ❑ Documents
- ❑ Distractions and bribes
- ❑ A roll of toilet paper

Tons O' Baby Clothes

An hour before leaving for the airport on our first big trip *avec bébé*, Bill and I sat in the middle of a living room littered with baby clothes, road maps, two suitcases that seemed to have shrunk to gym bags, and seven-month-old Annie, rocking back and forth on her knees, thrilled by the chaos.

"Don't crawl," I told her. "Wait a few weeks. Please?" She smiled with glee.

"What clothes shall we bring for Annie?" I asked Bill.

We looked at each other mystified. We were off to a different continent for three weeks. What kind of weather would we face? What social situations?

In a flash of brilliance, Bill said, "Let's bring it all!"

It worked then, and that's what we always do now, though as Annie's body gets larger we're getting a little more selective.

- For a baby, I suggest bringing as much comfortable and easily washable baby clothing as you can cram in the suitcase. Doing laundry can be a drag (there are laundry tips in chapter 3), and your little dirt-ball won't become neat just because you're on the road. In most cases you'll be able to replace whatever you need, but you don't want to waste your valuable vacation schlepping from store to store for necessities. (Note for the continental traveler: though shopping overseas can be fun, the beautiful clothes in Europe are far too expensive for everyday use.)

- Toddlers and preschoolers need a lot of clothing, too. Dark clothing and denim can be worn until filthy without much visual evidence—kudos for using an item more than one day without washing!

- Bring at least one sun hat, and for cold climates, a winter hat that covers the ears.

- Extra shoes (lightweight, inexpensive tennies) are good insurance against puddles, deep gutters, or toilet-training accidents. They can double as wading shoes.

- Extra clothing to consider (depending on season and destination) could include bathing suits, rain gear, wool sweaters (sturdy, warm, and slow to show dirt), one "fancy" outfit, a winter coat, maybe a windbreaker, a warm hat, and light gloves. (For camping and snow clothing, see the lists in chapter 10.)

Just How Many Outfits Does One Kid Need?

Evaluate your child. Be honest, now. Some little angels never seem to get wet or messy. Packing for them is easy—pack up to seven little outfits—one per day of trip up to a week. For longer trips, plan to wash as you go, or hit a washer/dryer on day six.

Some kids, on the other hand, are like Annie, whose enjoyment of the world is based on sampling substances with more than one sense or body part. We're well acquainted with ice-creamed shoes, jellied T-shirts, and a little face that looks like it went nine rounds with Jackson Pollack. We pack every outfit she owns, tote our own laundry soap, and scope out laundromats with fierce radar.

Laundry Soap

Get the soap you can use in sinks as well as in machines. For a short trip, pre-measure load-sized scoops into plastic bags and seal with a twist-tie. In Hawaii, the condominium we rented had a washer and a dryer, and several times I found myself on my knees in front of the machines, grateful, grateful, *grateful*. (At Lake Tahoe, the condo was similarly equipped; unfortunately, the power went out in a blizzard, leaving a machine full of wet, soapy clothing—but that's another tale.) Generally when we're on the road, we do a lot of washing by hand.

Toiletries

Don't forget the things that you don't use every day, like the baby nail clipper and the rubber bulb-thingy to clear out nostrils (for an infant). Another important item: diaper ointments (even if your baby is not usually rashy)—keep in mind changing climates and all (review the rash procedures in Chapter 2). Special note: If you're flying, keep the clippers in the chck-in bags. Metal nail files may be considered weapons.

Fluids

Bottles, sippy cups that don't spill, canteens, juice boxes—bring some or all. At three, Annie became adept at drinking from a commercial bottle of spring water—the kind with the squirt top. Whatever form it takes, don't forget the liquids. Nothing is worse than searching for fluids with a screaming, thirsty child. Of course, if you're a nursing mom you have it easier—but bring along a canteen of water for you.

Snack Food

Bring a small amount of something high-protein and non-perishable for emergency situations—delayed flights with no food service, terrible traffic jams...anything can happen. Bring an eensy jar of peanut butter, a protein bar, fruit roll-ups...just try not to casually munch on it yourself, or you may find yourself sorry!

The Basic Baby First-Aid Kit

You don't need to buy a special kit. I suggest customizing your own based on your destination. A call to your pediatrician explaining your destination and circumstances is always a good idea. I've included a "starter list" of first aid items in chapter 14, Troubleshooting A to Z, under M.

Each family's customized first-aid kit will illustrate a particular "slant": Our accident-prone little friend Jay's parents suggest suture glue and butterfly bandages. (At three, we already call the poor guy "Scarface.") Of course, they're the ones who call the emergency room at every destination in advance to find out what the pediatric procedures would be should something happen.

My personal weak point is skin, and I highly recommend the anti-itch Benedryl ointment stuff available over the counter in your local drugstore. It is my friend. I'm the type that mosquitoes love. On any given rural twilight, Bill will get a mosquito bite—one—while I'll get swarmed. Then my bites swell, pop, ooze, and eventually scar. Annie, poor dear, has inherited my skin. This ointment, with a little hydrocortisone chaser, is great.

Sunglasses

Available for you and baby in a variety of styles, colors and (ouch) price ranges. Don't forget that baby needs them in the snow, too.

Kleenex

This is the kind of thing I never, ever would have thought about packing in my pre-motherhood days. Long ago, it was me, my carry-on, and the road at my feet. But ever since Annie was an infant, I go *nowhere* without tissues. Wow. I feel like I've finally become a grown-up.

Chewing Gum

For airplane rides with kids three and up. Annie tried gum for the first time on a flight from Oakland to Seattle and did pretty well...hey, by the way, did you know that you really *can* remove chewing gum from hair using peanut butter?

Bathing Suits

They're small—pack one just in case, even if you don't think you'll be swimming. You never know when it will come in handy, and buying a swimsuit on the spur of the moment can ravage your wallet. In Maui we learned the hard way—children's swimsuits were hard to find on the mainland in January, so we cast our fate to the trade winds, and the bitty scrap of Hawaiian orange-and-green fabric set us back twenty bucks.

Socket Protectors and Masking or Duct Tape

Quick baby-proofing for hotel rooms—small, cheap, and worth their weight in worry.

Sturdy Toys

Not too small, and not too many. Especially if you're spending time in a natural setting. Picture yourself traipsing through the underbrush looking high and low for Sammy's one-inch tall favorite doll. Sammy is sobbing, you're contracting a fierce case of poison oak...no thanks. Let Sammy enjoy the sticks, the rocks, the leaves, the dirt.

Plastic Bags

You can *never* carry enough plastic bags. Tote a wide selection of all sizes: large garbage bags for dirty clothes, medium bags for dirty diapers or food or shoes, small baggies for found objects (feathers and rocks), and all size gradations in between. They weigh almost nothing and take up limited space.

Sunscreen

Our little friend Jakob's parents call it "Sun Scream."

On the road, we're outside more than we usually are at home, so it's easy to catch a few too many rays. Daily deployment of sunscreen is a good habit to get into, especially as the ozone grows thinner. Slather it on yourself and your loved ones before you get dressed in the morning; that way it won't be an issue when you hit the beach and the little one wants to run. (A more detailed discussion of sunscreen is included in chapter 10.)

Books

Bring some for all family members—though there's a good chance you won't find the opportunity to read yours. Reading books at bedtime helps settle kids who are still a little too hyper from the excitement of the long travel day. Paperback children's books are small and very lightweight. Have your toddler help decide which five she wants to take—then stash away an extra few for on-the-road surprises.

For four- or five-year-olds, try chapter books (*Little Bear, The House at Pooh Corner,* the *Little House* books). Read one chapter a night or at naptime (or whenever your child gets wiped).

Camera and Film or Disposable Camera

Inexpensive, light, point and shoot or disposable cameras are a boon to society. In general, I suggest never bringing anything on a trip that you're not prepared to lose or have damaged, but there may be times when you'll *want* to take

your video camera. Weigh the stress of worrying about it against the pleasure of having it with you (and having the videos later), then decide.

Receiving Blankets

My friends Ailsa and Steven swear by these. They always bring along at least three to use for car sunshades, extra towels, or in case Shoshi or Ellie throws up in the car.

Diaper Wipes

Wipes for all ages! You'll need approximately one box more than your normal allotment for every four days on the road. This doesn't mean you necessarily have to lug them all—they are available (with slight variations) all over the U.S., and in many places around the world. (Diaper wipes come in handy for the adults, too. Get the unscented type, unless you enjoy smelling like a clean baby's butt.)

Wipes can be used for far more than little bottoms. Some other applications:

- Sticky hands
- Grimy faces
- Filthy feet (before climbing into bed at night)
- Backs of necks (saves wear on shirt collars!)
- Damp underarms
- Assorted other body parts
- Dusty windshields
- Washing dishes in the stream (more effective than a sponge, and reusable)
- Cleaning picnic tables
- Arts and crafts paper (dry flat)
- Shoe polishers
- Emergency coffee filters (just kidding!)

Flashlight

Useful outside when you're camping. Especially useful inside for reading in the motel room if you're having one of those awful nights where the baby tosses and turns and wakes up every time an adult switches on the light. What—your kid always sleeps through the night? I hate you.

Baby Tote Gear

Backpack, stroller, what do you need? No easy answer to this one. Where are you going? How much walking will you do? Weigh the benefits of having the item against the drag of lugging it around. Factor in the size and ages of your children. Can they walk? *Will* they walk? What's your primary source of transportation? If you have a big car and are doing a car trip, why not bring the stroller? A stroller is less manageable if you are going Greyhound. (Go back to chapter 5 for more in-depth discussion of tote modes.)

How Much Stuff Do You Really Need?

A friend of ours recently returned from beautiful Costa Rica. Bus travel in Costa Rica, though cheap and convenient, often entails changing vehicles. Buses arrive at one side of an unsafe, rickety bridge, the passengers disembark, carry their luggage across the gently swaying bridge, and board another waiting bus, which carries them ten or fifteen miles—where the same thing is repeated.

On the day our friend traveled, her bus was filled with locals traveling light, tourists with backpacks, and an intrepid family of five Americans—two parents and three children aged five years, three years, and eight months. Each time the bus stopped, the hassled mother hustled the cranky children out of their seats, down off the old bus, over the bridge and into the waiting (even older) bus. Meanwhile the father, sweating furiously in the tropical heat, unloaded and trekked back and forth over the bridge, lugging multiple suitcases, strollers, a baby backpack, and a playpen.

The family did not look like they were having fun.

Lovey Toys

Familiar friends are a welcome touch of home for sleepy children wanting comfort in a strange environment. We have a rule that stuffed animals are for inside cars, hotel rooms, and tents—just imagine dear little Lambykins, covered in creek mud, clasped to the tiny chest of your just-bathed tot.

She's Got a Stuffed Animal Jones...

Our family lore includes a story of my step-daughter Rachel, aged five and seriously addicted to stuffed animals. The family was on the way to Mexico and traveling "light" (car to the border and the train to Mexico City), so a strict, two-animal limit was imposed on the poor girl. How she agonized over which friends would accompany her! Finally, Owly and Betsy were carefully bedded down amidst Rachel's clothes and toiletries. The journey was long, but eventually the family arrived at the hotel. Out of the duffel bag came Owly and Betsy. Then, much to the family's horror, out came the stowaways: Donder, Rainbow, Kissy Bear, Sheepy, Sealy, Moosy, Big Moo, Little Moo, Dolly, Molly, and Spot!

Annie isn't quite so delightfully devious, so to honor the grand family tradition her sister began, we always pack at least one unexpected stowaway that we keep hidden until bedtime the first night. At the grand unveiling, her face inevitably lights up with joy and amusement at the sight of her unexpected friend, and at the silliness of it all.

Lovey Blanket

Bedtimes in strange places can be scary for toddlers. Bring a blankie from home. Annie's travel quilt is a zillion different colors and cheery prints. It accompanied Annie on all her early journeys. (If it was a person, it would wear a bored blasé expression: "Europe? Hawaii? Been there, done that.") From one corner of the quilt peeks a little bear. Annie and I used to play a game checking each of the corners for it. "Is it here? No. Is it here? Yes! Here's a little guy who wants to say, 'Hello, Annie, Hello!'"

When Annie entered day care, the quilt lived in her cubby and rested with her during naptime. She doesn't remember all the places it (and she) has been, but it still brings a sense of security. On trips, the quilt still often comes with us. In a strange place it is one more environmental factor that remains familiar.

Brightly Colored Band-Aids

Not strictly a first-aid item—carry a few in an easily accessible place. "Preventive medicine," says my friend Ailsa, whose little girls Shoshi and Ellie (ages three and four) often arrive at destinations with their legs and arms plastered. Stickers work wonders, too.

Documents

Don't forget your tickets! You may need some or all of the following: birth certificate, immunization record, passport (yes, your baby needs one), medical information, prescriptions, and insurance forms. You might also consider family zoo or museum membership cards (if you're a member of your local zoo, you may be eligible for entry into other zoos). For security reasons, some parents travel with photos and fingerprints of their kids to help in the very rare cases of natural disasters, lost children, or abductions.

Distractions and Bribes

Since we're exceptional parents who never, ever lose our cool or our sense of control, and Annie is a *perfect* child who *never* cries or whines, and never, *ever* throws tantrums, we don't need to stoop to such things as little gifts for distractions and/or bribery when nothing else is working. But we've heard from people who aren't as perfect as we are that it's always a good idea to keep a few hidden gems to pull out in dire circumstances when you absolutely need the little buggers to stay still. Things like tiny dolls, trucks, books, or even...no, I didn't say it, Mom...candy.

Toilet Paper
Bring an extra roll. You never know.

And Don't Stress

It's always best to take what you need, unless you like unpleasant surprises, hassles finding things, or spending lots more money than you should. But you can always make do. In our global economy, replacements for almost anything are available (unless you're in the wilderness or deep in an under-industrialized nation). Children really need very little to survive. Ultimately, all they require is food, shelter, clothing, and you. When you're on the road, you are their home, and their security. Little else matters.

A Final Note to Despairing Moms

When you feel desperate that last day before you leave, with the floor strewn with items and the baby teething on the first-aid kit, and you're biting your lip to keep in the *screams*, remember, moms, it's just like labor and delivery. It's just one day (albeit one painful day) out of your life.

CHAPTER 8

Up in the Air

Up in the air you go flying again,
Up in the air, and down!
—*Robert Louis Stevenson*

Up Where the Air is Clear

I love listening to parents recount their recent airline trips with the little fruits of their loins. "It wasn't bad at all!" they usually tell me, amazed that everything went so well after all their nights of worry. "Sophie loved the airplane!" "Henry slept during the flight and the grandparents were *so* happy to see him!"

Yet, sometimes their voices hush as they tell me a nightmare story of screaming kids and frantic parents. Airplanes can provide trying times, and airports can seem like giant pinball machines—and you're the ball. Knowing what to expect, planning ahead, and taking a few precautionary steps can help assure a positive experience.

What follows is a step-by-step breakdown of everything connected with air travel—from making reservations, through airports and flights, to collecting the baggage and getting the rental car. (If you're flying alone with the small one, read this chapter first, then get additional survival hints in chapter 11.)

Making Reservations

You can make flight reservations through a travel agent, over the Internet, or by telephone directly through the airlines. Package deals are available through tour companies as well—check newspaper travel sections for bargains.

Some things to consider when planning flights:

  🔑 Try to schedule flights during your baby's naptime. If you have a non-napper, avoid flights late in the day when your child is exhausted and cranky.

  🔑 Ask about off-hour, mid-week travel. The rates are often cheaper.

  🔑 Be aware of this difference between direct and non-stop flights: direct flights stop at least once. You might have a layover, though you won't change airplanes (use the layover as an opportunity for your toddler to run around). Non-stop flights are preferable because (like the name says) you don't stop.

  🔑 Build in "buffer zones"—ask how much time you'll have between connecting flights. There is an FAA minimum layover time between connecting flights, but if the buffer zone is too short and the first flight is too late, you might have trouble making your next flight.

Call the airline the week before your flight to confirm flight times, make sure notations in your record still exist, and find out about food service and whether your plane will have refrigeration. Not all do! Planes without refrigeration do not carry milk.

Seating Arrangements

Center bulkhead seats face the walls at the front of each section of the plane. They provide more leg room and a small play area right in front of you. I swear by them, though they have a few disadvantages: you have to stow your carry-ons in the luggage racks above you (no seats in front of you to stow stuff under), sometimes the armrests don't move, sometimes the seats don't recline, and sometimes you have to fend off other passengers trying to use the space between you and the wall as a shortcut across the plane. (This can be a particular drag when your baby is napping on the floor at your feet.)

Not all airlines allow families to sit in the bulkhead, and those that do don't allow you to reserve the bulkhead in advance. You can try! Call early and often, to have requests entered in your record; arrive at the airport with time to spare; and, if necessary, throw a small tantrum yourself.

If you have an infant, your plane is equipped with bassinets (ask the ticket agent), *and* the bassinets are the type that attach to the bulkhead (see "Bassinets and Sleeping Bags," below), you can try to land the bulkhead by reserving a bassinet. You'll still be bumped if other passengers have more need for the bulkhead than you do (the lady with triplets, the man in the wheelchair).

Special note:

Airplanes are germ-factories. The air is recycled and the oxygen content becomes reduced. To reduce your chances of getting sick, drink mass quantities of non-carbonated water, take Vitamin C, echinacea, and zinc lozenges before, during, and after the flight (consult your pediatrician for advice on dosages for little ones), and wash your hands frequently with soap and water or rub with an anti-bacterial gel. If you or your child are especially prone to contracting viral illnesses, get flu shots, consider wearing disposable paper surgical masks, and avoid flying during the height of flu season (drive, take the train, take a boat).

So, the Tantrum Didn't Work?

If the airline won't allow you to sit in the bulkhead, try asking for the front seats of a section. Or reserve an aisle seat. Sitting on the aisle guarantees access to the rest of the plane, a necessity with a toddler. If you're trapped in the middle with an antsy kid, you may be in for a miserable journey; and even though window seats provide a nice view (for *you*, your baby won't care), they can be a hassle as you try to get the bathroom yet again. ("Excuse me... I'm sorry... excuse me...")

If you're traveling as a family of two adults and a child under two in arms, try reserving the aisle seat and the window seat in a row of three. Unless the plane is very full, they'll probably keep that extra seat open.

Car Seats on the Plane

Here's the dilemma—pediatricians insist that the safest way for a baby to experience take-off and landings is strapped in her car seat. But where do you put it? If your child is under two, you're probably not paying for her to have her own seat, though some airlines do provide discounts for babies under two riding in carseats.

When you make your seat reservations, ask the ticket agent to enter in your record that: 1) You're traveling with a baby, and 2) That you want to bring your car seat. Ask them to try to leave the seat(s) next to you open (try the aisle/window trick above). When you call back to reconfirm, make sure the notation is still there. If the plane is too full, the attendants will check your car seat at the gate.

What's the Law?

Here's a summation of the current FAA regulations about babies and toddlers and car seats and such: if your baby is under two years old, you do *not* need to buy him a seat—you may carry him in your arms. If your child is over two, he must be in an individual seat and restricted by an approved seatbelt. That means, either in the regular airline seat with a regular seatbelt, *or* in a carseat approved by the National Highway Safety Transportation Administration (NHSTA). Your car seat must be embossed with the NHSTA logo (a sticker will not do).

Quick Tip:
Bottles

Mixing formula on airplanes can get very sloppy. Bring pre-measured water or make up bottles right before you board (go back to Chapter 2 for more on traveling with a formula-fed baby). For a baby *over* one year, bring along bottles with ⅓ cup of pre-measured powdered milk inside. Fill bottle to top, shake it, and Voila!

Negotiating Airports

I love airports. They're busy, they're crazy, and they can be the most challenging part of the trip. Here the masses converge, here humanity at its worst and finest can be found embracing, departing, crying, laughing, rushing, fretting, being bored...but I digress.

Time and Waiting

Leave lots of time. Arrive with plenty to spare. Post-September 11, most airlines now ask you to arrive two hours before a domestic flight and three hours before an international one, and to leave even more time if you're traveling with little ones. Arghh! I know, the flight itself might only be half an hour! At times, security lines and keeping your little ones sane in them (not to mention you) will make you reevaluate whether the driving trip is really that bad a thing. You may not be able to avoid the line but snacks, courage, and patience will get you through every time. If you're traveling solo, the stroller or luggage cart is a necessity (more below). If you're traveling with another adult, take turns standing in line and walking around with the baby.

Getting to the airport very early does have some advantages, though. Better to be bored than frantic. Many airports now have play areas, exhibits, and other fun things to do when you're not in line. Food is usually bad and expensive—try to bring your own snacks. If you have a long wait for a plane after security screening, consider stowing your carry-ons in a coin-operated locker. With only your baby, a lightweight stroller or luggage cart (optional), a wallet, and an extra diaper to hold, you'll be free to wander around and people-watch. Beware of the gift shop! It is designed to suck you in and steal your money!

The Trouble with Train Schedules

Experience can make one cocky. I speak from experience. On our most recent trip to Paris we had an almost four-hour layover in Amsterdam. We knew: 1) The train to Amsterdam takes twenty minutes; 2) Trains run every ten minutes; 3) Trains in Holland are very reliable; 4) The main train station is a brief walk from incredible canals and even more incredible fresh herring stands. The plan? A quick trip in, a quick walk, a quick gulp of fish, and a quick trip back out. We had plenty of time. Of course, all his happened a few months before September 11, when air travel became more stringent. All went well. We got back to the train station with almost two hours to spare. Then the nightmare began… the famously reliable trains fell down on the job. We boarded a train. It didn't leave. We dismounted and boarded another. An announcement: this one would be late as well. Four trains and many tears later, the train left the station—twenty minutes before the plane was scheduled to fly. The train, full of late airline passengers, flew down the tracks. The family, once there, flew through the airport, making wrong turns, yelling at ticket agents for them to call ahead and hold our plane, all three of us running flat out. I never knew a kid could run so fast. At the gate, we pounded on the locked doors—and made the flight. All that remained was the sweaty, red faced Walk of Shame to our seats. Yes, we were the culprits who held up the plane.

Porters and Valets

Airports in the U.S. and many other countries usually have porters available to help you carry stuff. They are airport employees, but it is customary to give them a tip. Have a few small bills easily accessible. You don't want to be digging through your bags while your toddler is running away.

Checking In

Get your seats pre-assigned, if possible. Then check your luggage curbside if your airport provides this service (it's worth calling ahead to find out). Even if you have to wait in line at the ticket counter, you'll have an easier time with less stuff to shove along with your feet. Putting identification tags on your bags *before* you get to the airport will save you time once you're there. If you check a car seat or baby backpack, you'll have to sign a damage waiver, but don't worry, they usually arrive at the other side intact.

Carts

Most U.S. airports have luggage carts available for around a dollar. Sometimes they're free. Either way, make sure to get one, even if you check your baggage. It will be invaluable for confining your child, for parking your carry-ons, for claiming airport territory, and for zipping from place to place. Most models have a place for little children to sit, similar to a grocery shopping cart.

Consider a Stroller

Lightweight, fold-up strollers are another approach, even if your kid usually walks. If you have *two* little ones, a double stroller is invaluable. You might look ridiculous, draped with baby gear and slowly maneuvering a wide swath across the crowded airport, but who cares? You'll get there slowly, but you'll get there. Arrive at the gate early. If there is no room in the cabin of the plane to stow the stroller, the (grumbling) airline personnel can check it at the gate and send it downstairs.

Reject the temptation to use your stroller as a luggage carrier; you'll increase your stroller's life-span.

Moving Sidewalks

Some allow carts and strollers, some don't. They can be dangerous for little hands—be aware!

Shuttle Buses

Hop on. If there are no seats available, look pathetic and desperate. If this doesn't work, ask the driver to ask somebody to move. If none of these tactics work and you absolutely have to stand, hold on and have your child hold on to you. If you have a baby, wear him—in a front pack, backpack, or sling. Stand with your feet wide apart for more support. Brace yourself against a pole—it's more secure than the ceiling straps.

Metal Detector and Security Screening

To get to the secure areas of the airport and the gate where you'll board your plane requires going through the metal detector and security screening. You'll have to unload all your stuff from the cart and put it on the moving band so it can be X-rayed. You may or may not be able to get your cart back. Ask. Sometimes they'll take it around the side. You may be pulled aside and questioned or searched. You might very well have your check-ons searched (remember to take all nail files and any other possible weapons out of your bags before leaving for the airport). All of this adds up to one thing—delays. That's why you got here early.

If you're a celebrity, you may not have to deal with the baaing and mooing of the rest of us as we slowly wend our way towards the security screening point. Waiting for Bill to return from a recent trip, Annie and I watched a dapper man in a wheelchair (garbed in fedora hat, cashmere shirt, leather coat, and $600 shoes) get wheeled by a porter swiftly past the line to the checkpoint where, with a nod to his admirers and a buck for the porter, he stepped out of the chair, walked through the metal detector, and strode casually away and up the escalator.

The Gate

Unless you're traveling internationally, you'll generally find fewer amenities here than in the main part of the airport. I usually delay our trip to the gate until shortly before boarding. On the other hand, if you're nervous about time, loaded with stuff, or ready to sit and rest, go to the gate area and claim a bank of seats. Toddlers can watch the planes take off and land. If things get too crowded, you can often find a nearby empty gate where you can still hear announcements and the little ones can run around.

Before Boarding

If your child is potty-trained, try to have him go *before* you get on the plane. Change diapers here, too. Airport bathrooms are usually easier to negotiate, and often cleaner, than airplane bathrooms. Many airports have nurseries equipped with changing tables, sinks, towels, and chairs to feed the baby.

On, Off, Up, and Down

You've gotten all the way to the gate! Alas, the journey has yet to begin. Here's the scoop on boarding, deplaning, ascending, descending, and the flight time in between.

Boarding

Most airlines have a pre-board option for people traveling with small children. There are two schools of thought on this one:

School of Thought #1 - Take advantage of your pre-boarding advantage. Settle in; take up space. Get greedy. Grab pillows and blankets and stow your stuff in the luggage bins. Ask for the seats next to you to be left empty as long as possible. Assert yourself. You're traveling with a baby—most people won't want to sit next to you anyway.

School of Thought #2 - Don't board yet! It's a long time before you actually leave, you know. You might get your seven-month-old all calmed down then wait forty-five minutes on the ground before taking off. The airplane ascends, and baby, refreshed from his nap, wakes up ready to boogie. (Caution: With this School of Thought you're risking your luggage bin space!)

Strapping In

If you're not using your car seat, your little one needs to be strapped into a seat belt or held tightly on your lap for take-off and landings. (Remember that the in-arm choice only works if your child is *under two*. Kids who are two and over *must* have their own seat and be secured with an approved restraint.) Some international airlines have children's belt extenders—they hook to your seat belt as the child sits on you. I haven't found them in this country and it's probably just as well—the guy I talked with about them at the FAA called them "death belts." He explained the physics, too. Ugh. Enough said about that. Don't use them.

Taking Off and Landing

Little kids have no natural fear of flying, but they will pick up on your tensions. Try to relax. If you're traveling with a toddler or preschooler, explain what is happening.

The Ear Thing

Many parents are concerned about the change in air pressure on take-off and landings, and how it will affect their baby or small child. Contrary to the horror stories you might hear, many pediatricians now believe that there is no relationship between flying and ear infections.

Ascents and descents with an infant should be relatively easy. Encourage them to nurse or, if they're in their car seat, to suck on a bottle or pacifier to keep their ears popped and pain-free. They may feel some discomfort, but it should pass quickly.

The slightly older baby—uncomprehending, unco-operative little dear—may have a slightly harder time, though his cry of dismay at the unaccustomed pressure is nature's way of adjusting. Do whatever you can to get him to swallow.

A small child, over two and communicative, can be worked with. She'll grab her ears or tell you of any discomfort: "Mommy, my ears!" Bring along a sippy cup. Encourage her to yawn. Make silly faces at her, and have her make them back at you. A drop of Vicks vapor rub or eucalyptus oil on a Kleenex held a comfortable distance under your child's nose also can help clear stuffiness. Children over three can chew gum to relieve the pressure (but make sure you watch where the gum ends up).

Bill says jelly beans do the trick—at least they did for Annie on their first solo daddy/daughter flight to L.A. Of course, he's only admitting this *now*.

Drugs

Drugs are a useful option for some families. Benadryl (an antihistamine) unstuffs noses and ears (and has the added benefit of helping kids relax and, potentially, sleep). Consult your pediatrician for advice and prescriptions. Test the drugs once before you go—they make some kids hyperactive. Exactly what you *don't* want. If your child has a history of motion sickness, talk to your pediatrician about Dramamine.

Whatever the drug, if you'll be on the plane a very long time (over four hours) you may want to weather the take-off and wait awhile before giving the medica-tion. If you do it right away, it will wear off near the end of the trip. You'll be at your most fatigued, and your baby will be wired for the rest of the flight.

If you want your child to relax but you're leery about medicating her, chamomile tea and milk is a natural sedative. Bring a small thermos already made up, but make sure it's not too hot.

Turbulent Times

We flew to Maui on a cold, blustery day when the rivers flooded over their banks. As we waited to board, we admired the fools returning from Hawaii, with their blissed-out expressions and wilting flower leis. Their tan limbs shivered in their shorts and teeny tank tops.

Once aboard, the crew triple-checked everybody's seat belt, the plane accelerated down the runway and took off at a steep angle, cutting sharply up through the storm, and the young flight attendant in front of me surreptitiously crossed herself. Never a good sign.

I took deep breaths. I turned to two-year-old Annie to reassure her and was met by a grin. All over the plane, parents grimaced and children giggled as we bounced our way over the Pacific. An hour into the trip the air cleared, the flight attendant smiled, and we were truly on our way.

In-the-Air Survival Skills

Merely getting yourself and your children aboard an airplane can feel like a victory. And it is! Yet there are a few things you should know before you go.

Dress for Disaster

Flying alone with kids, you may have juice dumped on you, and be thrown up or pooped on. The plane may be hours late. Think of it as a job, not a fashion show. Opt for sweats rather than silk. Bring two changes of easy-to-change clothes in a ziplock baggie for each child. Take off everybody's shoes—feet swell—and fly in slippers or thick socks. Make sure to bring sweaters or sweatshirts—airplane air is *cold!* Bring one change of clothes for yourself. Wet or dirty clothes can be stowed back in their baggie, keeping the rest of your stuff unpolluted.

Learning the Hard Way

Jessica knew well about bringing extra outfits for her *kids*, but half an hour into a full day of flying (with a two hour stop-over at Chicago's O'Hare), eighteen-month-old

Alexandra threw up on her. Not just a little, either—Jessica was soaked to the skin with vomit. With no extra clothes except for a sweater, Jessica had no recourse but to remove her shirt, put on her sweater, and spend another eight hours of traveling ignoring both the pungent odors rising from her torso and jeans as well as the strange looks from strangers.

Changing Diapers

This is another place where the space in front of the bulkhead seats comes in handy. Usually one of the bathrooms on an airplane has a fold-down changing table. Or look for empty rows of seats. Use the little vomit bags provided in the front seat pocket for dirty disposables and wipes—but don't stow them back inside the pocket. Give them to the attendant or throw them out yourself during your next trip up and down the aisle.

Treats, Toys, Bribery

Don't rely on the airline to supply entertainment— bring lots of things to occupy little hands and mouths. Play-Doh, plastic dinosaurs, lots o' paperback children's books, stickers, coloring books and marking pens, forbidden snacks…all of these things can be segregated into separate zip-lock baggies and whipped out one by one as the little one gets restless. Make sure you put things away as you go—you'll save yourself an end-of-flight scramble.

Lily once continuously read to Xavier, three and one-half, on a flight across country. Lily's voice grew hoarse, but Xavier sat quietly the entire trip (quite uncharacteristically for him), and the adjacent passengers got a healthy dose of children's literature.

Many airlines have complimentary activity packets. Ask the flight attendant. A tape recorder with headphones is a good choice for some children (the plane's headphones may not adjust small enough for a little kid).

Toys that are too tiny or have wheels are *not* good choices. Try to keep things around your seats fairly organized—and save yourself from the mad dash to get everything stowed as the plane descends and the seat-belt light begins to blink for landing.

The Long March

Be prepared to walk all the way to Chicago or Tokyo—sometimes pacing the aisle is the only way to calm your kid down. The other passengers are usually charmed. The exercise will help you avoid a bad case of jet lag, too.

Other Kids

If there are other babies or small children on the plane, you're in luck! Kids can play together, older ones can admire little ones, parents can give each other breaks.

Food

Don't ever rely on airlines to get your child fed. Meals are *not* provided on every flight. If you are traveling cross-country you may be caught in the twilight zone—two long flights and a layover but, because of flight times, you only get a small breakfast. Bring your own supplies of sandwiches, fruit, and snacks.

Airplane food is notoriously bad. Although it may not be edible, its arrival breaks up the monotony and provides some entertainment value. Special children's meals are sometimes available (at least one airline uses a famous fast food joint's kids meal). You can call at least a day ahead to request vegetarian, kosher, diabetic, or seafood meals. One advantage to ordering special meals is that you will often be served first.

Snacks

Normally forbidden snacks are fine as a special treat but try to keep the sugar level down and the energy level up.

Small bags of cut-up carrots or celery (watch for choking for the under two set), washed grapes, raisins, Goldfish crackers, home-popped or organic popcorn (doesn't have too much salt), tiny cookies (for treats and bribes), mini-bagels, fruit roll-ups, Cheerios, and cheese cubes are all good choices. Most airlines have switched from peanuts to pretzels for financial reasons—that's OK, babies and toddlers shouldn't eat peanuts anyway. You might want to review the travel snack information in chapter 3.

Water! Water! Water!

Airplane air is as dry as the Gobi desert. A lot of the symptoms of jet lag are caused by dehydration. An amazing fact about the human body—we have a feeble thirst mechanism. By the time you think about taking a drink, your body is already dehydrated. Avoid alcohol; that only makes it worse.

Bill and I always bring a liter of spring water and force ourselves to drink eight ounces per hour during the course of the flight. We have a separate bottle of water for Annie, and encourage her (frequently) to take sips.

Bassinets and Sleeping Bags

Bassinets hook onto the wall in the bulkhead section of some airplanes. They are for use only by small babies—and must be removed for take-off and landings. Sleeping bags are useful in the bulkhead section, too. Baby can sleep at your feet while you relax. I suggest asking about and reserving these items in advance.

Flying Baby!

On a long flight to Europe, we got lucky. Flying was exciting for seven-month-old Annie, not because of the gorgeous view of Iceland or the free drinks, but because of all the people and attention. Eventually she fell asleep, exhausted from smiling at so many friendly faces. And about the ear thing—we had no problems. Annie nursed during take-offs and landings, except during the final landing when she refused to nurse and sat quietly on my lap, occasionally yawning.

The Impossible Child

Your little angel is running up and down the aisles kicking people. Every polite request is met by a high pitched scream of denial. When you try to calm him down with Play-Doh, he throws it against the head of the man in front of you. You've never seen so many tantrums in a two-hour period. Your head is splitting. You suspect that the head of every passenger within four rows of you is splitting. Your kid has turned into a monster.

When a kid is this hyped up, you can try some of your bribes—but they probably won't work. Try not to lose it. Take ten deep breaths, letting each out slowly. Accept that the rest of the people on the plane hate you. So what? They'll probably never see you again. Firmly deal with your child (without screaming). This kind of behavior is not acceptable, no matter how miserable or excited he is.

Take him into the bathroom, kicking or screaming if need be, and keep him there until he is calm. Hold him. Assess the situation. Why is he out of control? He may be miserable *and* excited. Try to remember that crying is the only way your baby has of expressing himself. Is he hungry? Scared? Simply on overload? What can you do to lower his stress?

Take care of his bodily needs. Reassure him. Sometimes just the few minutes in private together will change your child's energy level. Sometimes it won't. Do the best you can—you're not the first parent who's had to deal with behavior like this and you won't be the last. Eventually the flight will be over.

On a trip to Seattle, Annie enjoyed the view of the mountains out the window. "Is the pilot driving very fast?" She surprised me by knowing the word for pilot. Two and one-half years old. Brilliant? I think so.

Dealing with Unsympathetic Fellow Fliers

There are adults who are intolerant of children—even children who are not acting out. You may even have been one of them once...I was. It's their loss. How do you deal with that man across the aisle who's been sending you withering glances while your baby screams? What do you say to the poor woman who's been kicked in the back for the thousandth time by your restless four-year-old? They look at you like you're the most terrible parent on the planet for allowing her be so out of control.

You may not be able to calm your kid, but you might be able to save your reputation. By translating the situation for the other adults, you'll let them know that you're aware of the situation, and are dealing with it. Verbalize your child's emotions: "I know, it's hard to be strapped in for so long. But the plane is going through a thing called turbulence, and we need to stay in our seats." Or, "I know, I know, you're tired and hungry. Just rest here, Sweetie. Lunch will be here soon." Or even, "Rosie-Posie, you're angry because Mommy got mad at you. But I need you to be more considerate and not kick that man's chair."

In dire cases or when you're feeling particularly flush or your boss is sitting, unexpectedly, in the row behind you, you might resort to bribing your fellow passengers. Buying drinks and/or movies for your baby's victims might be expensive but will lead to a lot more "understanding."

"We're There, Honey!"

Yes! You made it! Only a couple more hurdles await...

Deplaning

Resist your impulse to stand up and rush off the plane—you'll just end up standing in the aisle, smashed up against your restless fellow passengers. Stay in your seats as long as you can. Then gracefully depart, first

carefully checking around your seats for dropped toys, bottles, and tiny socks.

Baggage Claim

You've successfully negotiated the flight. Everybody is tired—but you still have to get your luggage and rent the car! Poor toddlers have been cooped up long enough, now they want to run. The baby is crying in your ear. Gird your loins. This may be the hardest part of the journey.

Rent a little cart again. Stop at the bathroom. While you're waiting for your luggage you may need to get tough and stick the kid in the cart whether or not she likes it. If you aren't in a rush, you can wait for a while before approaching the carousel. The crowds will be thinner, and your luggage will have already been unloaded.

Car Rental

Waiting in car rental lines can be a drag. If you can, arrange ahead of time for your car to be waiting for you. If not, grin and bear it, and save one or two high-protein snacks for the line.

CHAPTER 9

Baby-Friendly Lodging

Oh for a lodge in some vast wilderness…
—*William Cowper*

Sleeping—Part of the Adventure

Hotels, motels, hostels, friend's houses, and rental condominiums are more than just a place to park your weary heads; they're part of the adventure. For a little kid, there is magic in the Magic Fingers massager on the motel-room bed, the condominium closets provide secret hiding places, and face it, even for adults, room service is *fun!* This chapter focuses on how to find places to stay that are a blast for little kids, and affordable and easy for you, from fancy digs to down-and-dirty dives. It includes tips on making your stay in your "home away from home" less problematic.

> **It's the Novelty…**
>
> The first time my step-kids Aaron and Rachel stayed in a motel (back when Aaron was five and Rachel was two), they couldn't stop bouncing on the bed. For hours it went on—first one, then the other, then both of them, until the inevitable collision occurred and the giggles

turned into tears. They had beds at home and they didn't bounce there—what was so exciting?

Bathroom faucets—we take for it granted that they come in different shapes. Kids don't. A new style of window shade! For toddlers and preschoolers, there is little more thrilling than complimentary tiny shampoo bottles, use-once-before-they-dissolve shower caps, and lightweight fold-up travel toothbrush kits.

Assessing Your Lodging Needs

Before you jump into making reservations any old place, consider your family's needs. As you read this chapter, consider the following:

- It's cheaper to share a bathroom down the hall— but not a great idea for a child in potty training who, when he has to go, has to go now!
- Do you want or need a bathtub? A shower?
- Consider the noise factors. Is the hotel noisy? Is your child? Your baby screams all night? "Okay, okay, ixnay on the monastery idea."
- What kind of sleeping set-up is available? Will the place provide the equipment you need?
- What kind of other amenities will you like or need? Will you use the amenities provided? (If you'll never swim, despise room service, and won't use the baby-sitting, a place with a pool, fancy catering, and in-house child care won't do anything for you.)
- How long will you stay? What's tolerable for one night might be dismal after two.
- Does it really need to be swanky, or will "func-tional" do?

Combining Your Lodging Types

Nobody said you have to choose one type of lodging and stick to it. For me, the most extreme contrast of lodging types was a trip to New York City, years before wife-hood and baby. For the first three nights I stayed with my

Aunt Laurie and Cousin Jesse in the United Nations Plaza hotel, a gleaming metal and glass skyscraper. We indulged ourselves with room service, and enjoyed the dizzying view from the ninety-second floor.

Then Laurie and Jesse flew home, and I was on my empty-pocketed own. The taxi driver who picked me up in front of the swanky lobby asked my destination three times before he "got it." I settled into the back seat with my backpack and said loudly again, "The Uptown YMCA, please. "That's where I stayed for the next three nights, in the birthplace of the disco song of the same name, hiding in my roach-infested (but very cheap) room as naked men in towels roamed the corridors and TVs blared 'til dawn.

Staying with Friends and Family

Staying with friends and family can be the ideal travel set-up, and you certainly can't beat the price, but you do risk the relationship. Value the friendship, tread lightly, and consider the following before throwing the phone in the air in glee and shouting, *"Yes! Yes! Yes!"* when they agree to put you up:

- Do they have kids (ideally kids in the same age range)? If so, then they'll probably be set up with toys and babyproofed, and used to the racket and clutter you'll be bringing with you.
- Do they not only *like* kids, but *understand* kids? Is the house kid-friendly? Are they open to making baby-proofing adjustments? ("What a beautiful Tiffany lamp, Aunt Martha. Do you mind if I put it up here in the closet until we're gone? I'd hate Baby Maurice to cause the estate broker any distress....")
- No matter how great a set-up your friends have, and how much they beg you to come, if you have too many high-octane kids, you may feel like you are imposing. They may feel that way, too.
- Are your lifestyles, values, and schedules compatible? (Notice the word "compatible." They don't

have to match, but if they diverge widely, you may have a problem.)

- Do they have animals? Are animals an issue for your family (do they frighten your kids, do any of you have allergies)?

Renting a Room— Research and Reservations

As an experienced adventure budget traveler, I hold grim memories of walking up and down the streets of many a city looking for lodging. As a parent, I've had the experience a couple too many times (well, how do you think I *know* all this stuff?) of not reserving, of leaving it up to chance, and then, when the baby suddenly reaches her limit, being forced to find a place to stay *immediately*. A place usually can be found, but inevitably it's at least twice the expected cost. (There was that time in Italy...but then again, when do you have the opportunity to stay in a medieval fortress, huh? And it was late, and the baby was tired.)

When traveling with small ones, by all means try to avoid these scenarios. A little advance planning makes a big difference. Rely on all the technology available to you—we've set up lodging in France via Internet and email, and in Thailand via fax. I'm old enough to still think this is an amazing fact.

Booking on the Internet

Researching lodging on the Internet is fantastic, especially for seeing what hotels, apartments, and resorts look like (simply plug your destination into your favorite search engine and let the hits fly!). *Booking* hotels or lodging on the Internet, on the other hand, *can* be successful if you watch for pitfalls: Are the photos really representative? Is somebody available through email or on the phone to answer your many questions? Shop savvy, save agony.

Facilities

When contacting potential lodging places (hotels, motels, B&Bs), these are a few things to ask about:

- Ask for a full description of facilities. What kinds of rooms are available? Are they set up for children? Does the hotel *like* kids? (It's a good question to ask—they'll rarely admit to a "no," but you may be able to tell from their enthusiasm or lack thereof.)

- If you have more than one grown-up, more than one child, and the budget can stand the strain, ask about getting two adjoining rooms. Sometimes a two-room suite can provide enough privacy and yet enough togetherness. (In Mexico City, we stayed in a four-bed "suite" that cost little more than a "double" and gave us all the privacy we needed.)

- Ask about the availability of cribs, crib sheets, floor pads, or rollaway beds (if required). Do they need to be reserved? What size are the "big" beds? Some suites have hide-a-beds for additional flexibility. For us the ideal set-up would include a California king-sized bed—big enough for the *whole* family (no matter what sleeping arrangements we made, Annie, until the ancient age of six, always ended up in the bed with us anyway).

- Don't feel like taking the potty seat, the VCR, the rocking chair, the high chair, and the crib? If you stay at a destination resort, you may want to rent these things. "Baby's Away" rents baby equipment—daily, hourly, weekly, monthly—to visiting parents at more than thirty locations. Their number is listed under Equipment in the Resources Appendix.

- Some hotels and motels have "kitchenettes." Do you want to eat breakfast in? Have some late night toast and jam? Not a bad idea with a kid.

🐘 Where is the available room located? Unless the view is a draw and the hotel has good elevators, request a ground-level room to minimize the "schlep" factor.

Money Issues

Face it, money is *always* an issue, and unless you're staying with your parents or Great Aunt Sophie, lodging will always be one of the biggest expenses of any trip. (If you're considering staying with your parents or Great Aunt Sophie, weigh the emotional expenses against the financial expenses...for some people, it's "cheaper," alas, to stay in a hotel.)

Services and Amenities

So just what will you be getting? Find out.

🧱 Ask about special amenities for infants or children (some fancy hotels provide special welcome packages for the toddler set.)

🧱 Are they willing/able to help you discover local things to do with kids?

🧱 Is there a pool? Spa? What are the hours, and are children allowed? (Sometimes they are not, or the hours they are allowed are restricted.)

In General

🔑 Reserve as far ahead as you can.

🔑 Find out about payment. Do they take checks? Credit cards? Cash on the barrel head?

🔑 What is their cancellation policy? (Kids *do* get sick...)

🔑 Request written or faxed confirmation. And whatever else you forget, remember to bring the confirmation with you!

Fabulous Fancy Hotels

Look, when you're traveling with little ones, life is hard enough without trying to rough it, too. There is great emotional value in being pampered—and sometimes you've just gotta go for it. There are trade-offs—when you choose to stay in a fancy rather than a moderate or budget hotel, you are choosing to spend a big part of your traveling budget on lodging.

An Advantage of a Fancy Hotel

Sarah was three and taking a bath in the fancy Los Angeles hotel her mother and father were treating themselves to. They turned their backs, and she pooped in the tub. Life is easy in the fast lane—one phone call to Housekeeping, one moderate tip, one clean tub.

Scintillating, Scuzzy Motels

Old roadside motels retain a down'n'dirty, romantic, All-American charm, and though the bed might sag and the bureau may be scarred with ancient cigarette burns, the prices can't be beat. Slightly more upscale and newer motels provide the basics—a bed, a TV, a shower, maybe a pool—and sometimes that's all you need.

Kid-Delighting Motel Features

Kids *love* ice machines ("It's free!"), and most motels have them down the corridor.

Some old beds will, for a quarter in a meter on the side, give you a jiggling "Magic Finger" massage. Treat your kids to *one* a night.

Modern motels sometimes have super-duper play structures—and somewhere out there is an old-fashioned motel with the kind of fun-and-funky playground I remember from when I was a kid.

Go for a Swim

It's a driving day? Leave early in the morning, eat breakfast during rush hour, arrive by three in the afternoon, and take a refreshing swim. Motel swimming pools offer the perfect end to a long afternoon in the car.

Once in Port Angeles, Washington, we stayed at a seedy motel with an even seedier swimming pool.

Annie, who was *seriously* into wonton soup, must have had a craving, for she invented a game with Bill called Swimming to the Chinese Restaurant. Like a small flea on the back of a dog, she hung onto her daddy's neck as he swam lap after lap, back and forth across the pool. What this had to do with Chinese food, I've never been quite sure, but it didn't really matter—I left them to their delightful game, laid down on the motel bed, and stared into space for a blissful, solitary hour.

Quick Tip

Are your child's toilet habits still a little...*unpredictable?* Bring waterproof sheets.

Once You Arrive

Once you check in, you have a couple of things to do before you dash to catch the last half hour before the Louvre closes, or race to the lake before the wind comes up: you need to make the room livable; and, you need to make sure that it's babyproof.

Set the room(s) up so you'll all be comfortable. Does the room have everything you requested or need? Feel free to move furniture around, and if you can't move it yourself, ask for help from the management. If you explain that it is for safety and you promise to return things to their proper positions, they won't squawk about it. (If they do, you might want to gently murmur the word "lawsuit.")

Hotel and motel rooms are usually fairly easy to child-proof. Review the basic Babyproofing Checklist in Chapter 1. The suggestions below may give you some additional ideas.

- Have unsafe furniture or delicate objects removed from the room.
- Unless you bring your own toilet lock, it's a good idea to keep the bathroom door closed.

•⚓ Electrical outlet covers are cheap, light, and small. Carry several with you and plug those outlets.

⚓ Bring a small roll of masking or duct tape for sealing and shutting.

Hotel Baby-Sitters

Hotels often provide or arrange baby-sitting services for their guests. Sometimes these are hotel employees, though usually they are professionals hired through local baby-sitting agencies. (The advantage of agency baby-sitters is that they aren't just the proprietor's fifteen-year-old niece—they are experienced, and they've been "checked out.")

If you don't like the person the hotel provides, or if the baby-sitter acts like just a "maintenance" person— parking your kids in front of the tube and chatting on the phone or some such nonsense—tell the hotel management at once. They'll change your provider.

Room Service

Pros:

• Room service is fun! It's exciting hearing that knock on the door, seeing the cart wheeled in, and opening the silver lids on the dishes.

• At the end of a long day of travel when you can't bear leaving the room again, room service can save your butt.

• In a fullservice hotel, room service can be an excellent breakfast choice. Kids can take a long time to get ready in the morning, especially in a new environment. By the time they're washed and dressed, they're cranky for lack of food.

Cons:

• Room service is expensive. It is ridiculously expensive.

• Room service is not always available. Don't ever count on it. Carry emergency supplies.

• Quality can vary from quite good to "If you plug your nose, this is really quite mediocre."

Treat Yourself

Sometimes you just have to take care of yourself. Sometimes the traveling is too much. In New Delhi, I was sick with bronchitis, and the Indian streets with their people-cows-cars-chickens-trucks-taxis-monkeys were too much for me. My fascination had shifted to an agoraphobia induced by feeling physically crummy. The idea of going out for food filled me with a sense of doom.

We were staying in a middle-class business hotel—cheap by Western standards, expensive by "traveler" standards and this hotel had (oh joy!) room service! Brought to our room, the finest tandoori-and-butter chicken I've ever tasted, accompanied by beautiful buttered nan (bread). I was immediately happy—the world shifted focus, and I knew I'd be all right. Never before had four hotel walls felt so welcoming and warm. Food with no effort. Well worth every rupee (though, like everything in India when you have American dollars, it was *cheap*!).

Food Delivery

Many restaurants in the United States will be happy to deliver to hotels and motels. For a fallback, there's always pizza or Chinese delivery. In addition, in many major U.S. metropolitan areas, there are also restaurant food-delivery services. These companies usually publish a free listing of the restaurants available and their regular menus.

Craving that special pasta dish from the restaurant across town? Call the food-delivery company, select from one or more restaurants, and they do the hauling. There is usually a minimum charge, a delivery fee (about five to seven dollars per order—it varies by location), and, if you compare the menus in the brochure and the regular restaurant menus, you'll notice that each item has been slightly marked up. Plus, of course, you should give the delivery person a tip. Many companies will also pick up videos or booze on their way over. ("*Party!!!*" Not.) If there is no brochure in your room, ask at the front desk or manager's office for details and suggestions.

Beds with Breakfast

In this country, bed and breakfast inns are not always the best choices for kids. They are quiet, and precious, and charming, and often small with thin walls. If your kid is at all kid-like, you might want sturdier walls to bounce off of. If you do decide to go the "quaint and quiet" route:

- 🗂 Make sure to ask the proprietors how they feel about kids before making reservations.
- 🗂 Many B&B rooms are very small. Where will Junior sleep? Is there room for your porta-crib or for their rollaway bed? Do they have a rollaway bed?
- 🗂 Be prepared for some serious babyproofing and knick-knack removal.
- 🗂 Ask for a room as far away from other rooms as possible.
- 🗂 Find out what they mean by "breakfast." Coffee and a Danish are not the most nutritious way for a two-year-old to start her day.

Quick Tip

If they're reluctant to answer your questions, you should be reluctant to stay there.

Resorts

At a resort, the lodging isn't *part* of the vacation, the lodging *is* the vacation. Resorts are more than Club Med—there are places to take the mineral waters, places for singles, seniors, kids, and weight loss. There are beach resorts, city resorts, and great old rustic lake resorts where you can rent a row boat, cheap, and the squeaky cots in the cabins date back from 1954. Kid-friendly resorts often offer baby-sitting so the adults can eat a romantic dinner together, or even spend the day alone. Vacationing at a resort is a bit of a commitment. Query carefully before you sign up for a weekend or a week—let them know all about your family, and listen hard if they try to discourage you from coming. You should know exactly what you are getting, and so should they.

Family Youth Hostels

You don't have to be a youth to stay in a youth hostel. Youth hostels are an inexpensive way for families to stay all over the world. There are a couple of hundred hostels in the United States and Canada, and more than forty-five hundred hostels worldwide. Hostels vary tremendously, from a pristine chalet high in the Swiss Alps, to a lonely lighthouse on the Northern California coast, to a huge, gray institutional facility in a German industrial center. Wherever the hostel is located, it is always inexpensive, and there are always opportunities to meet and talk with people of all ages from all over the world.

Youth hostels, while not providing the amenities of a hotel, motel, or bed and breakfast, are usually great fun for kids. They provide a social environment and, quite often, lots of people to gush over Baby.

All hostels have dormitory-style gender-separate accommodations, and many have private rooms for families. (For more information on youth hostel membership, see the Resources Appendix.)

- ✓ Reserve!—some hostels fill up three months in advance.
- ✓ Hostels provide bare-bones lodging—beds, pillows, and blankets. You bring or rent sheets.
- ✓ Some have on-site laundry facilities.
- ✓ Family rooms are often available, providing more privacy. There is sometimes a surcharge.
- ✓ Youth hostels often provide shared kitchen facilities. (My mother traveled all over Europe a few years ago, cooking a pot of brown rice nightly in the hostel facilities. She called it her "security blanket.")

✓ Many hostels, especially rural ones, are closed during the day. It's called a "lock-out." (Sounds penitentiary-like, doesn't it?) For some early-rising families, this is fine—for some it can be an issue. Do you have trouble getting up and out in the morning?

✓ Be prepared for a "lights out" curfew.

✓ It's best to travel light when staying in hostels. In some places, security is an issue, but hostels usually provide lockers for valuables and other possessions.

✓ Kids under five are generally free, kids under twelve may receive discounted rate.

Special Note: Children under ten *must* be accompanied by a parent or guardian of the same sex.

On the day after Christmas in Quebec, we spent a snowstorm holed up in a youth hostel, the only guests in a facility that sleeps two hundred. Outside, the winds blew freezing cold off the Saint Lawrence River, and five feet of snow piled high against the hostel walls. Inside, the warm, radiator-heated air thawed our chilled bones, and we enjoyed the absurdity of choosing among yards and yards of beds.

House, Apartment, and Condominium Rentals

For many families, short-term house, apartment, or condominium rentals provide the best lodging solutions of all.

Condominium Rentals

For convenience and cost-saving, try renting a condominium. The cost per day will fall somewhere between Sleazy Motel and Fancy Hotel, but, ah...the convenience! Your own fully equipped kitchen! A washer and dryer! Extra rooms! (No more hiding out in the hotel bathroom with the flashlight, trying to get some reading done.) In the snowy winter, you can sit...or (*ahem*) whatever...in front of a roaring fire with your sweetie while the baby sleeps in the bedroom. In tropical Hawaii, you can breakfast on papaya and mango on your lanai, listening to the chirping of wild birds and watching whales leap in the ocean below.

✓ Condominiums are available at many resort destinations. Besides offering discounts and/or packaged activities (ski lift tickets, golfing, snorkeling trips), many condominium complexes have on-site shared barbecues, pools, Jacuzzis, and/or mini-gyms where you can work that body. (The Resources Appendix lists a place to start when you're looking for the perfect condominium. Also try the local chamber of commerce.)

✓ Ask about facilities and set-up. Many condominiums are built on multi-levels. Are there balconies? Could a small child fall through the railing? If there are bunk beds, are the ladders detachable?

✓ Condominiums usually sleep lots of people, and are a good choice for joint family vacations.

Having a kitchen to prepare at least some of your meals can be a huge boon. Eating out with a child three times a day is a challenge. (That's putting it mildly—review the restaurant tips in Chapter 3.) Eating out is also time-consuming and very expensive. (Multiply the number of days of the trip times three meals plus snacks and you'll feel like your family is the sole support of the region's restaurant industry.) Remember, you can *still* go out to eat...and you'll enjoy it more because you're doing it for pleasure rather than just because it's time to refuel *again*.

✓ Shop around; package deals (air, car, condo) through travel agents may be a better deal than buying separately—or they may not be.

✓ What's the deal with cleaning? Some places include cleaning in the price, some tack on an additional charge, some rely on you to scrub it down. Find out in advance.

✓ Some places provide sheets and towels, some provide them for a fee. Depending upon your travel mode, you may want to bring your own from home. (For little ones, familiar bedding can ease the stress of being in a strange place.)

✓ Condominiums are often privately owned, and decor, style, color, and furnishings vary widely. *Some* are quite tasteful. Condominiums usually provide dishes and cooking utensils, though the quality can vary here, too—from top-of-the-line microwaves to burnt-bottomed pots and pans and knives that struggle to cut the butter. You'll usually find an assortment of non-perishable food basics like salt, pepper, and spices, and often the cabinets will have oil, popcorn, chocolate pudding, or other items that previous guests have donated. When you check out, don't leave any perishables, and either replace the mac & cheese and the cans o' alphabet soup you borrowed, or donate a few non-perishables of your own.

At the Condo in the Tropics

Baked and relaxed after her days at the beach, Annie scampered around naked as Bill and I prepared dinner in the kitchen or grilled on the barbecue. Evenings, we watched the sun set between two palm trees on our lanai, dressed only in bathrobes. Annie loved our "Hawaii House" (as she dubbed it) and for months after our return would stop in the middle of playing and, misty-eyed and solemn, ask when we were going back.

Braving the Elements, Inside and Out

Things don't always *exactly* turn out as planned, but that's where adventure usually begins. We planned a weekend of sunny snow play with our friends Ailsa and Steven and their girls Shoshi and Ellie. But at the last moment, their girls were sick and the weather forecasters were predicting the worst storm of the season (chains required, sand bags available, "Batten down the hatches, Matey."). So we went alone. "Pack in a lot of food," the rental manager told us as we picked up the keys. "You may not get out tomorrow."

The condominium was built on four levels and could sleep eight to ten people, and we were only three. Annie and Bill played in the snow until the storm began in earnest. Then, Annie ran up and down the carpeted stairs, establishing territories in each bedroom. She established the School for Hard Plastic Animals in a walk-in closet, and a bed became the hospital (her stuffed Kitty was very sick after falling over the balcony). I spaced out on bad novels and took a bath. "Oooh! Super Nintendo!" Bill said, and except for groaning each time he lost another Mario, said little after that…until the electricity went off.

That's when we realized that the condominium was all-electric—stove, heat, water heater, coffee pot. When we tried to light the fireplace, the condo filled with smoke, and the smoke detector went off and wouldn't stop (*it* wasn't electric) until we opened all the windows and doors. The storm turned to blizzard.

Once we found and opened the flue, we built a roaring fire and shut the windows. The electricity came on just long enough to make dinner, went off, then came on again in the morning just long enough to make coffee. It wasn't what we planned, but the snow was beautiful, we were far from the hassles of home life, and we were having fun together. On the morning we left, I shoveled three feet of snow off the twenty steps down, cleared a passageway along a ten-foot path, then dug the car out of the garage. I felt strong, I felt resourceful—living in the San Francisco Bay Area where it doesn't snow, this was actually my idea of a good time!

Furnished House and Apartment Rental

Condominiums are available primarily in resort areas, but in many places around the world you can achieve the same benefits by renting a furnished house or apartment. Besides the comfort and savings (house or apartment rental is usually much cheaper than a hotel), you'll get a feel for the culture that you can only get by living there.

In Europe (I'm talking Paris, London, Rome, Madrid), this type of lodging, known as "self-catering," is very popular. Self-catering is a great idea for family reunions (you can rent a castle in Italy! The more the merrier—and the cheaper!). Houses and apartments are usually rented in one-week increments, though in Provence or Tuscany you may need to commit to a two-week stay. (Oh, poor baby. You have to stay two weeks in Tuscany? Shut up before I drool on you.)

International house and apartment rentals can be set up through family travel agencies or over the Internet (once again, see the Resources Appendix). If you're booking by Internet, you'll select your location and ideal apartment or castle, make the queries by email, possibly follow up by phone, and finish by snail mail (when the manager sends the key to you—often a heavy, ornate, iron thing that goes in an eighteenth century key hole and transports you instantly to your destination).

Numerous agencies in England provide "self-catering." Check out the listings in the *London Times* and the *Guardian*. (These newspapers may be available at a local independent bookstore or newsstand.)

Furnished apartments also are available in the U.S., if an area is at all touristed. Contact an area's chamber of commerce for the names of local real estate agencies.

Quick Tip

Just as television adds pounds, computers add square feet. Rule of Thumb: Rooms are always smaller than they look on the web page.

Home Swaps

A home swap is, simply, swapping your home with another family for a certain amount of time. You get the apartment in Bombay, they get the apartment in New York, everybody has a great time, and the washing machine is available day and night.

The advantages? Save yourself a lot of money, live like the locals, and make sure your home stays secure and your house plants watered while you are away. With small children and babies, establishing a known "turf" can make all the difference in the world. The disadvantages? Strangers are living in your house. You are not there to protect it. They may have misrepresented themselves or their home. You have to do laundry and clean up after yourselves, and while you're cleaning, they might be doing a really sloppy job (this may sound like a small thing, but varying standards of cleanliness is actually the primary complaint that house swappers express).

Can you imagine it? More to the point, ask yourself if you would consider it relaxing to save the vast amounts of money you'll need to find decent lodging, and live in a home that is already set up with all the necessary gear. You can cook and live the local lifestyle. For some people this sounds like a dream. For others, a vacation is a time to avoid cooking and cleaning; they would worry too much about accidentally damaging things and, worst of all, they would spend their time stressing out about what was happening back in their own home.

Home swapping is probably not for worry-warts; it relies on good will and communication, and setting it up can sometimes be complex. It's an intimate relationship. You need to find somebody whose home is roughly equal to yours, who has somewhat similar values, who lives someplace you want to visit, and is interested in visiting your place, and who, after copious communication (mostly through fax, mail, and email) you believe you can trust.

In the ideal home-swap situation, you'll have a bit of overlap and be able to meet your exchange family in one locale or the other. It is sometimes a good idea, too, to have a friend or family member meet the family that will be staying in your house and show them how things work—that pesky furnace, that toilet handle that needs to be jiggled, the timer setting on the sprinkler system. It's always good to have a friend or family member available in case of emergencies.

If you're planning on a home swap, it's best to begin early. Many home swaps are arranged up to a year in advance. (For information on how to set up a home swap, see the Resources Appendix.)

When the Hallinans (and their three kids) home swapped in England, they accidentally broke a teapot so they replaced it with a nicer one. They came home to discover that their exchange family had accidentally broken three wine glasses and replaced them with far more beautiful (and expensive) ones.

Pros:
- Live like the locals. Shop in the local markets and cook local food!
- Avoid the local laundromat. Wash clothes while you relax.
- Save a bundle of money. Can't beat the price—it's free! More bucks to spend on souvenirs!
- Sometimes the swap family will provide introductions to friends—and you will meet wonderful people you'd have never otherwise met.
- With all the communication back and forth, you may develop a true international friendship, and a family to exchange with for years on end...
- It's about trust.

Cons:
- Who goes on vacation to do daily chores? Plus, you have to leave the house cleaner than you found it.

- If money is no object and you hate washing clothes, the hotel or resort can always do the wash for you.
- If things don't pan out on the other end, you may end up spending that "saved" money on home repairs.
- Sometimes the swap family will provide introductions to friends—and you will meet horrible people you'd have never otherwise met.
- Things can get damaged. The people in your house might (and this is a true story, albeit third-hand) clog the toilet and flood the house with sewage water. You have to be okay with the idea that this might happen while you trip the light fantastic in Cannes, London, or Bucharest. Remember you hold pretty strong cards—you hold their house hostage, too!
- It does take a while to set up.
- It's about trust.

Assorted Odd Lodging

...or expand your mind and try a more unorthodox approach to lodging. Who knows? It might even be cheaper than the standard hotel or B&B.

Check Your Affiliations

Are you a member of the club? Local faculty clubs and national organizations often have reciprocal agreements with other local clubs and organizations. If you're a member of the National Writer's Union, for instance, your Local may be able to help you find lodging at another member's home in your destination city (especially if your journeys are Union-related). In Chicago, we stayed at the University faculty club, in a building festooned with gargoyles. Bill happens to have the same last name as the university president. They treated him, me, and Annie like royalty, assuming Bill was the president's brother or something. (Yes, we did set them straight. Eventually.)

Back to the Dorms!

Staying somewhere for a month or so during the summer? Any town with a college will have dormitories and apartments available off-season, and usually they will rent or sublet them on a monthly basis. You'll need to set this up a few months in advance. Call the university housing office and follow the phone tree until you reach the right person. University "conference services" often rent dorm rooms on a nightly basis—much cheaper than a hotel.

Monasteries and Convents in Europe

Actually, you *can* stay at that monastery or convent, even without taking a vow of silence. People who have done so in Europe swear by the experience—it's a chance to stay in a historic and beautiful setting, with meals often included and young children often welcomed. Monasteries and convents often have minimum and maximum stays, or other restrictions.

Guest Houses

They're known as "guest houses" in Thailand, "losman" in Indonesia, "gite" in France, and other names around the world. These are basically small, family-run inns, often in developing nations, providing shelter to 'round-the-world-with-a-backpack, on-a-shoestring travelers, often in the family home. They are often the best way of gaining insight into a culture, if you are staying only a short time. Prices are inexpensive and lodgings range from rudimentary to quite nice. Many are listed in the Lonely Planet guidebooks—many others you'll find by listening to touts in train stations, or by word-of-mouth from other travelers. Some you need to book ahead on the Internet. As with other kinds of lodging, some are appropriate—even quite wonderful—for kids, and some are not.

You Mean You Want to Sleep Here?

Of course, hotels, motels, condos, castles, and guest houses are for more than parking your stuff in while you wander around town, take pictures, and buy souvenirs. Eventually night falls. It's time to sleep.

Expect a Little Meltdown

Evenings on the road can be hard when you've been cooped up in a car or sightseeing among strangers all day. Expect a little baby meltdown. The hotel, motel, condo, or B&B is a private place—there are no strangers here, this is time for just you and your kid, who really just needs some reassurance, no matter how awful she is acting.

- Rather than scold, try to comfort.
- Create a quiet time—try reading a book cuddled together.
- Try to focus on the child; this is not the time to get fed up and park him in front of the TV. He's giving you a very distinct message—"I need you, Daddy, and I need you now!"

> We always know when we've pushed a little too hard or far because our normally charming and delightful child suddenly turns into a small, demonic dervish. She won't listen, she screams, she hits, she laughs when scolded. What keeps us from despairing completely ("I'm a terrible parent, I've raised a monster!") or from losing it completely, is the fact that she is so obviously exhausted, tired, wired, maybe hungry. A firm hug, a small scold, and time alone with one of us seems to be the cure.

Maintaining Bedtime Routines

Try to maintain your normal bedtime routine. All the excitement of being on the road and in a new place can keep kids from falling asleep easily.

- Duplicate your home routine as much as possible. If you read before bed, make sure to bring some soothing favorites from home.
- Darken the room so he is less aware of how foreign the surroundings are from his room at home. (If he's afraid of the dark, pack along "Mr. Night Light" and plug it in near the bed.)
- Familiar sheets and blankets are useful—if you have enough room to bring them along. This is

the time to haul out the "stowaway" lovey toys for
cuddling.

🦋 Your baby or child might regress to a less-mature
state. This is normal (though sometimes a pain in
the patootie for the parents). Be kind—she is feeling insecure.

🦋 A newly potty-trained child might feel better in a
night-time pull-up.

🦋 A baby might wake more frequently for nursing.
Let her—the reassurance will help her sleep
better *tomorrow* night.

🦋 In desperation, we've been known to stick Annie
in the bed with us, and watch something banal
and boring on TV until she drops off and we can
transfer her to "her" bed.

What to Do Once the Baby Sleeps

OK, he's down for the night. You're stuck in the hotel
room. Now what? No matter how much you may want
to flee, do *not* leave Baby Boris alone.

🗝 If there is more than one adult, you can take turns
painting the town red. Or not.

🗝 Hang out in the motel bathroom—Annie wakes up
if the room is too light, so I bring the Powerbook
and write, sitting on the floor in front of the toilet,
using the seat as a desk.

🗝 Read your guidebooks. Plan tomorrow's itinerary.
("Go slow!")

🗝 Read, meditate, or do your stretching exercises.
This is "down" time. Remember, this is your vacation. Take a break, baby.

🗝 Watch pay-per-view TV at low volume.

🗝 Turn in early yourself.

Hotel-Room Horrors Quiz

Are you up for a challenge? OK, screw your courage to
the sticking place and get ready to hear—and resolve—
the following gruesome hotel-room scenarios.

Scenario A   *You hit town. It's late. You've been in afternoon traffic for three hours. The baby has been screaming for the last two. It's a town with motels near the train station, all geared to serve the train traffic—that's you. Your train leaves at 8:00 A.M. and you have to be there an hour before. An hour of cruising up and down the main drag follows. The baby wears himself out screaming and falls asleep—his third nap of the day, and he usually only takes one. Many motels sport No Vacancy signs. At the ones that don't, you stop the car, your companion hops out, enters the office, and is told that things are, indeed, full. Finally you find a motel. It's a dive, but it's home for the night. You drive in, pull up, and settle in.*

How could you have improved this scenario?

Scenario B   *It's 11:45 P.M., you're in a quaint and quiet bed and breakfast inn and your kid (or worse, kids) are still bouncing. Wild. They refuse to sleep, your throat is hoarse from yelling, you hate your spouse, your spouse hates you, and the neighbors are about to get you evicted. How do you deal with it? You cannot A) Let them scream and run (for your sake as well as the neighbors—you're exhausted and you have that 8:00 A.M. ferry to catch!). Wild, evil fantasies enter your head. However, neither can you B) Take up child abuse (besides the obvious immorality of it, this is a very quaint and very quiet bed and breakfast). You cannot C) Lock them in their room and head to the kitchen for a well-deserved cup of herb tea or to the bathroom for a bubble soak—because the kids don't have a separate room, you don't have tea, and the bathroom is right in the middle of the fray. You cannot leave. There is nowhere to go. It's late, you're tired, and in your nighties.*

Any ideas?

Scenario C   *It's Paris, Paris, Paris at last! You reach the budget hotel, but you cannot find a parking space. Your traveling partner runs to the banque to change your greenbacks into euros to pay for dinner; you double-park the rental car and carry the baby and a suitcase upstairs to the small concierge's office, where a large green parrot stares from a* *cage and a kindly lady scoops the baby out of your arms and says, "I watch. Pas de problem, no problem. You get ze luggage, I hold zis bébé." You agree. Snookums doesn't look unhappy, and the concierge looks so kind, and has so much authority in her voice. Twenty minutes later, hassled out of your mind from fighting Parisian traffic (and worrying about your baby), you return to a screeching parrot, a screaming child, a frustrated looking concierge. Your travel partner isn't back with the money yet. Baby stares at you with large, bloodshot eyes and hiccups loudly—you know she's been crying for at least ten minutes.*

How could you have avoided this?

Answers to Hotel-Room Horrors Quiz

There are few real answers when you are in the middle of horrendous (and true-life, I confess) scenarios such as these three above. Much of the solution is in the prevention.

Scenario A OK, things aren't going as planned *at all*. Time for a little attitude adjustment. Time for an adjustment of plans. Stop driving. Commute traffic is bad news. Call ahead to the train town and make a motel reservation. (Get motel names from the phone book, if you are close enough, or the chamber of commerce, if open.) You might also revise your plans, find a motel in the area where you are stuck in traffic, turn in early, and drive to the train station at dawn. (I'm not going to pick on you for not having a motel reservation in the first place.)

Say you wait out the screaming baby and tied-up traffic and hit town, as in the scenario, only to find yourself cruising the main drag. This is a time to split up—one adult takes the baby to a park or cafe, the other gets major brownie points for doing the driving and motel-locating. There's no reason for a tired, cranky baby to put up with an hour-long motel search, too. And by letting the baby scream his way into his third nap, you're setting up a nightmarish night.

Scenario B   Well, maybe B&Bs are not the best idea for the next few years. But did you try the bathtub? Water has tremendous powers to entertain and soothe and—most of all—to change the mood. We all have 20/20 vision in hindsight, but once things are calmer, analyze why the kids went ballistic. Did they get over-tired during the day? Was there a lack of stimulation? What foods were involved?

Scenario C   Yeah, I know you're excited by Paris, but you blew it, chéri. You risked having the car towed and you risked baby's life and limb. You shouldn't have let your partner go to the bank. The hotel would have changed enough money for the evening—and even if the exchange rate was higher than the bank, it would have been worth it. Never leave the baby with a stranger. It's not just a matter of safety (the concierge *was* a nice lady), it's a matter of the *baby* being comfortable. You could have left the baby in the car, and taken turns shut-tling the luggage upstairs (with one person guarding baby and car at the same time). The parrot should have given you a shiver of anticipation—you can never tell how an animal will react to a child, and visa versa. And in Paris or any other major city, traffic is always unpre-dictable, and it always takes a while to park.

PART THREE
On the Go with Baby

CHAPTER 10

Outdoor Adventures

It is always sunrise somewhere: the dew
is never all dried at once: a shower is forever
falling, vapor is ever rising. Eternal sunrise,
eternal sunset, eternal dawn and gloaming,
on sea and continents and islands, each
in its turn, as the round earth rolls.

—John Muir

Inviting Wonder

Children belong outdoors. I live in a city where the night
sky has no stars, where I must drive to hear the crash of
an ocean wave. Yet it is vital to me that my daughter feel
a connection to—and a reverence for—the natural
world. That she can put her hand in spring water and
know that water is more than fluid from a tap. That she
walk, even occasionally, on ground that isn't sidewalk
and cement. That she know the moon. That the natural
world is natural to her.

There are too many telephones, cars, and walls in
our lives. Bring your toddler into the garden, to the
beach, to the mountains, into the woods; watch as she
changes, mellows, responds to the elements. And for
you too—a couple of hours or days in nature and something inside releases. Gone is the city's frantic energy,

the "Come-on-baby-we're-late" pace of busy life. This chapter is about visiting the Outdoors.

Gardening with Little Ones

An avocado seed or a potato propped with three toothpicks into a glass of water, a container of tomato plants on a sunny fire escape, a small plot of land amidst your larger plot of land—toddlers love to garden and no garden is too small. Outdoors? Begin with peas, beans, carrots, and herbs—the easy stuff. Indoors? Even a two-year-old can help hold the watering can over the potted plants. Besides an educational lesson (here's how *food* and *flowers* happen), mucking about in the dirt and water is endlessly fun.

Toxic plants

Be aware: glossy daphne, gorgeous foxglove, the stunning red of poison oak. Even wild lupine runs you a risk—the seeds are poisonous. Supervise children in the garden. Better yet, plant only benign plants.

Day Trip to Nature

Tired of the runaround? At or away from home, you can do nature as a day trip. City dwellers can find solitude in regional parks, urban streams, and botanical gardens. Venture a little farther—a day hike, a walk in the woods, a day at the beach, a trip up a volcano—the change of pace will do everybody good. These day trips feel like vacations, even if they're only a few miles from home. You'll return feeling that combination of refreshed and exhausted that only a day in nature can provide.

Once in Maui we rose at 4:00 A.M. to drive thirty-seven miles from sea level to the ten thousand-foot summit of Haleakala, the ancient volcano. Our goal: a breathtaking sunrise over the crater. The moon shone full, etching Maui in silver, black, and white. At the summit, the eerie landscape was barely visible through the waning darkness. Frost covered the ground. A mini-bus belched tourists in shorts who hopped from foot to sunburnt foot, wrapping themselves in beach towels in a futile attempt to warm up. Despite her sixteen layers of clothing, Annie's nose turned beet red. "It'll be beautiful, honey," I promised, teeth chattering next to her icy ear.

The sky turned pink. "Almost time!" somebody yelled. "Here we go," I told Annie. The expectant crowd leaned in. And just then the fog socked us in, a hard rain began, and, freezing, foiled, and frustrated, we all ran for our cars.

Awe of Nature

How many miles had we traveled to get to this Hawaiian beach? Yet Annie took one look at the gently lapping ocean, broke into frightened hysterics, and refused to have anything to do with it. We talked to her. We carried her to the water and dabbled in one small foot. We tried to see it from her perspective. Awe of nature is a good thing, I told myself. The bravest of us all fear the sea.

Finally, Bill and I had to be *flexible*. We dug a huge hole for Annie to sit and dig in, threw a T-shirt over her body, tied a hat on her head, and took turns running to the waves. By day two, she was giggling with us in the surf—she just needed a chance to process the new scenery.

Beaching It

There is magic where water and land come together. For me, the word "beach" elicits memories of walks along the Northern California coast, Annie's face buried in my chest against the wind, of wading with her at Lido, Venice, far across the Adriatic from the war-torn Baltics, and of lazy days of white sand and warm waters in Hawaii. There is something magical about digging holes in sand with a child, searching for shells, and collecting green, brown, orange, and

blue jewels of ocean-smoothed glass. There is something that defines summer about a long hot day on a
lake beach. There is something lulling about the sound
of foghorns as you fall asleep after a long day of ocean-
gazing.

Beach Toys

You can do very nicely with nothing but what the
beach provides, but a single bucket and a shovel are
fine things. Old yogurt containers are exactly the right
shape for castle turrets. A few largish, hard-plastic
animals are fun for toddlers—make sure that they're
not too important to the child (they may get lost in the
sand or the sea).

Can you and your preschooler make doggy foot
prints? Walk on your tiptoes in the wet sand. Look
back. Woof! Woof!

Tidal Awareness

Children are rarely immune to the mysteries and
power of the sea. The tides rise and fall twice daily, and
if you'll be beach hiking, it's a good idea to know
where in the tidal cycle you are. Walking along the
beach at low tide, the sands are full of natural treas-
ures, and you can get to magnificent hidden places—
but be careful that when the tide comes in, you don't
find yourself stranded! Check the tide tables before
doing extensive hiking.

Beach Recovery

When it's time to leave, do some sand removal before
climbing into the car. Shake out shoes, if you've been
wearing them. Sit your kid in the car with her feet
dangling out, and gently brush off as much as possible. Sand is abrasive, and can hurt tender skin if you're
too rough.

Quick Tip:
Removing Sand from a Toddler's Bottom

When it comes to sand, no place is sacred. The best solution is to march quickly, little one tightly in arms, into the showers available at most public beaches. Enjoy a scream and a giggle in the refreshing (read: cold) water, and let some run down the inside of her suit. Then strip and wrap inside a big beach towel, and either carry her in the towel or re-diaper her, sand and all, and hightail it back to your lodgings. A short warm bath will rinse it all out. The offending sand will swirl down the drain, leaving you with a clean child—and maybe some guilt about the building's plumbing.

Small Boats and Safety

There is little more thrilling than a boat ride on a smooth-as-glass lake or bay. Yet, on small boats, safety is everything. Children need life vests, but not just any life vest will do! Finding a safe PFD (personal flotation device) will require a little research, but when you consider the frightening statistics you'll realize there are no shortcuts for this vital piece of equipment:

- Eleven children drown in the United States every day.
- Nine out of ten drownings occur in inland waters.
- Most drowning victims own but are not wearing their life vests.
- Some PFDs float a child on her stomach rather than on her back.

A life jacket (PFD) should be designed like a vest. Make sure it's comfortable, fits well, and doesn't ride up. It should also be fitted with quick release crotch straps. Most importantly: the vest must be designed so that the majority of the flotation material is in the chest area—look for asymmetrical flotation that will float the child onto her back, keeping her head and face above water within six seconds.

Josh and the Power Boat

Every summer, our extended family spends a week at a cabin on Pinecrest Lake, in the Sierra, North of Yosemite National Park. The cabin is accessible only by motor boat, or by forty-minute hike. On a warm day, in calm waters, ten-year-old Josh was allowed to help steer the boat across the lake. Annie and I sat on the dock and watched the lesson.

Here was the scene from my perspective: one empty lake and one solemn boy, flanked by three watchful adults ready to wrest the wheel from his hands at any hint of danger. Here was the scene from Annie's perspective: Josh—who wasn't too old to play "doodle bug," "hide-and-seek," and Legos with her—in charge, actually steering the boat across the lake! She looked at me, eyes big with hero worship. "Mommy, when I'm four, can I drive the boat?"

The Snow

On a sunny day, there is nothing as beautiful and fun as a romp in drifts of fresh, mountain snow. On a blizzardy day, snow is best admired from the comfort of a warm room.

You don't need fancy sleds, skis, or saucers (which can be dangerous for little kids, anyway). Beach and sand toys make great snow toys. Playing, throwing, digging, rolling, sliding, and building snowmen, snow-women, snow bunnies, and snow giraffes can keep toddlers giggling.

Resist the desire to stay out too long. Playing in the snow is tiring, and cold. Keep it to less than an hour—return to the drifts after hot chocolate, or at least a rest in the warmth of the car.

Be aware of the dangers of snow glare. Baby and child sunglasses are vital.

Once out of the snow, check to see if Bubbala's socks are wet. Dry those little footsies and change socks. Bubbala will probably need a complete change of clothing. Plan for it.

Full Speed 'til Meltdown

Last winter, Saill and I took Alonza and Annie and the dogs up to Emigrant Gap, the closest snow to the Bay Area. Saill, who had done this before, said, "They'll last an hour." The well-bundled girls romped. The dogs, Mollie and Sarah, romped. Saill and I stood and snacked and took a few turns on the saucers. After fifty-eight minutes, both girls' giggles suddenly turned to howls; the snow had worked its way in. We piled them back in the car, peeled off their cold and soggy clothes and shoes, and passed them dry clothes and blankets. On the way home, we stopped for hot chocolate.

Snow Clothing Basics

Leave lots of room in the suitcase for clothing. Sweaters are bulky, you'll want to layer, and you'll need to have many outfits available for when Wee Willy gets wet. Keep warm, but if you're from a non-snowy climate and venturing into the cold for an occasional weekend, there is no need to spend a fortune on fancy-schmancy snow gear. The five extremities—head, two hands, and two feet—should be well covered.

- Layer your child (see layering information, later in this chapter).
- In cold weather, long underwear is a must. Some experts suggest winter underwear should be constructed of several layers of fabric.
- A hat that covers the ears (and not the eyes). Most heat is lost through the head.
- Waterproof mittens and a warm scarf.
- Waterproof shoes or boots. Oversized rain boots with two pairs of socks will work in a fix. Non-waterproof shoes or boots will ensure that snow play is very short.

🧺 Waterproof or water-resistant pants, or "snow bib" to go over insulation pants. (Check used baby and children's clothing stores—these are frequently outgrown before being worn out.)

🧺 For extra protection, a standard, flexible raincoat or parka to go over all.

What a Difference a Year Makes…

When Annie was three, we drove into the mountains for our first snow adventure since she was eighteen months old, too little to remember the fluffy white stuff. To our surprise, she was too scared to touch it at first—she wouldn't step in it, she clung to our necks like Velcro. It was twenty-four hours before she relaxed—and then she couldn't stop snow-angeling and giggling. A year later, it was a completely different story. Annie was like a racehorse at the gate, a champion boxer at the bell, a…you get the picture. Every bit of her said, "Let me at it!"

Camping

Just a three-hour drive from our house in the city hides our favorite national forest, one hundred square miles of rarely visited mountains, creeks, and wilderness, uncrossed by paved roads. In the forest, days can go by without contact with other people or cars. Here, my city child can listen to the birds; pick wild fruit; swim in clean, rushing water; and sleep under the stars. Here she can learn the dangers of the forest—fire pits, splinters, sunburn, rattlesnakes, poison oak. Annie thrives here. She bounces in the tent, watches caterpillars, watches butterflies, and begins to understand the relationship between the two. She laughs at hopping frogs and points out small fish in the creek and birds in the trees. She sleeps well, lulled by the murmur of the nearby water.

Each summer we venture in, fording flooded streams and navigating miles of rutted forest service roads in our four-wheel drive vehicle. The trip is well worth it, for hidden within the scrub oak and cedar pine, bitter watercress stands in the bubbling granite-lined creeks, tiny strawberries hide underfoot, and black raspberries grow plump in the summer heat. High on the mountain, cold water springs fresh from the split root of a fir tree. The green meadows are dotted with flowers, and wildlife is everywhere: lizards, bears, deer, turtles, water snakes, frogs. Circling above the campsite, a single lazy hawk by day, bats by night.

You don't have to start big—your backyard may be the perfect place to pitch a tent or lay down the sleeping bags. Bring out the barbecue and roast hot dogs and marshmallows for dinner. (No! Let the answering machine get that phone!) Listen to the crickets, and sleep soundly in the cool night air.

Trailer Camping and Motor Homes

Many families use their trailers to get out into the outdoor world and still have the convenience of having it all with them. Trailers make weekend getaways easy—just grab kids, clothes, and food, and hit the road! The little ones can run in the woods, fish, and swim in natural water, yet still have the security of a "home." Resist the impulse to take the TV, the boom box, the cell phone (except for emergencies. Promise?). The United States is covered with trailer parks and campgrounds. Contact your local AAA office for more information.

Where to Find Wilderness

In the United States, we are fortunate to have access to beautiful and accessible national, state, and regional park systems. Choose your adventure and then venture in—to the rain forests of northern Washington, the Florida Everglades, the high mesas of the Southwest. Explore low deserts, rugged mountains, gentle redwood forests. State and regional parks are inexpensive and family friendly. Plan a trip to Yosemite, camping easily on the valley floor. Backpack into the true wilderness, where sometimes days pass between sightings of other people, and the only thing that reminds you civilization still exists is the trail of an airplane, miles above, scratching a white trail in the blue sky.

Distance from Civilization

Car camping runs the gamut from KOA campgrounds with hot showers and plugs for blow dryers in the bathrooms to back-country sites with rudimentary clearings, an established fire pit, an outhouse not too far away, and no water except what you lug along or purify yourself from the local creek. Backpacking, you'll often have no established campsite at all.

- When choosing a wilderness destination or campsite, remember the equation: distance from city + lack of amenities = true wilderness. Establish your priorities. How far are you willing to travel? What kinds of amenities do you want or need? How far from medical help are you willing to go?

- When you have kids of different ages, you should gear your trip for the lowest common denominator—the youngest one. That doesn't mean you can't do a wilderness trip—it just means set reasonable goals and go slow.

- Call your pediatrician and tell her about your plans. If your child has a chronic medical condition, find out what she recommends, and if you should limit your activities.

- Take a trip to the library, local bookstore, or camping supply store and browse the camping books for inspiration and location.

- Don't make your trip too short! Novice campers should plan longer trips closer to home. Huh? Sounds backwards? Unless you're a well-oiled camping machine, camping requires a tremendous amount of prep-work. A one-night camping trip is too much work for too little reward. Also, if it's a first camping trip, the kids may take one or two nights to adjust to sleeping in the tent.

🐾 The moment you enter the campsite, forest, or wilderness, you're in ranger domain and the ranger is your main source of information. Whenever possible, call the ranger station or camp office to find out about poison oak or ivy, nettles, thistles, mosquitoes, snakes, weather, roads, and so on *before* you pack up for a trip in the wilds. When you get there, check in at the station.

Quick Tip

When camping, try to include at least one adult per preschool child.

Equipment for Camping

Cut up that credit card—you don't need to buy out the camping store! If you've never camped before, get supply advice (and maybe a few loaners) from experienced friends, visit an outdoor equipment store and browse (this is a really fun thing to do with kids!), and visit a Sierra Club bookstore or your public library. There are many excellent books on camping that will give you wonderful equipment suggestions (hit the public library). Go light—you need less than you think, and you can make do with little. chapter 7 has the basic packing list—here are some notes and amendments:

🧳 Always carry a good, comprehensive first-aid book with you. Even if nothing happens—and probably nothing will happen—it will be worth its weight in reassurance. Most accidents and incidents are not serious, but even casual bumps and scrapes can cause anxiety if you're away from medical care. A good first-aid book will give you the detailed information you need, at the time that you need it.

🐾 Bring a good first-aid kit. No need to buy a special "camping" kit, you can customize your own (I've got some ideas under M in chapter 14, Troubleshooting A to Z).

🐾 Take a backpack to carry your child. Toddlers don't always want to walk, and your hikes may turn to snail-paced strolls as the little one examines every fallen leaf, twig, bug, rock, mossy patch, and gray lizard.

🐾 An extra tarp can create a play area, and an extra old blanket or two provides warmth on a cold night (or spread it on the extra tarp for good napping).

🐾 Bring extra boxes of diaper wipes, even if your child is toilet-trained. You'll need approximately one box for every four days you'll be camping. Kids get dirty in the woods—and they should—so you'll need to swab down their hands and feet before they climb into the tent with you. (Diaper wipes come in handy for the adults, too. Get the unscented type unless you *like* appreciating mountain air through a cloud of chemical freshness—or smelling like a clean baby's butt.)

🐾 Bring a bottle of disinfectant gel for pre-food and post-bathroom clean up. You'll plow through it, so bring enough.

🐾 Don't forget the special lovey toys for *inside* the tent. Keep them hidden until bedtime. The familiar friends will be a welcome touch of home for sleepy children wanting comfort in a strange environment.

🐾 If you have room in the car, pack a tot seat to hook onto the picnic table.

🐾 Bring a few containers (old plastic yogurt cups, egg cartons) to collect small objects for inspection at the campsite. (But remember, leave nothing but footprints, take nothing but photos.)

🐾 A day pack for dragging diapers—not your good "around town" one; bring one that can get dirty, 'cause it will.

♣ Plastic bags, assorted sizes. For everything.

♣ A sleeping bag for the child. Baby bags are quickly outgrown—consider getting your child a regular one.

♣ Snack food, high energy and non-perishable.

♣ Special cups that don't spill, the kind with covers. Spilled juice attracts insects.

♣ Sturdy, easy-to-clean toys; not too small, and not too many. Let them learn to play with nature's toys—sticks, rocks, and shells. Bring glue and cardboard to make nature collages from leaves and pine cones and moss.

The Three-Layer Approach to Outdoor Clothing

How should you dress your kids for camping or snow? Try thin layers that can be shed for heat or put back on for cold or bad weather or to protect from bug bites. Here's how to layer effectively for rugged outdoor adventuring:

The Inner Layer: This layer should stay dry from outside moisture, keep baby or child warm, and wick perspiration away from the skin.

The Insulation Layer: This layer should continue wicking moisture from the skin, and provide insulation. Wool, down, and synthetic fleece retain their warmth even when wet. Lightweight, synthetic fleeces dry quickly and are soft as, well, fleece.

The Outer Layer: Gore-Tex shells, parkas, raincoats. This is the waterproof, snow-resistant layer. Some raincoats are stiff and hard to walk in. Try to find a flexible fabric that covers the body, and the head.

Sleeping Arrangements

To tent, or not to tent? Tents are not *strictly* necessary, though they are a good idea for small kids. Tents confine, reassure, and prevent insect and animal bites. They also provide shelter from morning dew and rain. Consider borrowing or renting one for your first few trips until you figure out what you need. Large family tents are relatively inexpensive to buy, and each year's model is easier to set up.

Bill never used a tent until I came into his life with my little green pup tent (which we now bring along as a special "Annie Play Area"). Bill camped under the stars with his older kids every year from the time Aaron was three weeks old. Occasionally he hung a tarp over a tree limb to protect them from dew, and the kids always slept between the adults for safety.

Nights are even chillier in the woods without the confining warmth of a tent. Socks should be thick, pajamas should be warm, and sleeping bags should be warmer. If it's really chilly, consider a stocking cap.

There is nothing more magical than waking in the night under a black sky full of stars.

Tents

Sheila, Peter, and their very active eighteen-month-old daughter Julie loved to car camp. Julie was (and is) a very active, curious child—into, and out of, everything. How would they keep her safe? Solution: a family tent with two rooms. The family slept in the inner room, Julie between her parents. Sheila and Pete figured that with two sets of zippers between Julie and the outside (plus climbing over at least one parent), they could relax enough to sleep.

Quick Tip

When they go camping, Sheila and Pete are careful to explicitly assign "Julie Duty" at all times. Pete might say, "I've got Julie." Until Sheila and Pete verbally agree that Sheila is the one in charge, Pete is the man. By clearly communicating, Sheila and Pete are avoiding potential disaster and the awful conversation no parents ever want to have:

"I thought you had her..."

"I thought *you* had her!"

Camping Clothing

Pack clothing carefully. You'll be outside all day: it's cold and drizzly in the mornings, it's hot at noon, and the mosquitoes come out at dusk. (See The Three-Layer Approach to Outdoor Clothing box.)

- Generally, bring ugly clothes you hate, and stay away from pastel colors; after five minutes in the woods they'll be wet, muddy, or covered with berries and roasted marshmallow debris.
- Bright colors, while rather ugly, make your child easy to spot if you lose him.
- Sturdy shoes are a *must*. This is no time for sandals or jellies.
- Jeans and overalls can be worn until filthy (remember, this is *natural* dirt).
- Bring long sleeves and long pants to help protect Hunny Bunny's delicate skin from sun, mosquito bites, ticks, and poison oak.

Campfires

There is nothing more heartwarming than sitting around the campfire in the evening, singing together, telling stories about the Glow People who live in the embers. If well-supervised, even a young child can learn about fire safety—how to collect kindling, and build, light, and watch over a fire. Make it into a ritual—teach her the rules. A campfire touches something deep in all humans, no matter how young.

No Safety Gates in the Wilderness

"It's *hot*," I told her. "No, no, very *hot*." As my only darling daughter examined the campfire's glowing coals with fascination, I reminded myself that children have survived open fires since the dawn of humanity. In some pre-industrial cultures, mothers watch their crawling babies approach the fire pit and say nothing. "They have to learn for themselves," they say. I tried to be pre-industrial. I held my breath as Annie investigated. Then, as she came within four feet of the scarring, searing embers, I swept her up in my arms, terrified.

Camping Cuisine

Camping stimulates the appetite. What you'll eat while camping depends on your family and child's eating habits and pleasures, but the simplest menu tastes twice as good in the great outdoors. Growing up, my family brought jars of flour and sugar, spices, bags of potatoes, and more on our camping trips. Bill and I love to cook but we aren't always so ambitious—though we rarely open cans of food at home, we depend on them when we go car camping. We want to relax too, you know. Plan ahead, and bring a lot (unused cans can go in your emergency box).

- We bring a cooler with one or two blocks of ice (it lasts longer than cube ice) when we can find it in the supermarket. Half-and-half for coffee stays fresh for at least two days if kept next to the ice. Eggs and butter will keep even longer. Drain the melted water every day, and store in the shade while you're out at the water hole.

- You might also try plastic quart bottles of drinking water and using them in the cooler to keep food cold. Once melted, drink.

- Powdered milk for the kiddo is a good, non-perishable alternative—be careful of the water (read W in chapter 14, Troubleshooting A to Z for more on water safety).

- Canned beans are always good (for the first few hours after dinner, at least) and kids usually love them. Canned tuna makes a great lunch. (Pair with a crispy green pepper!)

- Fresh fruits and vegetables last for days and days—if kept cool. Vegetables taste delicious steamed over the fire. Corn on the cob is a hit with the younger set.

- Rice is hard to do, even over a camp stove. Stick with boiled potatoes, pasta, or bread.

- Bring olive oil, vinegar, butter, salt, pepper, garlic cloves, spices, and onions. Sautéed onions spice up anything. Don't mention them, and kids will usually eat without complaint.

- Roasted marshmallows and s'mores (roasted marshmallows smashed with a chocolate bar between two graham crackers) are better in memory than in their sticky reality. They're a family tradition, though, and who can argue with a good tradition?

- For the child who eats only various versions of pasta, you're in luck—open-air spaghetti tastes great!

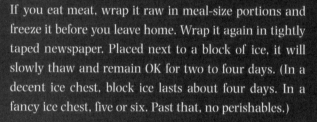

Quick Tip:
Attention Carnivores

If you eat meat, wrap it raw in meal-size portions and freeze it before you leave home. Wrap it again in tightly taped newspaper. Placed next to a block of ice, it will slowly thaw and remain OK for two to four days. (In a decent ice chest, block ice lasts about four days. In a fancy ice chest, five or six. Past that, no perishables.)

Washing Dishes

If you're cooking over a fire, put on a pot of water to heat before you sit down to eat. Campgrounds often have spigots of cold running water. Scrape the dishes and rinse in cold water. Add a little biodegradable soap (if you have it) to the hot water, and give the dishes a quick go over. Rinse in the cold. You really don't need the soap, though. The hot water's what does the trick.

If you wash dishes in a stream, scrape them well away from the water. Squat near the stream. Make sure another adult is watching the child. Only use biodegradable soap (and not too much)—and don't worry about getting the dishes too clean. The sponge will get scummy, the dishes will be greasy, but come on, this is camping! Lay each completed dish or utensil well away from the water, or you risk having your possessions float away. Dry them with a dishcloth to polish off residual grease and scum.

Childproofing a Campsite

A campsite will *never* be childproof. The first hours before your child understands her boundaries will challenge you. Be watchful of where you put the stove, fuel, matches, axes, knives, lanterns, first-aid kit, and other items that might be dangerous. For parents, the woods become a world of NOs.

Minimize the dangers by keeping knives, axes, stoves, lanterns, and so on as far away from temptation as possible. (You might want to keep them locked in the car, except when in use.)

Define the campground danger areas in terms your child is familiar with: "This is the stove; this is the fireplace. They get *hot*." Then watch your child *like a hawk!*

Garbage

Leave your environment cleaner than you found it. Campsites are rarely as well maintained as they could be, and there's nothing worse than finding a beautiful site that somebody has trashed. After our camp gear is set up, we move around, noses to ground, and collect garbage—old pop tops, bottle caps, broken glass. For preschoolers, make it into a game. Who can find the most garbage? (Not good for kids still in the pop-it-in-your-mouth stage.) Paper can be burned in the campfire, but make sure everything you put in a campfire burns. Never burn disposable diapers. Don't leave garbage in the fire pit. At the end of a camping trip we're like Santa Claus, packing a "ho-ho-ho" lot of garbage out.

Quick Tip:
Car Camping Abroad

All over Europe (not just in the more rural areas) sites are available for cars and trailers. They're the best way of meeting families with kids. Car camping abroad varies quite significantly from car camping in the American wilderness. In some spots, campsites are little more than a parking lot with water, pit-toilets, and a place to pitch a tent. Yet, you'll also find spots of incredible beauty—a beach below a castle outside Barcelona, the gorgeous farmland outside Amsterdam with a trolley line into the city that runs every half-hour. Almost all of them have a little store where you can get coffee and marvelous bread in the morning.

Washing Clothes

For short camping and backpacking trips, you can avoid doing laundry by bringing enough clothes, and planning on being a little dirty. For longer trips, washing by hand may be inevitable, but splashing in the water can be a fun family affair (keep the kids away from the poopy diapers).

- ✓ Wash clothes well away from streams.
- ✓ Bring clothesline with you.
- ✓ Always use biodegradable soap.
- ✓ Toddlers can help wring out clothing.
- ✓ If you'll be washing diapers—and do try to avoid this—bring a lightweight plastic bucket.
- ✓ Disinfect your hands with disinfectant gel after you're done.

Dirt Tolerance

What feels natural in the woods can feel disgusting the minute you hit paved road. Don't plan on dinner in a fancy restaurant on your way out of the wilderness. That first hot shower will feel blissful, and there is a delightful feeling of satisfaction watching the dust and dirt swirl down the drain.

Camping, Just Camping in the Rain

Rain can be great fun! A light rain clears the air and flat-tens the dust. Children delight in clomping in their rain-boots, squishing through mud, watching worms squirm. Kids are waterproof (and so are you). If the weather is warm enough, there is no need to stay inside just because of a little wet weather. Toddlers can play in the rain, get soaked, and be fine—as long as dry clothes are available for quick changes. Getting rain-drenched is not a great idea for a baby who isn't moving around enough to keep from getting chilled.

A cold, heavy rain, on the other hand, can dampen any outdoor adventure. Getting too wet in cold rain puts kids (and parents) at the risk of hypothermia. Use rain gear, seek protection, and change into dry clothing. Cozy up in the tent or car and read to the sounds of the pattering precipitation. If it's too soggy, you might want to head for an alternative place.

A family tent is a cozy hideaway in the rain. Well protected, you can snuggle down and read together, tell stories, and nibble on snacks.

- Never use a heater or kerosene lamp inside a tent.
- As long as you're dry, you're less likely to be miserable.
- In some older tent models, if you touch the sides, the rain will come in. Your mission, should you choose to accept it, is to keep your kid from bouncing off the tent walls.
- Drag the extra tarp that you used as a play area for your baby over the picnic table with all its gear.

Backpacking

Hiking in the woods with a baby on your back, you are both with your child yet alone in blissful solitude. Baby, high on her perch on your back enjoys the elements and the gentle rocking movements of your walking, and she looks around peacefully or dozes, comforted by your warmth.

- Unless you are a very experienced backpacker, start small with a few day hikes.

🎒 If you plan on taking a hike or a real backpacking trip with Baby on your back, practice wearing the pack around town, around the house, and maybe a few long evening walks in the neighborhood. That's also a good time to break in new hiking shoes.

🎒 Before you take off for a few *days*, do a day hike with a fully loaded pack.

🎒 The joke of trimming a toothbrush to get it thinner and lighter is not a joke—every ounce counts.

🎒 Plan carefully—get a topographical map and plan to go slowly.

🎒 Your child is not a parasitic growth on your back. No matter how young, he's a participant. Keep him in mind.

🎒 If you're backpacking with a walking/hiking child, make sure the little one is willing and able to hike, and that you're in good shape, too.

🎒 If your little ones are walking and carrying their own packs (some four-year-olds are up for this, some not), make sure that their pack weighs no more than 20 percent of their body weight. Be prepared to heft both kid and pack if necessary.

🎒 If it starts to rain, hike with a waterproof tarp as a little shelf over Baby.

Quick Tip:
Backpacking Ratios
The more people per baby the better—an excellent ratio is four adults per one child.

When Nature Calls In Nature

Easier to care for a baby outside? Some say so. You'll probably use fewer diapers a day. If you swim in a creek, baby can be bottomless (with lots of sunscreen on that little tush). For long camping trips and backpacking journeys, use cloth diapers and hand-wash them daily. Baby waste is biodegradable, but make sure you wash *well* away from streams to avoid the spread of disease. Drying diapers in the sun both bleaches and sterilizes them. For shorter trips, you can use disposable diapers and lug them out. (Aha—another use for jumbo plastic bags!)

Potty Training and the Campsite Outhouse

Some well-appointed campsites have bathrooms with flush toilets, but at many your only option is the outhouse or porta-potty. These facilities can be frightening for little ones who are just getting comfortable on a standard toilet—they stink, and it's a *loooooooong*, dark way down. I confess, I was a little nervous about Annie using an outhouse, too. I don't know how potty training occurred when all facilities were in out-buildings. Maybe children were tougher then. Maybe outhouses were simply a rough introduction to Life-with-a-Capital-L. Here are some options:

- Hold the child while she goes. Reassure her (and yourself) that she won't fall in.
- Pack a potty seat. This is a drag, because you'll have to clean it under rustic conditions.
- Revert to diapers—also a drag because you'll have to wash them or lug the trash out.
- Have the child be like a bear and go in the woods. This isn't a good solution in well-populated areas, and it's best not to bury human waste unless you have no choice.

Here's the official way to do it: dig a hole with a stick at least six inches deep and at least 150 feet away from water, then bury the waste thoroughly, covering the spot with topsoil and leaves. Burn the toilet paper or put it in a ziplock baggie and pack it out. Wash your hands well with disinfectant gel or with soap and water, or rub with a wipe, a stub of soap, and another wipe.

Wildlife

Animals, large and small, live in the wilderness. Teach your children how to gently collect bugs, snails, and slugs—put them in a jar with holes in the lid and examine them briefly before releasing them back to their "homes." Watch for birds—Jays, Gulls, Chickadees, Hawks, Robins. See the little chipmunk hiding in that tree?

Teach your children to observe but not disturb wild animals. Most animal and snake bites occur because the animal feels threatened and tries to defend itself. Kids like to touch things. As a parent, your job is to know the potential dangers, and supervise your child.

Rule Number One: *Don't feed the animals.* It's bad for them, and potentially bad for you. If you are in bear country, tree your food. Contact the ranger station for information about local wildlife and how to deal with the food situation.

Rule Number Two: *Don't ever pet the animals.* (My friend Tilly saw a visitor in Yellowstone actually sit his child on the back of a wild buffalo.) No matter how cute or sweet they look, wild animals are wild. They may bite or charge, and they carry diseases. If you or your child are bitten by a wild animal, you may need rabies shots.

Avoiding Outdoor Disasters

Yes, the wilds are wild, but by taking a few precautions, troubles can be minimized or avoided.

The Sun

Protecting yourself and your baby from the ravages of the sun requires a three-pronged approach: sunscreen, sunglasses, and protective clothing. Remember that a fair-skinned child will burn more quickly and more severely than a child with more skin pigment, but *anybody* can develop skin cancer. The skin of all kids should be protected from the sun.

Sunscreen: Thirty minutes before your child is exposed to the sun, apply a hypo-allergenic sunscreen or sunblock of at least #15 SPF with both UVA and UVB protection. If she'll be swimming, go for the waterproof stuff. If you can, avoid PABA, fragrance, and mineral oil. Lipbalm with #15 SPF is also available. Reapply sunscreen every two to three hours, or after swimming, sweating, or toweling. When camping, the white lotion will blend nicely with the brown dirt covering your child's body to form a protective camouflage. If your child's skin is very fair or the sun exposure extreme, apply the white goop—zinc oxide or titanium dioxide—on her nose, ears, and lips.

Sunscreen is not recommended for babies under six months—his skin is very sensitive and burns easily. Keep him out of direct sun between 10 A.M. and 3 P.M., and dress him in lightweight clothing that covers his full body. Babies should never be deliberately exposed to the sun.

Quick Tip:
Beach Protection

Beach sun is bold sun. The sun reflects off the water and sand, making sun protection even more vital. Try a beach umbrella and hang out and nap in the shade. Slather your child in sunscreen half an hour before you hit the beach to allow it to fully soak in and dry. The sight of a toddler completely coated in sticky sand is a sad, sad sight.

Sunglasses: "Cool, Baby!" Those sunglasses are for more than the hip and happenin' look. Because of the thinning ozone layer, sunglasses should be a part of every baby's outdoor gear. Inexpensive baby sunglasses (and straps to hold them on) are available in many sizes and styles. Use 'em.

Protective Clothing: Combine thin clothing with sunscreen, and your child should be fine. In very sunny climates, or between 10 A.M. and 3 P.M. when the sun is strongest, combine sunscreen with a more textured weave.

Hats—Broad-brimmed hats shade heads, faces, and necks. Hats are particularly important for bald babies. It may be a battle to keep a hat on a baby or toddler, but the more accustomed they are to hats, the more they'll learn to deal with it. (If you wear your hat, baby might wear his too!)

Long Sleeves and Pants—Lightweight cotton blouses and shirts make sense to protect delicate limbs, especially those fresh from the ravages of cold winter weather. Lightweight cotton pants offer comfort from breeze and sun.

Sunburn can be very serious. If your child has a mild burn, coat the burn with aloe vera gel. Try cool compresses or a cool bath with baking soda. Cover with something really soft and stay out of the sun. Use Ibuprofen for pain relief. Administer plenty of liquids. Seek medical attention for blisters.

Snakebites

Snakes are scary, but though over seven thousand people are bitten every year by poisonous snakes, only a dozen die each year. There are only four kinds of poisonous snakes in the U.S.: the coral snake, the copperhead, the water moccasin, and the rattlesnake. See chapter 14, Troubleshooting A to Z under C (for Critters) for more information on snakes. (You'll also find information there on little crawling and flying things—mosquitoes, spiders, and so on.)

Never Poke Your Fingers into Gopher Holes

Annie was almost two. One morning in the forest I glanced down beneath the camp picnic table to see a four-foot-long rattlesnake, with twelve rattles, gently sleeping inches from my feet. Annie's feet never touched the ground in that campsite again. Trying not to impose my own prejudices on my child's wildlife experience, I held her in my arms and backed away slowly, saying, "See the big snake, Annie? Look, isn't it *big*?"

We retreated to the safety of the car, doors locked, while Bill, protective testosterone raging, transferred the entire camp to another, less snake-friendly campsite in ten minutes, stopping only to take a picture for posterity and to lecture the innocent serpent. I waited until Annie's attention was diverted before turning my back to silently scream, remembering her little fingers exploring small "gopher" holes in the ground the day before. Gopher holes? Squirrel holes? *Snake holes! Aaahhh!*

Poison Oak, Ivy, and Sumac

Gnarly contact dermatitis results from these allergenic plants. If you know you've touched a poisonous plant, you may be able to stave off the reaction if you rinse well with cold water and detergent or wipe the skin with alcohol within five minutes. Baking soda, cold compresses, and calamine lotion may relieve mild symptoms. Hydrocortisone cream also helps. Keep fingernails cut short, and contact your doctor if the case is severe.

Safe Drinking Water

Giardia, a microorganism that can cause severe intestinal health problems, is a major problem in wilderness areas. (Interesting note: giardia is also a common problem in child-care centers.) Never drink untreated water from a creek, lake, river, pristine mountain spring, waterfall, and so on. Some campsites have running water, and signs should be posted if it is unsafe. For our car-camping trips, we bring a couple of five-gallon containers of spring water. For information on making your drinking water safe, see W in chapter 14, Troubleshooting A to Z.

The Pay-Off

The hassles of arriving, setting up camp, and adjusting to the wilderness are fleeting. By the second day, you've decided to stay. The sun comes out in the morning. Dew hangs on spider webs, the creek bubbles, the camp coffee tastes divine. By afternoon, something has transformed within you all. The silence of the forest enters your bones, the sun bakes out the city stress. The toddler runs in endless happy circles, falling frequently on the soft pine needle floor and solemnly dusting her hands off before resuming her spinning. In the late afternoon, she spends quiet time on her play space under the trees, staring up, up, up.

"Trees, Mommy. Sky."

"Do you see any birds?" you ask.

"No."

"There," you point at a Stellar Jay on a cedar pine.

"Bird!" she says. "Hi, Bird!"

Your partner, chopping garlic for dinner on an old stump, smiles over at you.

Late in the evening, the baby sleeps in the tent and you play gin rummy on the picnic table by lantern light. A toad the size of a cantaloupe galumphes out of the bushes. The crickets sing.

CHAPTER 11

Traveling Solo with Children

I have a little shadow that goes
in and out with me,
And what can be the use of him
is more than I can see.
—*Robert Louis Stevenson*

Alone with the Monster

Secret adventures, special uninterrupted time together, a chance to carve out a separate relationship away from the daily hullabaloo—these are rare opportunities in our rush, rush, rush lives. Yes, there are big benefits to traveling alone with your small child. (Plus it can be fun!)

Yet (and now we enter the Dark Side), the idea of traveling solo with babies or small children seems to bring out intense fear and trepidation in many parents. Being a single parent, even briefly, brings its own concerns. Traveling solo with a kid or kids can be daunting. But hey, don't get all housebound, or anything. This chapter brings you face-to-face with traveling alone with the lovely little monster.

Just to Clarify: I use the term "solo" to mean anybody traveling alone with a child, regardless of their marital or partnership status at home.

The Zen of the Traveling Parent

Traveling solo with baby? Pack up your endurance, store up your sense of humor. You may need both. There may be times when the baby is screaming, the plane is delayed for six hours, your rental car gets a flat tire, the hotel loses your reservation, and your twins suddenly develop the stomach flu and throw up all over your last change of clothing.

This type of travel is challenging by nature. You have no other adults to help you. Nobody to spell you when you're tired and cranky. You are the bottom line. It helps if you expect it to be hard. Little kids don't usually understand when things aren't working out. They take their cues from you; they feel your tension. Hard moments become harder when you overreact. Take ten deep breaths and try to step back from it all. Give *in* to the experience. Get Zen about it. Laughter is sometimes the best and only response.

Quick Affirmation

Actual traveling and transitional times tend to be the hardest. Think of them as obstacle courses to be navigated. Lower your expectations. If you can get there with everybody reasonably intact, you're doing great.

Tools for Successful Solo Travel

The secrets to successful solo travel with little ones are *lowered expectations, flexibility, delight in small things,* and *tight organization.*

Expect the Worst, Experience the Best

By expecting and planning for difficult situations, you'll probably be delighted by the surprise of a wonderful trip.

Bend Like a Blade of Grass in the Wind

First, let's do the '70s chant—"Cosmic. Trippy-and-a-half, man. Groovy, cool, I can relate. Sausalito Sunset. Zoid." Now, let's take it to heart. No really—you have to take it as slow as you can, allow *tons* of time for everything in the world to go wrong, and let your baby be your barometer.

Tighten Your Organization

Before you leave, try to anticipate problem areas. There are certain things you can do to lower your stress and help ensure smooth seas:

- Try to minimize what you bring. The less you have to lug and balance, the better. Can you pick everything up at once, and the baby, too?
- Choose destinations where you will feel comfortable. (Perhaps a visit to friends or relatives—you do want to show off that gorgeous kid!) And if you can splurge a little on comfort, now is the time to do it.
- Consider traveling with a friend, perhaps another parent.
- ID your kids with dog tags (available at your local pet food store). If you're staying at a hotel, make sure they have the hotel's business card secreted on their little bodies.
- Stay where you might meet other adults or parents traveling solo with kids. Consider youth hostels where you'll share common dining and living areas with other travelers. (This is not a suggestion for finding romance—you probably won't look your best with that frazzled expression and cookie crumbs adorning your hair.) A little adult conversation is a good thing.
- Know that you may need to enlist help from passersby.
- Plan to eat early, before kids get hungry and desperation sets in; you'll save yourself some heartache—and maybe even cash (see "Saving Money" on the next page).

🧳 Take resource materials (maps, guidebooks). This can save time and stress, and give you something to do during those long, lonely hotel nights.

Quick Tip:
Taking Just One

If you have kids plural, you might consider taking a trip with just one of them. You'll enjoy special time with your child that may be hard to come by at home, and avoid situations caused by sibling rivalry. Take the older one—let Melanie know she's still special. Or take the younger one—give Danny the rare experience of being alone with Mommy or Daddy. The one who stays home also gets special solo time with a parent, and both kids might find, to their surprise, that they even *miss* their sibling.

Saving Money

There are practical benefits to solo travel with little kids. Fewer adults means less money spent.

🐜 If your child is under two, most transportation is free.

🐜 Consider sharing travel and room expenses with other single or solo parents.

🐜 Breakfast is often the least expensive meal in restaurants, so plan that as your main meal. Eat lightly from your own food stores when you get up, then if you time it right, you can eat your breakfast right before lunch time.

🐜 Hoorah for lunch specials! Eating your main meal in the middle of the day is better for the digestive system anyway, I've been told.

🐜 Many restaurants offer Early-Bird dinner specials.

🐜 Do Juniorette and you eat more than one meal, but not enough for two? Consider all-you-can-eat buffets. Kids often eat free or for only a few dollars. The casual atmosphere is ideal for toddlers and preschoolers, and everybody, even the pickiest eater, usually can find *something* to eat.

🐜 For cheap lodging, consider state or national park campsites (go back and look at chapter 10). When traveling solo, never camp unless there are two or more other cars there.

No Breaks for the Weary— Combating Fatigue

You're thinking for two (or three, or four) so don't skimp on your own sleep. Nap when the little one naps (or just lie down and close your eyes). Avoid the temptation to drive on in the blissful silence. You need to stay fresh.

Remember, you're not crazy, you're jet-lagged.

Take a break! Hire a hotel baby-sitter, visit relatives, take a rest. You deserve time to yourself. Relax!

Some people think traveling solo is *easier* than traveling with a partner. Leslie, who has done a number of trips alone with her two-year-old and three-month-old, prefers to go without her husband, who tends to get more stressed than she does. Leslie does it by being totally organized, and giving herself pep talks when the going gets rough: "This is not going to be easy, don't expect it to be easy, you can manage, you can do it…"

Airports and Airplanes Alone with Little Alfie

The tips below are *especially* important if you're doing it solo. For basic airport/airline information, read chapter 8.

🐜 If your child naps, plan flights around nap time.

🐜 Leave lots of time to get to the airport. *Lots of time.* An extra *hour* even. I mean it. It's really, really important.

🐜 Before you get to the airport, stash a few easily accessible dollar bills for valets and porters, and for renting your little cart.

🐜 Cut a deal with your toddler. Jonah can either hold your hand or sit in the stroller or cart. He cannot run around or walk by himself. It is too dangerous. If Jonah is a very good boy, he can have _____ (insert small bribe here).

🐾 Carry your tickets, money, and important documents on your body. Strap your camera around your neck. Your bags should contain nothing irreplaceable; there may be times when Emily breaks free and bounds across the airport. She's your first priority—you must feel OK about leaving things for a second, and possibly losing something to a thief.

🐾 Once in flight, give up on the idea of magazines and movies—unless the little booger falls asleep.

🐾 Stay hydrated. I'm a firm believer in drinking lots of water on flights, but traveling solo with Annie means I simply can't lug an extra bottle of water with me. I use it as an excuse for exercise and defeating boredom—Annie and I make frequent trips up and down the aisle for water.

Our three-year-old friend Gus flew from California to Michigan and (blissfully for his soloing mom), fell asleep before take-off and slept the entire flight. As they disembarked, Gus looked around puzzled and asked, "Why are we back in the airport again?"

Quick Tips:
Schlepping Solo Across Airports

Help! The first leg of your two-leg flight is arriving late. You're still in the air; you've been circling for thirty minutes. Your connecting flight is leaving in ten, and the gate is half an airport away. The baby and toddler are hungry, you're going to have to balance two diaper bags plus your carry-ons, and you anticipate having to sprint through the airport to make your next flight. What can you do?

🧷 Sweetly explain your plight to the flight attendant (who, with luck, doesn't hate you already). Ask if they can call ahead for an electric cart to assist you (they do it for people who have physical disabilities). With any luck you'll find yourself gliding high above the fray in a little electric cart that goes "Beep! Beep! Beep!" and scatters travelers like chickens.

🗟 You can also ask an airline-gate person to call your departing flight's gate to tell them you're on your way, and to please hold the plane for you. Then grab the kids and the carry-ons, and *run*.

🗟 Ask for help. This may be a good time to rely on the kindness of strangers. Get them to carry your *stuff*. You carry your child.

🗟 If you miss your connection, first laugh at the absurdity of life. Then feed your kids a snack. *Then* start raising a ruckus to get on the next available flight. If you missed the plane and it's not your fault, the airline might: a) Give you a voucher for free or reduced travel next time, b) Get you on another airline's flight, or c) Put you up in a hotel until another flight is available. If they give you an option that is unacceptable, gently press a little harder. They may accommodate you, and it never hurts to ask. (Sit your gooey-faced little pookie on the ticket counter while you negotiate—charmed or repelled, the staff will steam into action!)

Flying Solo with Two or More

When you're flying with more than one, you may have a built-in ally—your older child! Treat Big Brother or Big Sister as a fellow adventurer who you can't manage without, and they'll often come through. A three-year-old can hand you Baby's bottle, a four-year-old can sing to the baby while you readjust your load.

Entertaining little ones at different stages in development can also be hard.

🗟 Enlist the flight staff as allies. This means being extra courteous.

🗟 Ask for meals to be served early.

🗟 Don't order hot beverages on the plane. They may end up on a lap.

🗟 Rely heavily on bribes and treats (though keep sugar treats to a minimum or it may backfire on you!). Pack enough doo-dads so that you can surprise each child every half-hour or so.

- Accept that you can't always contain them; sometimes you'll need to let them run.
- Forget about what other people think. You're doing the best you can.

Doing the Driving Trip Alone

Traveling solo, you won't be able to hand off food and drink when the whining gets intense. You won't be able to soothe a screaming baby as you cruise down the highway at sixty MPH. You'll have to pull over frequently. You'll have to take it slow. (These tips are in addition to the information provided in Chapter 5.)

Here's where that flexibility comes in handy. If you're driving alone with a nursing baby, plan to stop frequently for nursing breaks.

- Mark forty-five minute increments on the map ahead of time. When you get to the marked places, *STOP*!
- Don't drive during rush hour.
- Try not to travel late in the day when kids get cranky.
- Travel a few hours into the night while they are sleeping.
- Make reservations ahead of time, and have your daily travel goal in mind. This is not the time to cruise up and down city streets at dusk looking for the Vacancy signs.
- Always bring along food and water (chapter 3 has snack suggestions).
- Don't push your limits. If you or your kids are tired and cranky, take a little break. Stop and sing a song. Splurge on an ice-cream cone. When people get tense, bad moods get amplified. Do something silly to break the tension.
- Remember that it is *always* further than it looks on the map.

Family Reunions Alone

Any trip "back home" to the bosom of your extended family can be both wonderful and emotionally draining. A family reunion can be a great choice for the solo parent— you'll get a break from duty from loving relatives who can't wait to spend time with your little darling.

Know that you're doing your child a wonderful favor by exposing him or her to historical links. Family bonds are cemented by shared times.

Though you may feel at home, your baby may get nervous. Imagine what it's like: "All these screaming strangers keep *grabbing* me!" Familiarize your child with who they'll meet ahead of time. Look at photos of relatives on the plane, or pin them to the back of the seat so baby can see them as you drive.

The rules of your extended family may be different than your rules at home, and if you assert *your* rules, you might open up old family tensions. Yikes. You may have to fend off unwanted, unneeded parenting advice. That's hard to do when you're the only one marching to a certain beat. Remember, as the parent, you are the authority. You owe it to your kids to maintain some consistency.

At the same time, this is a good opportunity to teach your children that different people do things in different ways. Be flexible where you can. You might say, "At home we all eat together at the big table, but when we're at Aunt Stacey's the kids all eat at the little table and the grown-ups eat at the big table. While we're here, that's what we'll do. At home we'll eat together again."

Be aware that you might inadvertently slide back into old patterns of behavior that you thought you'd grown out of. Without a partner or spouse to keep you centered on who you are now, maintaining your adult identity can sometimes be difficult. This temporary personality alteration might confuse and upset your kids. ("Who is that weird woman who looks like Mom?") Make special time for just you and your children. They need the security of knowing that you are still the same old Mom or Dad. You probably need that security, too.

Hotel Rooms Alone

Read Chapter 9 for general advice. Below are some "solo" specifics.

Safety

Always make doubly sure that the room is safe for the baby (review the "proofing" information in chapters 1 and 9). Have the management remove anything you feel is dangerous.

Hotels and Dining Alone

You've settled your stuff in, now it's time to go out for dinner. Your baby or toddler is tired from the long travel day, and will enjoy the chance to check out the new environment. You'll probably enjoy an early evening stroll. But sometimes it is really too much to go out. If everybody is exhausted, cranky, and unwilling, take the night off and explore other options. Traveling solo, you can't send somebody to the store while you stay with your children. Kids must eat when they're hungry, and you should, too. Now's when you dig into your supplies (and have a *big* breakfast tomorrow), or order from room service or a restaurant or delivery service. (chapter 9 has more information.)

Sleeping Arrangements

Since you're the only adult, there should be plenty of room in the bed. Annie and I happily share. Many people don't like their kids to sleep with them. Get a hotel room with two double beds, ask for a crib, cot, or roll-away, or create a bed on the floor.

Bedtime Rituals

As exciting as travel is, you and your child may become lonesome for the ones left at home. Bedtime rituals are even more important if the kids are away from—and missing—the usual loving caretaker. If you're going to be gone more than few days, the half-hour before bedtime is a good time to play tape recordings sent by Mom or Dad, read or write letters and postcards, or make phone calls.

Lonely Nights

Bring along things to occupy your time after the baby falls asleep. Unless you hire a hotel baby-sitter (there's more on this in Chapter 9), you won't be doing the big boogie at the disco down the street. Plan tomorrow's itinerary, watch a movie, read a book. Or catch up on your sleep. You have a big day ahead of you.

Testimonial

Gizelle and her two-year-old daughter Arielle took a special vacation together, just the two of them, to San Diego. Yes, there were complications—getting across the airport was hard, it rained, and Gizelle got the flu. Despite all this, Gizelle insists, "I'd do it again! I wanted to go so badly I didn't let my fears get in the way, and it was wonderful. I loved being there with my little girl—she's so cute and funny! Arielle was like my little date for five days. She was entertained just by being out, and she picked up on my mood—everything was exciting to her. One day she sang from 3:00 to bedtime. Six months later, Arielle still remembers and talks about the trip."

Dealing with Anxieties and Fears

It's perfectly normal to feel anxious about being alone with the kids on the road. Anxiety alerts us to the need for caution and preparation. Plan, prepare, and take the normal precautions (avoid deserted alleys, lock your hotel room at night, don't volunteer too much information to strangers—you know the drill). But don't be so frightened that you shut yourself off from adventure. Some people find themselves so fearful that they experience extreme anxiety and fear, or avoid the experience altogether. If you're considering traveling solo with children but feel overwhelmed by the idea, go back to chapter 1 for a pep-talk, and try the following:

- Try verbalizing your fears or writing them down. It's like opening the closet door at night for your toddler—in bright light, the monsters often disappear.

- Assess your fears. Are you worried about personal safety, or about your ability to handle difficult or scary situations?

- What are some potentially scary situations? What would you do if they occurred?

- Now might be a good time to talk to other parents who have traveled solo with kids. What were their experiences? What was the worst thing that happened? What was the best? What surprised them? Let somebody you trust help you assess the real dangers. They're probably fewer than you imagine.

Safer Among Strangers

"You take your baby overseas? Isn't that dangerous?" Crime statistics worldwide show that most places in the world are safer than the United States. And, everywhere, most crimes occur between acquaintances. You may be safer "out there" than you are at home.

Learning Strength

Being a single parent even for a day can be an exercise in self-assertion. You are your kids' ally, their buffer against the real world. Nowhere can this be more evident—or necessary—than when you are outside your controlled home environment. If asserting yourself is hard for you, practice ahead of time. Nicely contradict somebody in public. Tell yourself you don't care what other people think.

How Close Is Too Close?

I was alone with Annie on the streets of Venice one evening. Annie was seven months old. We were standing outside a restaurant when a young woman came down the narrow cobblestone street. She approached us and lifted Annie out of my surprised arms, murmuring endearments, "Che bella! Bellissima!" I simply stood there, unable to move. Should I grab my baby back? The woman didn't seem to mean any harm. This culture has a different sense of personal boundaries, my thoughts raced. Will I insult the woman if I remove Annie from her arms?

After a moment, the woman handed my baby back. After another moment, she had disappeared down the dark street. Though the woman had been kind, I was shaken and upset. Without another adult with me—one I knew and trusted—I had found myself unable to judge the danger level or appropriateness of the situation. All I knew was that I had felt intensely uncomfortable.

Since then I've tried to pay more attention to my personal comfort level, and to Annie's. Now when strangers come too close for my comfort—when they tweak her cheek, touch her hair, or try to hold her—I imagine that I'm a mother lioness protecting my cub. "Thanks for being so friendly, but you know, that's her body, please respect her privacy," I say. Sometimes I try to spare their feelings: "Uh…you probably don't want to touch her, she's still contagious." Sometimes I just react: "No!!! Put her down!"

Even when they might not understand my words, they understand my tone of voice and back away. I tell myself that Annie's getting a lesson about personal boundaries and asserting herself, too. And if people get huffy ("Well! I was just being friendly!"), I remind myself of the majesty of the lioness, growling at strangers as she gently places her velvet paw on her baby's head, claws sheathed.

For the Parent Staying Home

I watched them disappear through the sliding glass doors of the airport—tall Bill and tiny Annie, with her castle-shaped backpack, off on her adventure with her Daddy. The airport guard smiled, but firmly waved me back into my car. I drove on. Life for the parent staying home alone can feel mixed. I'd been looking forward to the time alone, but I felt a little lost, and a little jealous—of both of them on their upcoming adventure, and of Bill for getting to watch Annie discover new things in the big city of Los Angeles.

Then time...four days of uninterrupted *time*...stretched before me, and my heart beat faster with the possibilities. I got work done. I gabbed on the phone. I read a book and took a two-hour bath. I got a lot, *a lot*, of blissful, solid, uninterrupted *sleep* (and I can tell you that sleep is highly underrated in this society). But I missed my Annie.

When Annie was two months old, a separation of more than two hours felt agonizing to me. Now when she's away, I get occasional pangs of longing, as well as occasional pangs of guilt for not feeling more longing. It's important that Annie and Bill have special experiences together, and it's worth the wait to see the look on Annie's face as she comes racing down the airport ramp yelling, "Mommy! Mommy! Mommy!" delight, excitement, and love jumping from her face.

CHAPTER 12

Baby Business

If I see something good, I will fax it to you.
All right, Annie?

—Emma, age 3½

The Fax, the Phone, the Pacifier

Enough of the fun stuff: the day trips, the castles in Italy, the woods. This is the millennium, man. Kiss the kid good-bye, dry your tears, and get back to work. But wait, you forgot something important! You forgot the baby!

Part of incorporating *"le kid"* into everyday life means bringing him into your work life, as well. More and more people are doing it; trying to merge all the diverse elements of their lives into one cohesive, happy whole. Doing business with Baby means sometimes you take Baby with you on the road, sometimes you and Baby try to "work it out" at home, and sometimes Baby goes to the office. This chapter discusses all those possibilities.

Working on the Road
with the Little Poopsie

Besides the guilt I feel, I get *lonely* on the road—the long hotel nights, the impersonal coffee shops; each town seems the same to me, the movies and the factory remind me that I'd like to be ho-omeward bound....Oops, sorry Art, sorry Paul. Start again, Ericka.

So, you need to do some business out-of-town. Here are some reasons to bring Baby along:

- You just want to. No, you're not *weird* for wanting your child near you; she wants to be with you, too. If you bring her with you, you won't miss each other. Until much later in your child's life (when she'll spend her time trying to be as far away from you as possible), you are your child's universe. Whither thou goest, she wants to go.

- Be trendy! More and more parents are doing business with a baby. Time was when, female or male, you were considered a lightweight if you brought your kid with you. The times, they are a changin'...Sorry, Bob.

- Though you probably won't be spending your actual work hours with Small Sam, you may have *more* time with him than you would at home. He'll be happy, and you'll be happy. (Doesn't a nice cuddle with your baby sound like the perfect cure for the hotel blues?)

- You'll avoid those rough "Daddy's leaving" and "Daddy's home again" transitions, and your child's separation anxiety will be reduced.

- Your own "worry-quotient" will drop—you'll know exactly how she's doing, because you'll *be* there.

- If you travel regularly to the same places, your child will get familiar with the routine. Babies who travel a lot do it more easily than those who do it occasionally.

- Child-care logistics can be tricky—but child-care logistics are *always* tricky, on-the-road or not. Don't stress out; we'll discuss child care at home and on the road a little later in this chapter.

Planning the Business Trip

When you plan your schedule, try to limit your activities more than you would if you were by yourself. If your organization is doing the planning, try to negotiate a

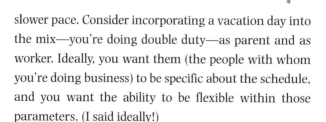

slower pace. Consider incorporating a vacation day into the mix—you're doing double duty—as parent and as worker. Ideally, you want them (the people with whom you're doing business) to be specific about the schedule, and you want the ability to be flexible within those parameters. (I said ideally!)

Special Packing Requirements

Sensible or not, you really shouldn't wear your stained sweats on the plane. You are on a business trip. Also, try to leave the silk and cashmere at home (or change once well away from baby burp and sticky, jammy hands). Your challenge is to find special clothes that look professional, feel comfy, and are easily cleaned. I strongly recommend rayon—hang it in the bathroom while you shower and the wrinkles should steam out. Unlike other business travelers (poor dears; calm on the outside, pining for their children on the inside), you have double requirements clothes-wise, and with all the baby gear, you probably can't get away with just a carry-on bag.

Working on the Plane

Probably not, unless baby sleeps. Apple juice and laptops are an unfortunate combo.

No "Drinks with the Guys" After the Board Meeting

Unless you're on the kind of trip where the "real" business occurs after hours on the golf course, you should probably keep your trip a little more "all-business" than you would if you were alone. (Life is long. You'll be back to Chicago another year—you can hear blues at the Blue Note then.)

"Mama's on a Business Call, Sweetpea"

Scenario: The first round of meetings went quite well, you *think*. You have to prep for tomorrow's round after Baby Heather goes to sleep, but she's a little agitated—the travel, the strange place, the baby-sitter... The phone rings. It's the Big Client calling to go over those figures. Suddenly the baby goes ballistic! Screams! What can you do?

Solution: Unless Heather is screaming from pain (in which case you say, "I have an emergency, I'll call you back," and hang up), maintain your calm tone and Plug that Hole. A baby with a full mouth cannot scream. Use a bottle, a banana, a cracker. If you're nursing, whip up your shirt and offer your breast. A nursing baby will usually nurse when offered the opportunity, and this is no time to worry about feeding schedules.

If nursing is not an option and bananas, bottles, or pacifiers are not working, calmly explain that you are very sorry, but you'll need to call back in ten minutes. The key here is the calm, professional voice that says, "I'm so together that nothing can faze me." Get the number (don't trust yourself to remember!), hang up, and deal with the situation. You've bought ten minutes, and ten minutes is a long time in babyhood. You can deal with almost anything in ten minutes.

Try to remain serene—if you're freaking out that you may have blown the most important deal of the century, you'll never change your child's mood, let alone her diaper. Comfort, caress, kiss. Set baby up with enough distractions to carry you through the call and, precisely ten minutes later (demonstrating how organized and professional you are to the client—they can't see your formula-drenched clothes), call back. Apologize briefly (without details) and continue to sell, sell, sell!

Child Care for the Business Trip or Home

Who will take care of the baby during work hours? Perhaps the ideal situation is for the whole family to go—you work, and your loved ones play. This is not always economically or logistically feasible—perhaps you're a single parent, perhaps your partner can't take

time off. Maybe you have available and appropriate friends or family at your destination (you lucky dawg). Usually you won't. When you bring baby on the road for business, you have options in addition to the hotel baby-sitters (we talked about those in chapter 9).

Conference Child Care

This only applies if you're going to a conference—and not all conferences provide this option. Conference child care is usually provided on-site for parents who bring their children. Before you jet off with Junior, get information about *who* is doing the care, *what ages* they will accept, *where* the care facility will be, *how many* kids they will take, and *when* the child-care center will be open. How long can you leave your baby? Two hours? All day? Then ask yourself, "How long do I *want* to leave my baby?" Have a back-up plan, and get information about hotel baby-sitting before you go. That way, if you get there and get a bad vibe about the place, you can remedy the situation and not miss that important paper on "The Sexual Secretions of Lower Invertebrates."

Bring the Baby-Sitter

If you have the bucks or the client or conference will pay for it, it may be worth it to bring child care with you. The care-giver doesn't have to be your full-time or even regular baby-sitter (though that would be ideal). Are any young adults in your life eager to get somewhere and willing to work in exchange for transportation? Back when I was nineteen and my cousin Jesse was four months old, my Aunt Laurie had to give a couple of speeches on the other coast. The people who hired her ponied up the plane fare for a baby-sitter—me!—and I got a free trip to Boston and New York, spent some time with my delicious nephew, and stayed on by myself for a week of adventure and fun before flying home. (OK, I'm busted. Remember back in the introduction when I said I'd never held an infant before Annie was born? I exaggerated. So sue me.)

Nancy, who worked part-time at home, hired a teenage "mother's helper," somebody slightly less than a baby-sitter, to come in the afternoons (with Mommy present) and play with her son, do odd chores, and remove the baby from the room *immediately* if the phone rang. This young man also accompanied her on a number of almost-local business trips. They all drove together in the car, and Nancy was able to nurse Jasper right before and after seeing clients.

Nannies and Au Pairs

Hiring a full-time care-taker for your child—for home and/or the road—can be agonizing. That's because it matters so much! It can be scary, too. Nanny horror stories abound. (Remember that movie about the psycho baby-sitter, *The Hand that Rocks the Cradle*? Actually, I never saw it. Who needs nightmares?) Less often, we hear the very common success stories of friendship, bonded families, and the joys of bringing a new person to respect and love in your lives.

Interviewing for a Nanny— For Travel or Otherwise

For my friend Ailsa with a three-year-old, a four-year-old, a career, and a husband who worked very full-time, the nanny was an essential piece in the logistical puzzle of her family's busy life. When hiring a nanny, she suggests that you:

- Interview with your head *and* with your heart. References are vital, as is your gut feeling about whether or not you like somebody, and whether you think they will be good for your baby or child.
- Decide in advance how many hours and how much you're willing to pay (ask other parents to determine the going rates in your community).
- Contact agencies. You give them your parameters, they set up the appointments. Agencies are more expensive than hiring independently, but they also

will be in charge of taxes, be responsible for your satisfaction, and will check out employees' records.

🐞 Advertise independently in local newspapers, religious papers, neighborhood newsletters. Try putting up signs in kids stores, preschools, bookstores, or other appropriate places (try the child development office at the local college or university). Many communities have email lists providing parenting information and resources. They often post child-care ads.

🐞 Speak with the potential nanny on the phone. If you like her (or him), set up an interview time and get her references.

🐞 Call references *before* meeting with the potential nanny. In a forty-five–minute, face-to-face interview, it's hard to get all the information you need to trust that person with your child.

🐞 References can give you facts (when did the person work for them, for how long) and also answer vital questions: Are they usually punctual? Are they messy? Do they sit in front of the TV all day? What language do they speak (there are pros and cons to bilingualism)? How do they display their temper—were there any odd or uncomfortable incidents? How do they handle criticism? Are they flexible? Do they need to do everything their way? (Of course, using this criterion, Mary Poppins, who did things her way and never explained, would not be a good nanny candidate.)

🐞 References can also alert you to potential trouble areas and help you prepare your questions.

🐞 If it doesn't feel right after talking to the previous employers, cancel the face-to-face appointment before you've both wasted too much time.

🐞 If the references are glowing (and the facts the potential nanny gave you check out), continue the process. Watch how the person relates to your children, and how the children respond to the potential nanny. The interview is the time to assess the potential match.

🐞 Ask the nanny to baby-sit for a couple of hours. See how it goes, how your kids do, and how the nanny feels. Will she or he like working for you? Does it feel right to you?

Quick Tip:
Who Are You Looking For?

Some say, "Look for somebody who parents like you do." But if you're a new parent, you may not *know* your own parenting style. Others suggest choosing a child-care provider to *augment* your care; somebody who can offer qualities or skills that you cannot. Here's a mental checklist:

✔ Is he responsive to the child? Experienced?

✔ Can she both nurture and foster autonomy?

✔ How does he handle conflict? Are you comfortable with his approach? Will he listen to your requests regarding conflict and discipline?

✔ Does she hold religious, political, or cultural beliefs that run counter to yours in terms of day-to-day care? In other words, her religion, politics, and culture are her own, but if she'll be teaching your child activities or habits that make you uncomfortable, then it probably isn't a good fit.

Nanny Taxes

Part of the process of hiring your nanny, full-time baby-sitter, or au pair is setting up pay. You'll probably contract for a certain range of hours per week, and you'll arrange how you're going to pay them—in cash or by check, and whether or not you're going to be withholding taxes for them.

Since you'll be taking taxes out for them (come on, it's the law and you don't want to blow your chance at elected office over something so small), you need to call

the IRS (I've included the number in the Appendix). Give yourself a pedicure while they keep you on hold. When you reach them, they will set you up as an employer and provide you with a wage book with instructions and a schedule of taxes.

In Support of the Au Pair…

Many moons ago, I was an au pair in an old chateau in France. The chateau was gorgeous and the grounds phenomenal—chestnut trees arcing over the long drive, hedgehogs scuttling, a long misty view from my window over pheasant-filled fields down to the Loire River….Sounds romantic, huh? Hah. More like slave labor. Taking care of three kids (ages three, six, and seven), polishing the silver, ironing Monsieur's underwear….What good is Paradise if you're on your knees scrubbing out the bathtub, crabby kids hanging on your back, while Madame takes a leisurely nap? How can you enjoy the French lifestyle when the nearest small city is fourteen kilometers away and your only transportation is a bicycle?

My purpose telling this story (other than *revenge*, should they ever read this—down, Ericka, down!) is to put in a word for the au pairs of this world. Please, I beg you, do not abuse them. Do not take advantage. Yes, they are living in your house, traveling with you, getting the opportunity to visit Baltimore and Hawaii. Yes, they are part of your "family." But they need a life, too. If they are kind and accommodating and love your children, and you are tired and stressed, it is easy to forget that *they really do need that day off—no exceptions!* Polish your own silver and iron your own skivvies. Stay focused. Light housekeeping does not include windows. An au pair is there for the kids. (End of rant.)

The Office at Home

More and more people telecommute or freelance from home, and home offices have gone from being a rarity to a norm.

The Fantasy: As a scribe-for-hire, I've worked at least partially at home since 1990. It took me years to learn how to ignore the piles of unfolded laundry and dirty dishes during work hours (or at least save them for a "coffee" break), but I eventually learned to focus, do my work, and mentally put on a whole new hat when it's work time.

"This will be a piece of cake," I thought when I got blissfully pregnant. "How lucky it is that I'm a writer—I can write when the baby is asleep or in a playpen next to my desk!" I had images of a sunny room (never mind that my office is a little dank); a bubbly, cooing baby batting at toys near me; and great prose streaming from my fingertips into the computer. Yes, I planned to mother and do great art at the same time. Well, I told you I hadn't spent much time around babies!

The Reality: The reality is that I need child care to be able to work more than occasionally. Parenting is work—it is intensive, disruptive, and not conducive to the quiet, uninterrupted stretches of time I need. The other reality is that, even with top-notch child care, there may be times when I need to work and take care of my baby. Sometimes the universe cooperates and I can, indeed, parent and work at the same time. At other times, "@*#&!$@!#!!!" (Your experience will also depend on the type of work you do. You might be able to nurse a baby and type with one hand—it is harder nurse a baby and conduct a psychotherapy session, or do a massage, or video-conference a board meeting.)

Home Office Survival Tips

- Expect—no, *allow for*—extreme flexibility. If you telecommute, it helps to have a flexible boss.
- Don't count on the nine-to-five thing. You may find that your best work happens between three and five A.M. when the house is finally quiet. Or, you might work best in two-hour chunks scattered throughout the day.

🪆 Try to establish a schedule, no matter how odd. It will be better for the baby—she'll get a general sense of when you're working and when you're not, and it will be better for you. Part of the challenge of working at home is legitimizing your work day. Scheduling regular work time helps. This might mean taking a lunch break at the same time everyday, or quitting at the same time.

🪆 Keep in mind that a toddler needs more attention than a baby.

First Day at Roots and Wings

It was the ideal day-care solution: three blocks away, in a loving, well-recommended family home with Maribeth, a great child-care provider. The night before Annie's first day, I had a vivid nightmare of seeing Maribeth drunk, eight months pregnant, and crying. I awoke with a start. I got Annie out of bed, got her dressed, and, trying not to let her see how traumatized I was, drove down the block.

Maribeth was so nice (and neither drunk, pregnant, nor weeping). I sat in the kitchen, steeling myself to leave my one-and-only child. The aroma of toasting muffins and fresh-cut peaches filled the air. I had a deep urge to stay all day, to sit down on one of the tiny stools and join the kids for honey muffins and hard-boiled eggs, to play with paint and books and animals, to snuggle down on a little pad at naptime. But it was time to go. Annie—ready for her own adventures—kissed and dismissed me, and I wandered out into the sunlight, teary, empty, and bereft.

Day Care While You Slave at Home

Let's face it—good parenting is a full-time job. You cannot concurrently work two full-time jobs and do a good job at either. While you will need an individual caregiver for your business trips, if you are working at home, you can explore other options—swapping with other parents, family home day care, infant centers, and preschool.

Kids of the New Millennium

Two-year-olds Stella and Andrew were making mudpies in the sandbox at their preschool and Andrew got sloppy and wet. Stella ran into the classroom, "Teacher Debbie, can you email Andrew's mommy and tell her to bring some new clothes?"

Working with Baby in the Room

Well, you can try. It may be an exercise in frustration, particularly if you're trying to do a task that requires extended concentration. Keep in mind that the child's needs will always be more real and more pressing than the report you *have* to finish—and that is appropriate. A small child needs attention, and he is not "bad" for asking for it.

- Much of your baby-tote travel gear—the front pack, sling, and backpack—will prove essential for working in the house or office, though be careful when you swing around with a backpack on your back (those things are *wide*).

- If you're trying to take care of a baby and work at the same time, you might find yourself standing up with Baby strapped to your body much of the time. If you're using a sling, make sure you switch sides often or you'll end up feeling as lopsided as Quasimoto.

- If you work at a keyboard, set up your desk so that it is ergonomically comfortable and safe for your body. This is especially important if your baby will spend some or all of the day on your body. In some areas, an ergonomic expert can come to your office, assess your working area, and make suggestions for raising or lowering your chair, positioning your keyboard if you work on a computer, and so on.

- A preschooler can sometimes sit near you and do activities with parental input from time to time—but don't count on it.

🧸 Pediatricians, child-development experts, and movement therapists are all very concerned about the damage that results from putting babies in swings, "jump-ups," walkers, crawlers, or other devices that put a child in a position or allow her to make movements she is unable to make on her own. Though they may free your hands for working, these are not recommended solutions. (Walkers are particularly unsafe because babies can move at speeds they're not ready for and accidents can happen very quickly.)

🧸 You can try a playpen for limited periods. Part of its success will depend on the temperament of your particular baby—some babies and small children simply require more constant physical contact than others. Even if your child seems "independent," never leave him in a playpen for more than twenty minutes at a time (unless, of course, the little angel is asleep).

🧸 Children *need* to move their bodies for proper physical, neurological, and emotion development, and keeping them physically restricted is inappropriate and wrong.

🧸 For the mobile baby, try babyproofing your office. Yes, that includes dealing with all those computer cords.

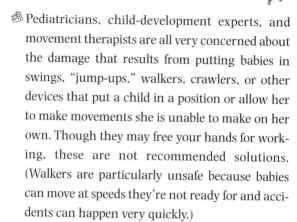

Quick Tip:
Planning on Playpenning?
If you introduce your baby to the playpen before they become mobile, they're more likely to accept it when they can crawl or walk.

Emotional Challenges of a Home Office
Once she is past babyhood, working in a home office with Kiddo in the house becomes both easier and more challenging. On the plus side, she can play with a

baby-sitter or another parent and you won't feel the same driving urge to run and cuddle her each time she cries. The challenge comes from Kiddo herself. She just can't understand that sometimes Mommy or Daddy needs to be left alone. "But I need to be with you...I'll be very quiet...I won't bother you, Mommy!" The little eyes run with tears, the baby-sitter stands feebly at the door waiting to see what you'll do, and you feel like an ogre. Yet you must work. You can explain and explain how lucky Kiddo is, not to have a parent gone all day every day, but a three- or four-year-old cannot comprehend. All she knows is that she needs Mommy or Daddy *now*.

Step One: Don't be angry at your child: she's just being honest about her desires.

Step Two: Have a private talk with the baby-sitter. It is his or her job to make sure that you are undisturbed.

Step Three: Provide as much physical distance as possible—a door that locks, another part of the abode.

Step Four: Be clear that sometimes your kid does need you, and need you immediately. Your task is to figure out when it can be avoided, and when it is real.

The Home Office— Tools of the Trade

A home office can be a separate room, with a private entrance and a lock on the door, or a cabinet where you keep your stuff and...the kitchen table. Of course, the more privacy the better, with the added incentive that you won't be able to deduct your "office" from your taxes unless it really is a separate room used only for office purposes.

Cordless Phones—More Than an Office "Must"

Cordless phones are a must. How else could you dash from room to room following a toddler in destruction mode and schedule appointments at the same time?

Come to think of it, this is far more than a business tip. Hanging out with a baby all day can be isolating, and chatting on the phone while performing mundane duties in various rooms can make the hours go quicker. When Annie was an infant, my phone calls with friends or my sister sometimes lasted through a couple of baby naps, sinks full of dishes, and loads of laundry. Attention to a baby is vital—attention to yourself, and to life outside the home cocoon, is vital, too.

Be Aware of the Isolation Factor

Working at home with a baby or little kid can be a double-whammy: people who work from home complain about feeling isolated, and parents alone with their children all day complain about feeling isolated. Imagine this: you have a major project due and the baby has colic. You haven't talked to a grown-up, let alone a colleague, for what seems like days, and you are getting very depressed. Well, who wouldn't?

- Can you do some of your work in the park? In a café? In a restaurant?
- Take your baby to work one day a week (we'll go into that in a minute).
- Get some exercise on your "lunch break." Take baby to the gym (many gyms have child-watch facilities—remember that section in chapter 6?), or strap him on your back and take a vigorous walk.

Taking Baby on an Office Visit

If you're working off-site from your home office, you may need to get into work occasionally, for meetings, to keep "in touch," or to alleviate your isolation. Part of the problem is that out-of-sight (or off-of-site) is often out-of-mind, and unless you make an occasional appearance, you may find yourself completely out of the loop. (This applies only to people who have jobs. Freelancers like me need to find other ways to communicate with others in their field: conferences, meetings, writers' support groups.)

If the site is safe (no babies at the nuclear power plant, please), drop by. Make up an excuse, if necessary.

Beware: the reality shift may be disconcerting. You're spending your time at home, dealing with very primal, beautiful, and deep issues of new life and development, and they're still in their cubicles, sneaking forbidden games of Matrix and emailing their e-pals in between dishing the dirt on the clients and whining about the workload. Walking back into the worksite may feel weird (everything in *your* life has changed, everything there is just the same), but it can also feel grounding: "Ah—*there* I am, the 'me' I was before I had a baby!"

Make an effort to talk about work, not Junior. The anti-child contingent will appreciate that your brain hasn't turned into creamed banana, and the baby-lovers and other parents will respect your seriousness and loyalty to the job. (Yes, a little cooing and beaming is allowed.)

The Office Baby

Depending upon the level of support you receive from your coworkers and management, working on-site with a baby, while certainly not appropriate for all situations, is sometimes possible. When my niece Emma was born, Jessica took a few months off of her arts administration job and then returned full-time—with Emma. Her office filled with diaper pails, toys, and baby totes. Life wasn't easy—but until Emma began crawling like crazy and there was an opening in a day care center a few blocks from Jess's office, bringing Emma with her was the best solution for all. When Alexandra was born, she too came to work with Jessica until she began to crawl.

Having babies in the workplace is still a new phenomenon in our society—you'll be a pioneer, so be considerate and conscientious about smoothing the way. The tips I've provided for working with a baby in the room still apply, but here are a few more suggestions:

　Rearrange your office furniture so that the area where the baby plays or sleeps is out of sight. Babies are messy, and you're there as a worker, not a professional parent—your coworkers shouldn't have to look at baby-clutter. Make sure all toys are stored at the end of the day and that the office looks like an office.

🐾 Babyproof the office just as you would your home or hotel room.

🐾 A baby, no matter how teeny, *needs* your attention. You may end up feeling like both jobs—the paid one and parenthood—are suffering. Plan for a lighter work load for the first six months.

🐾 The baby doesn't just enter your office, she enters the entire building. She (and you) will be better received if you invite the rest of the building into your baby's life. Bring her around for visits when she's in a particularly giggly, cuddly mood, or invite people to drop in—"Whenever you need a baby fix." Baby is your ally among those who might feel some resentment. It's hard not to like a baby. They might not like *you*, but who can resist that little yummy tummy?

🐾 It helps to have a baby-friendly coworker who is willing—and able—to whisk Little Porky away for a few moments when the Big Boss calls, the client drops by, or when you have to sound very professional on the phone and having babybabble in the background doesn't help.

🐾 If you're bringing your baby to a meeting, it's common courtesy to let people know ahead of time.

🐾 Be considerate of the janitorial service that cleans the office at night. They are paid to empty trash cans full of paper and paper clips, not baby waste. Jessica brought her own trash bags and removed them daily.

🐾 If you're in an office where you need to look presentable, your baby should, too. Appearances do matter, and you want your baby to be welcomed. Don't leave her in stained, smelly clothing or—and this probably goes without mentioning—wet or stinky diapers.

🎐 Jessica swears by food treats. A box of organic O's cereal can go a long way.

🎐 Keep a tape player and some lullabies or other soothing tapes handy. Turn on the music when the baby cries—even if it doesn't calm her down, the sound of soft music may mute the crying and keep your coworkers from getting too irritated.

🎐 Know that your pace *will* be slowed. Talk with your boss ahead of time about how you'll handle the job on days when your child is having a really hard time. Plan on your work taking longer and your production being lower.

🎐 Once your baby is mobile, keeping him at the office may no longer be feasible. How about agitating for on-site day care? Many corporations are going this route—you can visit at the center on your "coffee," "bathroom," and "lunch" breaks, and having baby on-site usually leads to more output, less absenteeism, and a generally happier staff.

Finding and Keeping Your Balance

If you do business with a baby around, you're one of many parents trying to balance their lives and get it all done. Baby business requires the same three skills that parenting and travel do—*flexibility, humor,* and *a sense of adventure.* Here's the deal—if you learn to do it effectively, you'll be able to do anything, go anywhere, be a star! Here are two survival tips:

🧳 Get thee to the gym or the dance class. Take a brisk walk in the warm, spring air. Physical expenditure of energy will give you *more* energy, not less.

🧳 Strongly encourage your best friend to get to know your baby better—and encourage them out the door and all the way to the playground for an hour. Grab a book, some chocolate, and fill a bathtub with hot, bubbly water. Now sit in it.

Note to the Overwhelmed: If your life includes working for money (and the majority of our lives do), you're probably running a constant game of catch-up, living too many lives. Try to slow down, rearrange your financial priorities, rent a smaller apartment, arrange for a job share, ask for birthday gifts of child care, splurge on a massage, or take a mini-vacation. Remember that this is an *era*. It will change. Coffee will go out of fashion, warm milk and meditation will come back in. It will! Too many people are complaining too much of the time.

Doing Business with a Baby

When Annie was twenty months old, I brought her with me to a job interview. The short flight was painless—Annie slept. I collected the rental car with ease. With Annie strapped in the rented car seat, I negotiated the long drive to the home of Dr. V, an esteemed man who had written a three thousand-page autobiography he needed whittled down to something publishable. I hoped to be the whittler.

Dr. V lived in a fabulous house with fine furnishings and a great art collection. We sat in his sumptuous living room. Annie played at our feet. The impressive man was charmed—he frequently interrupted himself to play peek-a-boo with her. Again and again he handed her priceless objets d'art to play with, murmuring, "It is nothing, it is only a thing. If it breaks, it breaks. It only matters that this little darling has a good time." Again and again I carefully pried my daughter's fingers from Fabergé eggs and pre-historic relics.

The interview was not going well. "This project will take a special person with wisdom, grace, life experience, and sensibilities that match my own," Dr. V pronounced. I nodded, trying to look wise, graceful, experienced, and sensible. At about this point, loud sounds emitted from the bottom half of Annie's body, and she began to cry. Dr. V's nose twitched, "I think you maybe need to make a little change?"

"Oh. Oh!" I said. "Excuse me, I have to get the diaper bag." As I said this, I had a horrible vision—the diaper bag left propped up against the car rental kiosk.

"I'll watch the precious baby," said Dr. V.

"No, no. I'll change her in the car," I smiled nervously. Holding Annie, I backed ungracefully out of the house, hoping I was mistaken. I could tell already it was a disaster. Annie had been constipated for a few days—now she clearly wasn't. I balanced her against my shoulder as I opened the car door. I quickly looked through my stuff. No luck—no diaper bag, no diapers, no wipes, no extras in the carry-on or purse.

This was no time for panic, I clearly needed supplies. "O.K. Sweetie, into the car seat," I said, plopping her right on her leaky diaper. I raced a mile and a half to a supermarket, unstrapped and grabbed Annie, ran into the store, grabbed a package of diapers and a box of wipes, waited impatiently while the checkout clerk corrected an over-ride, ran with Annie back to the car, changed her, clicked her back into her car seat, and roared back up the hill. I composed myself carefully and checked the time. I'd been gone twenty-two minutes.

Hoping that it had been so long since Dr. V had been around babies that he didn't know how long it took to change a diaper, I sauntered back in. Gracious Dr. V continued where he'd left off. I looked down at my white blouse, and casually pulled my blazer over a small brown stain.

Ah, Life. All of us mess up sometimes—diapers and diaper bags are replaceable—and at least I hadn't left the *baby* at the airport! As for Dr. V, well, I guess our sensibilities didn't match.

CHAPTER 13

Overseas Adventures and Long-Term Travel

"Travel with kids is different. Much more people-centered than activity-based. You have to change your expectations of what you can accomplish in a day and alter the pace. The rewards are definitely worth the effort. You see the country through very different eyes than the regular backpacker. People who would never normally engage with a Western traveler are much more open to you—particularly women and families. You gain greater respect as a family and attract a warmer, more intimate, welcome."

—John Eyles, world traveler and father of Ava, age 5, and Salila, age 2

Expand Your Horizons

Will you wait forever to see the majestic Andes, to safari in Kenya, to taste tropical fruit on a tropical island with white sands and blue waters? Listen to the wind. Stand on the shore of the Pacific Ocean and gaze out—the vast clamor of China awaits you, the spice bazaars of Java call. Adventuring overseas is not about being wild or irresponsible, it's about learning, growing, experiencing, and incorporating your children into your life. It's about responsibility. If you believe the world is one planet, teach that to your kid—by example, by experience. Bringing your baby along will open the cultures of the world to the entire family. And it's not as hard as you may think.

Baby as an Ambassador for Peace

All of humanity loves a baby. In a small town in the backwoods of the small Indonesian island of Sumba, Bill met a French couple with a two-year-old who had been on the road for almost two years—through Europe, Thailand, Australia, and now Indonesia. Wherever they went, other travelers would come and go in a few days, but they would stay a few weeks or a month, settling in, learning the community. When Bill got to Sumba, the family had already been there several weeks. Evenings, they'd go to a small restaurant where the proprietors' children loved little Veronique and whisked her away to play while the couple ate in peace. In time, the French travelers were invited to the restaurant proprietor's home, and the two families—one French, one Sumbanese—became quite close. This was a common experience for the couple—this slow-moving budget travel, this true opening up of a culture, aided by shared love of the child they escorted.

I want to put in a few words for traveling overseas on a budget, for slowing down and avoiding tourist locales, for being, in a word, a *traveler* instead of a *tourist*. A tourist is a contained unit, a short-term visitor, carefully protected by tours and hotels. In general, the tourist only meets people in the tourist industry. The traveler aims to get away from the "beaten path," to meet the natives, to experience the culture, and, in doing so, to share a bit of the traveler's own culture with the culture being visited. The traveler does not sit in air-conditioned tour buses, watching the sights silently through tinted windows, as if in an aquarium. The traveler has an impact, because the traveler has the contact.

Benefits for You and Your Family

Adventure travel, traveling long-term, and living abroad are ways of expanding your horizons as a human being. Bringing a small child along only deepens the experience. Traveling with a baby lets the traveler experience different ways of loving. The baby enjoys and benefits from the consistency of having her parent(s) with her all the time. The toddler or preschooler begins to learn about the world and all its possibilities.

Tolerance

Travel in developing nations requires a certain relaxed attitude. So there are ants in the sugar? Pick them out. Electricity only between 6 and 10 P.M.? Time for bed. The bed is lumpy? Adjust your body. Children tend to be more flexible than adults—*you* are the one who will be freaked out by the ants, the toddler will quickly learn how to remove them, and unless you act upset, she will be completely casual about it.

Tolerance of other people and their cultures is similar. Baby has the advantage. No child is born a racist. Human behaviors and attitudes—including hate—are learned, and there are countless ways to live a human life. It is easy to criticize another nation simply because they don't do things the way we do at home, but what you may find odd or distasteful your child, who hasn't had time to learn your prejudices, will simply take in stride. The world needs tolerance, and being exposed to differences from an early age will help create a kinder, more tolerant adult. And you may learn from your child's open-minded example.

Whose Tolerance?

Dealing with Cultural Reactions to You

Things are smoother with children along. It sounds simple, but the logic is this—wherever you go there are people, and people are basically helpful and kind. People all over the world have children, and people all over the world love children.

Annie's favorite aspects of Thailand: the fun, the golden Buddhas, her Thai friend Joi who lives on Koh Lanta, and the food. Least favorite?: being called "baby" (she's *not* a baby!) and having to tolerate the stares and occasional touches.

Toddling around the World

Many hard-core "travelers" gallivant aimlessly from country to country, taking a job here, an excursion there, topping each other's stories of hellish bus rides through India and landslides in Bhutan. With a family, it is inappropriate to be so boundary-less or budget-minded. You can go for the upgrade and skip the rock-bottom traveling, while still using public or smaller forms of transport instead of tour buses. If you spend a little more time and a very little more money, if you open yourself to the world and savor it slowly, the experience will last a lifetime.

You're in for a treat when you take your baby overseas. To many people of other nations, the United States is not considered a very child-friendly place. This doesn't imply that we are *un*-friendly, simply that many other countries are *more* tuned in to and accepting of children as a part of daily life.

Staying Safe and Defeating Fear

Ericka says, "Preparation *is* reassurance." Trepidation about travel, especially adventure travel is normal (so is excitement). Information and preparation can quell most of your fears—fear of inadequate medical care, language barriers, malaria, jet lag—but some of your normal nervousness will not dissipate until you actually get out in the world. For gaining confidence and information, check out chapter 14, Troubleshooting A to Z, as well as the books in the Recommended Reading Appendix. Don't be afraid to start small. Plan to take a month in Bali—where the tourist amenities are well-established—before moving on to the jungles of Sumatra in search of the wild tiger.

Testimonial

"Traveling around Costa Rica is a little rugged. Many of the buses are old Bluebird school buses, most of the roads unpaved and windy, and most of the bus windows stuck open to enhance the heavy smells of diesel dust and too many people on a bus. The exception is the ride to the Caribbean Coast from San Jose. These buses are all Mercedes with plush seats, air conditioning, reading lights, and some with bathrooms! You know conditions are a little austere when a bathroom brings such joy!"

—Annie McManus

Basic Overseas Maneuvering

When you're traveling with a baby or tot, you must have all your papers in order. It's easy to get casual and forget (after a year on the road, our friend Linda was so relaxed that she forgot to get a visa for India and was stuck on the Nepali border for two days before bribing an official to let her through—but she was traveling solo. Border guards are far more stringent about people traveling with kids).

Getting a U.S. Passport

If you're a U.S. citizen, you'll need a passport to travel in all foreign countries except Mexico, Canada, and a few selected Caribbean islands. You can obtain your passport from the State Department or through your local post office. Adult passports, good for ten years, cost $60. Passports for children cost $40 and are good for five years. Allow four to five weeks for processing. If it's urgent (and you'll have to justify yourself and pay more money), passports may be issued within a few days from a passport agency (located in larger U.S. cities). To get a passport you will need:

- Two 2 x 2 passport photos. There are a variety of requirements for passport photos, including "no hats allowed," so it's best to have a professional passport photographer do them—check your phone book. Always get extra—you'll need them for visa applications.
- Passport application (available at the post office or on-line at http://travel.state.gov/download_applications.html)
- Picture identification (this is for you—you will vouch for your child)
- A certified birth-certificate for you and for Baby or other proof of U.S. citizenship or naturalization
- The U.S. will soon require the signature of *both* parents on your child's passport application.

> Read, read, read up on your destinations before you go. The Lonely Planet Guidebooks are a great resource for on-a-shoestring travelers. Hang out at your local youth hostel, and listen to the foreign travelers compare notes on their travels. Invite a hosteler home for dinner. Chances are they'll return the favor when you're in *their* country! Ah, dinner in a Romanian village!

Getting Visas

A visa is a permission slip stamped into your passport. Many countries require tourist, work, or student visas, and visas often take time to process, so start early. It's usually best to apply from home. (Though if you're in Thailand, for instance, and you suddenly decide to go to Nepal, you can get your visa in Bangkok through a travel agency. It's a little scary because you have to leave your passport for a few days while it's being processed, and it's not a great feeling to be without your passport overseas.) Visas require passport-sized photos, so always carry extras.

> You'll know you've found a *real* traveler when one of the first things out of his or her mouth is the blasé query, "How long have you been out?"

Other Permissions and Paperwork

- In general, if you are traveling solo with your child, carry a notarized letter from the other parent authorizing international travel. In a number of countries (including our neighbor, Mexico), if you are traveling alone with a child, you must have written permission from the other parent before you can enter the country. (What if you are a single parent? Different countries have different policies; always check with the consulate or embassy before you go to find out how much red tape you'll have to wade through.)

- Many countries require proof of immunizations.

- If your name is different from your child's, it's worthwhile to carry paperwork that reflects that fact. Since my last name is different from Annie's, I carry copies of her birth certificate as well as her passport, even if we are just going to Canada.

Bodily Functions, Overseas

Well, it's diapers again (with a baby it's always diapers). We're back to the great debate: cloth or disposable—remember chapter 2? Here are some additional thoughts for overseas adventuring:

- Supplies of "your kind" of disposables may be unreliable overseas. When you find a brand you like, fill a duffel bag. Once empty, fill it with souvenirs.

- An infant under six months will need up to fifteen cloth diapers per day (carry a three-day supply). An older baby will require fewer. Bring a half-dozen diaper covers and/or plastic pants and safety pins.

- Disposal of disposable diapers can be a problem in areas where trash is burned. The gel in gel diapers releases hazardous fumes when burned. Always bring garbage bags in case you need to lug them out. In the Himalayas, for instance, where garbage is burned or dumped into a landfill, you'll be polluting the air with dangerous fumes or leaving non-biodegradable material in the most beautiful mountains in the world. Stick to cloth (which you can rinse and dry as you hike), or triple-bag the waste and hire an extra porter.

Pre-folded cotton diapers take longer to dry—stick with the regular ones. Many places provide inexpensive washing services. Always let them know that your laundry includes diapers. Rinse out feces ahead of time, and store damp, dirty diapers in a well-sealed plastic bag.

Disposables wick away moisture better than cloth and can prevent a prickly heat rash (also known as milaria—not to be confused with malaria). A more earth-friendly (and tush-friendly) option for avoiding diaper rash is using cotton and leaving baby bare-bummed for as much of the day as possible. Review the information on Rashes in chapter 2.

Quick Tip:
Disposable Diapers and the Metric System

When I was a kid, we had to learn metrics in school because the U.S. was about to join the rest of the world in that measuring standard. They lied, and I still can't remember how many centimeters make an inch. Buying disposable diapers overseas makes me wish I'd paid more attention to Mrs. Stamper, and less to Leon Johnson making faces at me from across the room. Here's the metric conversion—1 Kilo = 2.2 pounds. (That means that if you have a twenty-two pound baby, you're talking ten kilos.)

What to Expect: Squat Toilets and No Paper

You know that extra roll of toilet paper I suggested you always bring in chapter 7? In Asia, bring more. Very few places supply paper at all (some supply a bucket of water and a scoop). Toilet paper is commonly available for large sums in tourist areas (and comes in three styles—bumpy, raspy, or waxy).

Many places have "squat" toilets instead of the sit-down style we're used to. For those of you who have never used a squat toilet, there is usually a platform (or concrete footprints) for squatting over a hole. While there is medical evidence that this style of toilet is physically better for your body (and more hygienic), it can be hard for a little child to learn how to effectively perch, and kids are sometimes terrified of falling in. Stand or squat facing your child and hold their hands. Always supervise little ones.

> Interested in toilets? Eva Newman's book *Going Abroad* will tell you everything you ever needed to know about toilets around the world—and more.

Immunization and Disease Prevention

Many countries, including those in Europe, require no immunizations. Once you select your destination(s), contact your local Public Health Department, the Center for Disease Control (see the listing in the Resources Appendix), or your pediatrician to find out about immunizations and disease prevention of diseases such as typhoid, hepatitis, malaria, yellow fever, and cholera. Look at chapter 14, Troubleshooting A to Z, under M for medical, and R for "The Runs." You'll also find sections for water and food safety. Check it out—W for water safety, F for food safety. Maureen Wheeler's book *Travel with Children* also has a good breakdown of health risks and preventative measures for overseas adventure travel.

- Sterilize bottles and cups frequently by boiling them for fifteen to twenty minutes.
- Drink lots of water in tropical climates.

❧ If you'll be in a tropical climate, remember to protect those little bodies (and your own) from the sun with long shirts, hats, and sunscreen. The sun-protection recommendations in chapter 10 (that's the outdoors chapter) apply to overseas adventure travel as well.

❧ In malaria country, bring flying-insect spray to spray sleeping areas before bedtime. More details about malaria are under M in chapter 14, Troubleshooting A to Z.

❧ Before you go, know your child's blood type.

❧ If you're bringing prescription medications for you or your child, make sure the drugs aren't illegal where you're going. Have your doctor write a letter that describes the medical condition and prescribes the medication (with both brand and generic names). It's a good idea to contact the customs department of the country you'll be visiting to find out any gnarly details. And always carry your medications in your carry-ons—don't check them through.

❧ Carry your own packet of sterile hypodermic needles and syringe when traveling in *seriously* developing nations. You will have to get a prescription (and a doctor's permission slip) for them. Many diseases, including AIDS, may be transmitted through unsterilized equipment. If you or your child needs an injection, it's best to be prepared.

On-the-Road Experiences

Here's the "Core" of "Hard-core" traveling. Most kids are amazingly flexible—you'll be surprised at how easy it can be.

Establishing Home Base When All You've Got Is a Suitcase

"Where do we live, Mommy?" When you are traveling overseas for a long time, your child's sense of "home" may change. Family—by definition—is familiar, but when you are shifting locations frequently, little else may be. For a child, you are your child's home.

Travel with familiar items—a blanket that Shawn always sleeps with, Katie's special lovey toy. Bring pictures of people, places, and things from home. Photograph your house, your neighborhood, your local store. These pictures will comfort your toddler and fascinate the people of the cultures you'll meet.

Bring a child's sleeping bag. Hotels (especially the budget kind) and guest houses are not always equipped for children. Go the "extra dollar" and get a little more floor space so the baby can crawl—you often won't want him crawling on the ground outside, and those little limbs need exercise.

Bring Your Rhythm with You, or Develop It There

Develop a rhythm to your aimless lifestyle, and everybody will do well. How about this? Leisurely breakfasts, mid-morning playtime, afternoon adventures, evenings of hanging out, and traveling no more than every fourth or fifth day. If you let it, your family will fall naturally into a routine—and sometimes you'll remember the routine (like our daily Balinese breakfast of sweet black rice, bananas, and papaya) long after the individual events fade from memory.

Lugging It

No doubt about it: with a baby, you'll have to bring more gear than you would if you were on your own. We like to do what I call "satellite" travel—park most of your stuff at a hotel or guest house (they'll charge a small fee), load a backpack of necessary items, and adventure light for a few days. This means you don't lug your winter jackets (which you'll need next month in the Alps) all the way through the Greek Isles.

Language Issues

English has become the international language of travel and commerce. It always helps to speak the local tongue, but it really isn't necessary. (How many of us can quickly pick up Serbo-Croatian, Mandarin, Javanese, Tamil, and Nepali?) Traveling with a toddler or preschooler, you're in luck—kids pick up a language called "Pidgin Child" very quickly. Learn the words for "Thank you," "Hello," and "Beautiful." Always, everywhere, good will, hand signals, and smiles go a very long way.

A Small Child's Experience

Little kids don't have the same social barriers adults do—they easily make friends wherever they go. Kids on the road also don't need as many toys as the bored toddler at home—they're getting stimulation from exterior sources. Kids improvise—a twig becomes a magic wand, a sarong draped over a chair becomes a secret cave. Bring art supplies, a ball, some animal figures, and maybe some small musical instruments—you'll pick up more along the way.

Incorporating Your Child into the Global Village

Who will you find when your family hits the road? Not only the locals. All over the world an informal fellowship of Western expatriates and travelers have paved the way for you—from Germany, France, Canada, Russia, Holland, Israel, Brazil, Japan, Mexico, Australia, Greece, Britain, Egypt, Surinam, the United States, and everywhere else. You'll meet them while journeying from place to place on the trains, boats, and buses. You'll meet the same ones, a week later, in a budget hotel at the other side of the jungle.

The stereotypical long-term traveler stands out in any crowd—ethnic pants weathered from hand-washing, hair a bit shaggy, passport stuffed with extensions—but look again—these are not just aimless hippies longing for a return to the '60s. These are accomplished souls: bankers, artists, unemployed dot-commers, psychotherapists, merchants, writers, dentists, students—out for a couple of months or a year to take a closer look at the world. And yes, there are more babies and little kids than you can imagine.

The travelers are your lifeline, your source of information as to the best guest house in Cuzco, the finest pediatrician in New Delhi, the best place to buy bottled water and toilet paper in the next town. One day you'll find yourself at a table waiting for fresh green mussels with people from four nations in a slow-serving restaurant on a Thai island. You'll play backgammon and talk about democracy, dysentery, and Celine Dion. The baby will play in the sand at your feet, and you'll suddenly realize that you're comfortable anywhere in the world; that you've joined the world's community.

Finding the Familiar

There are things your family will miss from home. Mass market peanut butter. Roast Beef. In Southeast Asia, we craved cheese. The acrid tang of a good dried parmesan and melting, oozing Gruyere over sourdough bread. Ripe Camembert. Expatriates and travelers compare notes and obsessions: "Chocolate," the American says. "Oh, don't talk about chocolate," says the Austrian. Then after a pause he chimes in, "Have you ever had...Toblerone?" The group sighs with remembered pleasure.

Your picky three-year-old may take a while to adjust to his new diet. Let him eat plain rice, and supplement with vitamins. He'll soon catch on. If you'll be spending numerous months overseas, you may want to arrange to have the occasional care package of "familiar" food sent. In larger cities you may be able to find much of what you crave, though you'll probably pay for that familiarity. Don't worry—when you get home, you'll have a preschooler sobbing for mangosteen or gado-gado.

A Taste of Home

My own obsession with Goldfish crackers began long ago when, most of the way through a year in Asia, Bill and I spent three aching weeks in India. There I was—sick and tired, in the bus station in the city of Jaipur, surrounded by beggars with no fingers hounding us for money

("Baksheesh, Madam, baksheesh") and by heartbreakingly beautiful children with no parents in sight.

Then, through the misery and hordes, I spied a Western woman holding a large bucket of Goldfish crackers with the familiar label. The yellow bucket shone across the station like a beacon. The smiling fish called to me. I homed in, moving as if in a dream, approaching and politely introducing myself to the British woman who, it turned out, was on her way to help Mother Teresa in Calcutta.

"Would you like a couple of these?" she finally asked me, taking pity, no doubt sensing my X-ray eyes trying to penetrate the container as we talked. Only years of socialization at the hands of my polite parents kept me from snatching more than a handful, though I wished desperately that my hand would suddenly grow much, much larger.

They tasted delicious. Something about the comforting, slightly salty crunch of the tiny crackers loosed something inside me and brought tears to my eyes, and I think it was then that I gave up, and decided to leave India, go back to Thailand, and begin the long journey home.

For the average American kid, Goldfish crackers are just part of childhood, but who knows to what length these toddlers might go when, years later, they are faced with their comfort food calling to them from across a scary, sad, place like the Jaipur, India, bus station.

Transportation in Developing Nations

Most of the transportation basics we explored in chapter 5 apply overseas, too, but there are a few odd permutations.

Buses

In some countries, buses are the only way to get from point A to point B, though there are times when going a few miles will feel like going from A to Z to B, what with the bus breakdowns and the uncomfortable positions your body is forced to take when they cram in double the seating capacity—and then bring on the livestock. With a little one, you may get more room, or you may not. On the other hand, little kids don't often have the same need for personal space as adult Westerners, and may enjoy the sensuous quality of all that body contact. They may also enjoy (or at least not be offended by) the sometimes pungent smells. And finally, they're smaller and more flexible and find it far easier to squish.

Play It Safer with a Little One? YES!!!

We learned fast. For our first developing nation travel with Annie, in Guatemala, we chose our usual mode of transport from the capitol to Antigua—the cheapest one. Twenty minutes into the public bus trip, Bluebird bus brakes squealing metal on metal, diesel fumes in our faces, we realized that we should have gone the extra couple of dollars and taken the private mini-bus. We were fortunate—the ride was short and we learned our lesson.

Banana Boats, Elephant Rides, Yak Backs

When you're adventuring, you'll have lots of opportunities to experience alternative forms of travel. Always assess the safety element—there are no guarantees in life, but some "exotic" forms of transport are actually safer than some "regular" forms of transport (such as motorcycles and cars).

Quick Tip

Large plastic garbage bags are vital for keeping backpacks dry on small boat trips.

Trekking

For experienced travelers or a family that likes to backpack, trekking—which is like backpacking without the camping part—is a terrific adventure.

If you've never backpacked with a baby or toddler before, start *small!* In the Himalayas, there are many beautiful and gratifying two- and three-day treks.

Consider hiring a separate porter to carry child-supplies—and the toddler when she gets tired of hiking.

Always consider the distance from medical treatment. You'll be walking slowly, but can a running porter get there in half a day or less?

If there's more than one adult on this journey, consider splitting up for a week or so. One adult takes the baby to a resort area and hangs out while the other treks. Then switch—it's the other adult's turn for wild adventure. Perhaps a camel ride through Rajhasthan?

Long-Term Stays Abroad

The best way to learn a culture is to live there and explore at your leisure. Living in a foreign place with a small child, you'll have great opportunities to meet your neighbors—baby provides the best opening there is.

Creating a Home Base

If you'll be staying somewhere more than a month, consider renting a house or apartment. Renting is much cheaper than hotels, and you'll be able to establish a sense of familiarity and security for the kids (and yourself). You may not be able to rent a place before you arrive—arrange for a hotel or find a guest house to tide you over, then spend a few days getting oriented and deciding where you would like to live. At that point, you can contact a local real estate business (check the tourist office for referrals). Here are some things to keep in mind when renting:

- How close is it to public transportation? To the market? To the expatriate community hang-outs?
- Check out the bathrooms in any rental units. Are they shared? Pay a little more for private bathing (except possibly in Japan where the public sentos are a treat).

🔖 Is it furnished? Do a thorough check of all utilities and furniture, and make sure you and the rental agency agree on the condition of any appliances and furniture.

Staying in Touch with Home

It's now possible to call, email, fax, or send letters from almost anywhere in the world. Even the small towns in the most remote countries seem to have a local cyber-café or two where you can sit, sip, and surf for pennies (in Crakow, Poland, an hour of access costs about 25¢. It's slightly more in Western Europe, about the same in most places we've been in Asia). Set up a free email account at one of the easily accessible commercial sites before you leave home and have all your email forwarded there.

If you know where you'll be and you want to get hard copy letters, have your friends and family send them to you c/o Post Restante in Wherever, Planet Earth. And spring for the occasional phone call. For preschoolers, staying in touch with loved ones at home is essential—it helps keep them happy and contented on the road. It's nice for adults to hear from home, too.

CHAPTER 14

Troubleshooting A to Z

A baby is an inestimable blessing and a bother.

—Mark Twain

A Troubleshooting Alphabet

Travel with a weeny one is not without its complications. But most hassles turn out to be minor hullabaloo over nothing, and the complications that do manifest are the stuff of life, the adventures that will *bond* your family. (After all, you need something to retell again and again in your old age, something with which to embarrass your kids and fascinate your grandkids.) This chapter has assorted odds and ends about emergencies and hassles—how to avoid trouble, and how to deal with trouble once it arrives.

A

Animals

A is for domestic Animals. Big animals like dogs and horses, small animals like rabbits and cats. Big animals can frighten small children, and some are dangerous—animals when threatened can bite.

An over-enthusiastic dog can scare a small child by jumping up and licking him. Then, if the child runs, the dog might think he is playing, and chase along behind. If the child falls to the ground, screaming and cowering in fear, the dog might think he is ready for a wrestle, and jump on, tail wagging furiously. (This happened to my niece Emma—it took years to get over her fear.) Teach your child to stand still instead of screaming and running, never stare a strange dog in the eye, and, if she is knocked down or falls, curl into a ball, covering her head with her hands.

Some kids are fearless—they may be more challenging than a naturally cautious child. Animals, when threatened or frightened, will bite. If you are unfamiliar with an animal—keep your child well away. Teach your child not to touch or pet strange animals without your permission, even if the owner says, "Oh, Bowser loves kids!" Yeah. For breakfast.

If your child is bitten by an animal, seek medical attention immediately. Make sure you know and can locate the biting animal—it may save you and Junior from a trip home and rabies shots.

Allergies

A is also for Allergies and Asthma (and its accompanying medication, Albuterol). Many kids are allergic to animals—ask about possible exposure to Persian kitties at the bed and breakfast before you reserve, and certainly ask that distant cousin in Fresno who would *love* to put you up. Is Amanda allergic to feathers? Check the hotel beds and request that they "dump the down." If your child is allergy-prone, carry any medicines with you—even if it isn't allergy season at home, who knows what strange plant might set a sensitive child's nose and lungs a-quiver?

B

Baby Bottoms

B is for Baby Bottoms, and the on-the-road, out-of-house diaper emergencies that can befall them (and you). When you're out of the house, away from Command

Central (the diaper changing table) lots can happen, much of it funny—in retrospect. Here are some tips on dealing with common Diaper Emergencies.

Problem

You use cotton diapers and your only diaper cover or plastic pant is hopelessly soiled.

Solution

Try a triple diaper. A double diaper will merely keep the leakage from running down his leg—a triple diaper will keep his clothes from being drenched. Leaky Larry will be bottom heavy but it will help keep him from crawling out of reach.

Problem

You're out of diaper wipes.

Solution

Use alternatives such as moistened paper towels, carefully wielded wads of bathroom tissues, or a clean, damp cloth diaper. Resign yourself to a baby bath in the *near* future. Warning: *Never* tear up disposable diapers—they contain powerful chemicals that can damage your baby's skin and lungs.

Problem

You use safety pins on cloth diapers, and a pin breaks.

Solution

Try paper clips. You can try folding and tucking. Folding and tucking requires frequent re-folding and re-tucking.

Problem

No wipes, no water.

Solution

Be aware of possible contamination. Say you're in the car, you're out of wipes, you've changed a poopy diaper with the roll of toilet paper you keep in the glove compartment for emergencies. Now, treat your hands as though they are a teeming mass of bacteria (they are!) and don't touch anybody until you can wash well with soap. Once you thoroughly clean up, wipe your steering wheel. Avoid this scenario by keeping a small bottle of antibacterial hand cleaning gel next to the roll of TP in the glove compartment.

Problem

No diapers. You've left the diaper bag at home.

Solution

Hit the store. Even if you're a cloth-believer, this is no time to be squeamish about disposable diapers.

Problem

Out of cloth diapers, it's midnight, and you can't get to a store.

Solution

Many fervent believers in cloth keep an emergency packet of disposables on hand. If you don't, it's time to be creative! Got any old towels? Create a loin cloth. Or let baby air out on an old, soft, washable something. What if you're in a rental car or Uncle Jack's borrowed Jag with the all-white interior? Are you really *that* attached to your shirt?

C

Cranky, Crabby Children

C is for Cranky, Crabby, Crummy, and Crass—which your kids will probably be, from time to time. While every trip has its down points, no vacation day will be more perfect than a normal day at home. You don't expect perfection (from your kids or yourself) at home, it isn't logical to expect perfection on the road.

To help prevent a Case of the Cranks, *slow down!* (I really mean it this time.) Give your kid a chance to adjust.

Try to keep it light. Go for the surprises—dip into your emergency stash of special "somethings" (and I don't just mean food—try stickers, Band-Aids, a miniature kaleidoscope). Sing that special song you only sing when things go wrong. You don't have one? Try "Trouble" by Cat Stevens, or for more sugary uplift, "Tomorrow" from the musical *Annie*.

Critters

C is also for Critters—Mosquitoes, Ticks, Bees, Wasps, Spiders, and Snakes. After reading this section, you may feel like sealing yourself and your child in a protective bubble for the rest of your natural lives. Resist the impulse—for the vast majority of people, for the vast majority of time, insects are a small nuisance, easily dealt with.

The best treatment for insect bites is *prevention*—light-colored long sleeves and long-pants garments (don't forget socks), and insect repellent on all exposed skin. Insect repellent is not recommended for small babies.

In this country, *mosquito bites* are largely a nuisance (see M for malaria information), though they can become infected if scratched with dirty little hands. Keep fingernails short and treat bites with antihistamine cream or calamine lotion. Over-the-counter hydrocortisone creams reduce swelling, but avoid using them on the face.

Most tick bites are harmless, but some ticks can carry Rocky Mountain Spotted Fever or Lyme Disease. If you're in tick country, you should wear long sleeves, pants, and socks. Tuck your pants legs in. Tick repellent can safely be applied to clothing. Check your child's entire body nightly, especially in the hair—ticks aren't always easy to see or feel.

If you find a tick, don't panic—and *don't* rip it out. Review the instructions for tick removal in your first-aid book. Firmly grasp the tick as close to the base as possible and gently pull straight upward with steady, even pressure. Make sure to save the insect for analysis. Watch the bite area for four to six weeks. If a circular rash or redness develops, contact your physician immediately.

Avoid bee stings by not looking or smelling like a flower (leave the perfume at home). Don't swat at a bee or run away—retreat slowly if necessary. Bee stings hurt. If your child is stung, reassure her; the pain is frightening, but only 1 percent of all children (and 4 percent of all adults) are allergic to bee venom. Remove the stinger by scraping with a long fingernail, apply an ice pack (if available). Give an oral antihistamine. Mud soothes, as does a baking soda and water paste, or calamine lotion. Observe the victim for thirty minutes for allergic reactions (see your first-aid book).

For *wasp* or *hornet stings*, Dr. Spock recommends rubbing a drop of vinegar into the spot.

Make a habit of shaking out shoes before putting them on to dislodge any little friends (spiders, scorpions) who might be hiding inside. *Spider bites* are nasty, and the venom of Black Widows and Brown Recluse spiders can be deadly. Capture the spider if possible, clean the area with alcohol, and seek immediate medical attention. *Scorpions* are rare in the U.S.

Though *snakebites* are rare, prepare for disaster by reading up on snakebite procedures before you hit the woods or wilds. Don't get too close to a snake—back away slowly so it won't feel threatened. Remember that Coral snakes are very colorful, with stripes of red, yellow, and black. Rattlesnakes are very slow and not aggressive; contrary to myth, they *don't* have to rattle or coil before they strike.

D

Traveling with Kids Who Have DISABILITIES

D is for kids with Disabilities. Of course you can travel with them! Any limitations will be specific, because every disability is different. You, especially, need to be prepared and plan ahead. Several organizations are geared specifically towards travelers with disabilities (see Disability in the Resources Appendix). And be aware that you may be dealing with cultural reactions to disability, not just physical limitations. If your child is old enough to be aware of the reactions of others, it might be a good idea to prepare her, to the best of her understanding (given her age), about what she might expect. "Some people are not very nice, Honey. Sometimes people might laugh or stare at you. We don't pay attention to people like that. They are not very smart or nice." (Also see U, Unwanted Attention.)

E
EMBASSIES and Consulates

E is for Embassy. When you're overseas, it's a good idea to know where your embassy or consulate is. Here is what your embassy and consulate will probably *not* do: bail you out if you're arrested for drugs; lend or give you money if you come up broke; fly you or your family home if you are ill. Here's how the embassy and consulate *can* help you out: register your absentee ballot; extend your passport; and give you valuable information about visas, travel advisories ("There's a revolution on the Northern border—please avoid"), medical care, and long-term schooling. If you're in a trouble-zone (and just why *are* you there with Baby Enrico, I ask you?) it's a good idea to check in with the consulate or embassy just in case.

F
FIRST Days, and FOOD Safety

F is for the First day of a trip. The first day on the road, plan for disaster. Inevitably, everything that can possibly go wrong on a first day, will. You'll be fighting the flu. The kids will come down with colds (and will not be gracious about it), the plane will be delayed, your luggage will be lost, you'll be stranded on the dock when the ferry pulls out early, the taxi driver will cheat you, and you'll risk herniating yourself trying to lift your daughter's luggage. There may be bed bugs, bad food, or rain (there will *usually* be rain). A word to the frustrated, the disappointed, the distressed: hang in there. Keep this in mind—the first day of a trip is not, is *rarely* an omen of things to come.

Food Safety

F is also for Food Safety. Food-safety issues can affect everybody—whether at home or on the way to Katmandu, Timbuktu, or Kalamazoo. Here are some guidelines for avoiding that nasty bacteria waiting to make you and your baby ill.

Always wash your hands before eating. It's not pleasant to think about, but most contamination comes from ourselves. Pay attention to where and what you eat and make sure you don't introduce disease. Busy toddlers get into everything ("Wow! There's something shiny on the sidewalk—right next to that pile of dog poop!"). Wash their hands frequently. (Dip into your diaper wipes, carry a little plastic baggie with a stub of soap, carry a small bottle of antibacterial hand cleaning gel.)

Food safety is of particular concern for infants. Their systems are vulnerable. Make sure formula is not contaminated. Powdered formula is better than concentrate (which spoils quickly), as long as the water is safe. Check out W (below) for more on water safety.

Be especially careful about any child with chronic conditions (including frequent ear infections), or any child who has suffered a gastrointestinal insult (like a serious bout with diarrhea). If your child is healthy, food safety is mostly common sense.

Many food-borne pathogens are carried in the high-protein foods—milk, meat, eggs, beans, and so on.

Make sure all juice and milk is *pasteurized*. E Coli and other nasties can live in unpasteurized juices. Tuberculosis can be passed through unpasteurized milk. In many countries, stick with powdered, condensed, or sterilized milk, or skip it. Your child needs milk, but only if you trust the source. Milk which has been vigorously boiled should be safe if consumed promptly. Better a few days with no milk than amoebas, diarrhea, vomiting...

Make sure meat is cooked through, and that the juices run clear. Skip the steak tartare experience.

Picnic foods are a known danger. No lukewarm mayonnaise, out-all-day chicken, or sitting-in-the-car-too-long deviled eggs. Bring a cooler, or follow the two hour rule—no more than two hours out of the refrigerator for meat, poultry, or eggs. Use your common sense—this depends upon the weather. Bacteria reproduce faster in a hot climate.

Discard food if you fear it might be contaminated or too old. Better safe than groaning in agony.

The best foods to bring on the road are canned food, dried food, bread stuff, starches, and fresh fruits and vegetables (peel them unless the water is safe to drink). Think of it like preparing for an earthquake, tornado, or big storm. Jarred baby food is great, but make sure the safety button pops up when you open it.

In general, commercially prepared food tends to be safer than home-prepared food. (It may not *taste* better, though some of it is pretty yummy.)

On the road, look for busy restaurants. Restaurants don't stay popular if they poison their clientele, plus, busy means quick food turnover—food has less of a chance to spoil.

In an "iffy" situation, cook it, boil it, or peel it—or don't eat it.

G
GOING Home

G is for Going Home Again. Whew, you made it there and back safely. Welcome Home! Watch out! It's amazing how fast the relaxing benefits of two weeks at the beach can disappear. Unlock the door and life crashes in. The basement has flooded. There are seventeen messages on the phone machine, and 223 email messages. The mail is overflowing the mailbox. The bag of garbage that you forgot to take out when the airport shuttle honked three minutes early is still by the kitchen door—and the ants have found it, and they've had a party while you were away.

You think *you're* overwhelmed—look at the baby. Poor dear is experiencing a flood of emotions—not all of them bad: he remembers this place, he likes it, he's *tired*, wow, he missed it and he didn't even know it! Here are some stuffed animal friends! He's happy, he's exhausted, he can relax, he can release, he can giggle, he can scream!

Step One: Sit down. Don't deal with the mail, the email, the garbage, the baggage, the flood, the calls from the office. Don't even *call* the office. *Sit!* Take at least fifteen minutes (set the kitchen timer if you have to).

Step Two: Breathe. Focus on the baby. Hug the baby. Take a few moments to play.

Step Three: Try to ignore the mess and take time to revisit your vacation in your mind. After the first flood of anxiety, you'll usually find that the benefits of those two weeks (or two months) have not disappeared.

Step Four: Now *deal* with it! (Refer back to Step Two as required.)

(Also see Z, Time ZONES and Jet Lag.)

H
HUMOR

H is for Humor—your best weapon against travel hassles. Traveling with a baby is inherently Hysterical. You're still the same person you were before parenthood, but now you have this little Hunk of living flesh that goes with you. Traveling with children, funny things Happen. All of this is Humbling, and puts you deeply in touch with your Humanity.

I
IRRESPONSIBLE Behavior and INFANT Seats

I is for Irresponsible Behavior and Infant Seats. There may be emergencies when you have to break the law. Say it's raining in Manhattan, and you *have* to catch a cab. You aren't carrying a car seat. Say you're in Sri Lanka, and the rental car has no seat belts. No seat belts mean no way to attach the car seat.

Sometimes you have to just *go for it*. Try to remain calm—panic won't help. If necessary, remember your own childhood, bouncing in the station wagon as your parents drove across country. I remember my cousins Rebekah and Toby zooming around town *standing up* in front of my Uncle Rob on his motor scooter. What you're doing is not safe, but you and your child will probably survive. That said—(and I shake my finger at you) don't make a habit of it.

If you're a rider, put the seatbelt around you (not the baby) and hold the baby or toddler tightly on your lap (using your strictest grown-up voice to make clear the importance of this) no matter how much she wiggles and screams. For toddlers who understand, you can stress that they are riding "like a grown-up."

Hope that the journey is short.

Be strict with the driver, too. Say, "I want you to drive safely and slow. I'm concerned about my child."

If you rent a car in a foreign country by phone or fax ahead of time, make sure to ask about seat belts, and specify that you *must* have them. (Try to get it in writing—not that it will hold up in any court.) It's worth being ridiculed for asking: "Of *course* we have seat belts, what kind of savages do you think we are?" or "Seatbelts? *Hah!* What do you think this is? America?"

In some countries the rental cars may not have seat belts. In this case, you won't be able to attach an infant or toddler car seat. There is no easy solution. I went through the phone tree at the U.S. Department of Transportation and talked to three experts. Some people (not the experts, who were baffled at the question) suggest bringing your own seatbelts, hiring a garage to remove the seat, and bolting in a set of seat belts. This is beyond most of us. Others suggest wedging the infant seat behind the passenger seat on the floor. I suggest taking the train. *Do not* put a child in an unattached infant or toddler seat. This is *treacherous and potentially fatal*. Better to hold the child than let an unrestrained infant or car seat bounce around. Special Note:

Never buckle two kids in one seat belt—it increases the chance of serious injury.

J
JERKS, and How to Deal with Them

J is for Jerk. People all over the world have ideas about parenting—and many total strangers aren't afraid to voice their opinions. Unsolicited advice can be annoying particularly because you know your child and your situation. Sometimes parenting differences are cultural. Be sensitive to cultural differences, but have confidence that you are the best parent for your child, and politely ignore, explain, or defend.

K
KID Time

K is for Kids, and their own sense of time and space. Henry David Thoreau wrote: "The man who goes alone can start today; but he who travels with another must wait until that other is ready." He could have been talking about recalcitrant toddlers.

Kids have their own agenda. Kids have their own interests. Wisdom—the ability to see the big picture—comes only with age. You'll find this is true out in the world with your child: Toddlers see the world in minutiae—you're admiring Half Dome and they're playing with a leaf. Try to find a marriage between their interests, sense of time, and your own. (Cruising through the French countryside, Bill and I oohing and ahhing over medieval villages, Annie looking up from her dolls to say "WOW!!!" and immediately turn back to her game.)

L
LOST Children

L is for Lost Children. The idea of losing a child gives parents nightmares, and terrifies children, too. The majority of the time, lost children don't stay lost very long. Abductions by strangers are extremely rare.

Nevertheless, even a brief separation can feel traumatic for all concerned.

Here are some ideas for getting and keeping your children found.

- Stress the importance of staying with Daddy, Mommy, or Aunt Sherry—and tell your kids to look for the red shirt, purple hat, or whatever you're wearing. (Annie knows to look for Daddy—Bill's tall, so he stands out in most crowds.)
- Dress your child in bright colors.
- Make sure your child knows her full name, and if possible, the name of the place the family is staying. ("De Cwown Hotew.") Her home address won't help if you're traveling in Southern Zaire. Most hotels provide printed business cards. We always tuck one in Annie's back pocket (or safety-pin it to the back-bottom of her shirt).
- Tag 'em. Many childrens stores sell inexpensive, disposable ID wrist bands. You can have a separate band for each destination. Annie wears, on a silver chain, a heart-shaped dog tag I made at our local pet food outlet.
- Teach your child to ask for help from "officials," (police authorities, shop clerks, security guards) or other parents, rather than strangers. Asking for help from women is safer than asking for help from men. (Sorry to be un-P.C. about this, but most criminals *are* men!)
- Learn to whistle. My dad used to call us with one long high and two low whistles—a whistle he originally developed for Sweet Harry, his old horse.

If Your Child Does Get Lost

Don't panic! Try to think logically, and *then* alert everybody. Was he casting goo-goo eyes at the horsy ride at the supermarket? Might he have wandered that way? At big, organized events (county fairs, theme parks), announcements can sometimes be broadcast. Some stores provide this service, too.

Once you find your child, you will probably feel angry and may yell at your wayward kid. This is normal—the worry is replaced by relief, yet those tense emotions have nowhere to go. Being aware of this tendency can keep you from screaming, hitting, or otherwise punishing already frightened little Fanny. P.L.C.S. (Post Lost Child Syndrome) will pass faster if you let your child cry, be clingy, and tell the story over and over again. As for you, don't vent on your child, but *vent!* Yes, it *was* scary! If the scare was severe (more than fifteen minutes), be prepared for Fanny to have nightmares, or to otherwise regress a bit.

M

MEDICAL Emergencies and First Aid

M is for Medical, Minor, and Major. Most illnesses are Minor. You get sick at home, and you'll get sick on the road, too. Your family may even experience less illness if you experience the day-care "Pass it around again, Sam" syndrome at home.

First Aid

Every parent should know their way around a first-aid kit. If you are doing adventure travel, you'll find it helpful for other people's kids, too—a Band-Aid in Belize, a splint in Srinigar. You are not a doctor, though (unless you are), so never give any strange child unprescribed medicine. Create your own kit, and consider including items from the following lists:

Basic Family First Aid Travel Kit

First-aid guide(s) include information on wilderness first aid; acetaminophen and/or ibuprofen—for both baby and you; adhesive tape; ace bandages; antibacterial cream or ointment; anti-yeast cream; antihistamine liquid; antiseptic towlettes; Band-Aids large and small; gauze bandages; butterfly bandages; Benedryl or other anti-itch cream; activated charcoal (for when a caustic poison has been ingested); calamine lotion; cotton balls; diaper-rash ointment; eye pads and eye wash; hydrocortisone 1 percent; hydrogen peroxide; ipecac (don't use without speaking with a doctor or poison control center); measuring spoon, dropper, or syringe for oral medications; motion sickness medicine; prescription medications; small scissors; splints; surgical tape; teething stuff (if teething is an issue); thermometer; tweezers.

Camping/Outdoor/Wilderness First Aid Kit

All of the above, but add:

Broad-spectrum antibiotics (erythromycin, sulfa, penicillin); baking soda to apply to stings; calamine lotion or aloe vera gel; codeine pain medication; injectible epinephrine (for bee sting or other insect bite allergies—this is a prescription drug but may save lives); insect repellent (5 to 10 percent deet for infants through preschoolers, 25 percent for you); moleskin for blisters; needles and safety pins; snake-bite and tick-removal kits; sunscreen (#15 SPF, waterproof, with both UVA and UVB protection); suction bulb; waterproof matches and compass (not strictly first aid, but vital); water filter, iodine water treatment kit, or water purification tablets.

Adventure Travel First Aid Additions

Items from both lists above plus:

Hypodermic needles, sterile syringe, and a note from your doctor explaining why you have them (for injections in foreign countries); PeptoBismol (chewable tablets); oral rehydration powder; sterile hospital gloves and IV drip (for those going to truly risky places).

Emergency Courses

Consider taking a course in emergency infant or child care before you go. Courses should cover practical tips and preventive measures including cardiac resuscitation basics, burns, poison control, and choking. Hospitals and the Red Cross often offer free or inexpensive classes, often in the evening. Parenting organizations are another resource. A group of families can often hire a certified instructor (check local parenting publications for resources). Hiring in a group has the added bonus of helping you build a parenting network/community.

Hospitals and Health Services Everywhere

Your best overseas resource for a doctor or a hospital is the consulate or embassy. Hotels and tourist bureaus can also be a source of information.

Many doctors speak English. Try to find one, so you don't have to worry about your sick kid *and* figure out how to say "chicken pox" in French. IAMAT provides a world directory of English-speaking, Western-trained doctors. Contact information is listed in the Resource Appendix under "Overseas Travel Resources."

For up-to-date care and equipment, get to a major metropolitan area.

Hook up with the expat community and find out who *they* recommend.

Fancy hotels can also recommend medical personnel.

You are always a plane ride from home—in extreme emergency, you may not be able to leave, but somebody can always come in.

Medical care in other countries is usually good—sometimes better, and often cheaper, than ours.

Malaria

Malaria is spread by the anopheles mosquito common in certain areas of the world. It can cause recurrent fevers, sweats, chills, headaches, delirium, and other unpleasantness. Malaria is curable. But if not treated, malaria can lead to anemia, kidney failure, coma, or death. The malaria-carrying mosquito bites from dusk to dawn, so take preventative measures: Wear light-colored long-sleeves and pants, sleep under netting, and use bug repellent containing DEET. Spray your sleeping quarters with flying-insect spray. Mosquito coils—which burn like smelly incense—are also available in Southeast Asia, but some people may be allergic to the smoke. You and your baby should be on prophylactic medication—yes, protection against certain types of malaria *can* be given to your baby (the Center for Disease Control in Atlanta has all the details—get their address, phone number, and website from the Resource Appendix under Overseas Travel Resources). You have to start your medication two weeks before you enter Malaria Country, and you'll have to continue for four weeks after you return. Seek medical attention if symptoms develop.

N
Where NOT to Take Baby

N is for No-No, Not *There*, and No Children Allowed. Is it your dream to scale K2 with a dagger in your teeth? Are you dying to push your survival skills to the limit? Re-evaluate—adventure doesn't necessarily mean endurance—there will be time for endurance travel later. There are places where small children don't belong. Be sensible. Risk death, dismemberment, and moral destruction when you are by yourself. Be understanding of Baby, be considerate of other adults, be safe.

O
OPTIMISM

O is for Optimism, both the need for it when traveling with a little One, and the Optimism that you'll gain from your experiences. Things can get complicated on the road—you'll need to hang on to your intrinsic belief that "things will work out." Try to remember that most of the time the hullabaloo is just that—a lot of hulla-baloo over not much at all. If you can keep your balance when the train has broken down or the hotel has lost your reservations, you'll enjoy your trip far more.

As for gaining Optimism—it's a funny thing. Long-term travelers—the ones who've been on the road for years, in the danger zones, the jungles, mountains, deserts, the harshest conditions on earth—often have the most confidence in the potentials and kindnesses of human beings, and have the best sense of the future to come. Perhaps travel will bring you this optimism, too.

OPTOMETRY

O is also for Optometry. If you or your child wear glasses or contacts, bring along an extra set or a copy of your prescription. One time Josh accidentally knocked Aunt Julie's glasses into the lake at Pinecrest and she spent a precious day driving into the Valley and waiting hours for the "one-hour" optometrist to make her a new pair. In Thailand we had knock-off prescription RayBan sunglasses made from our prescriptions—at about one-eighth of the cost. They sure were useful on that pineapple boat to the islands!

P

Traveling PREGNANT

P is for Traveling Pregnant. Let your body be your guide—some women feel perfectly fine and enjoy being pregnant on the road, some find it difficult and unpleasant. It depends on what you're doing—mountain climbing, or lying on a beach in Cancun. The best time to travel pregnant may be during the second trimester—not too early and not too late. During the first trimester, you may experience morning sickness and fatigue. In the last trimester, you'll want to stay close to good medical care. You shouldn't do any physically strenuous travel after about the fifth month.

Before traveling while pregnant, check with your doctor for restrictions and advice.

You can fly safely through your sixth month, and then you may need a doctor's note. Many airlines won't carry a woman in her third trimester. Call your airline for guidelines and restrictions.

When selecting a destination, consider the food. Choose a place with food you like, because when you're pregnant, you're gonna get very hungry. If pregnant, I personally would avoid Italy—the smell of garlic was utterly repugnant to me when pregnant. Maybe spicy food makes you heave—in that case, stay away from Thailand.

Drink plenty of fluids. It's easy to get dehydrated.

If you feel queasy, avoid boats or long car travel which only makes it worse. Try anti-nausea wrist bands, available in maternity shops. These operate on accupressure principals, and are "all-natural." Pack along ginger tea and/or ginger candy. They're a natural anti-nausea tonic that just might help.

If you travel to countries that require immunizations, get them before getting pregnant (ideally) and, if pregnant, avoid "live" vaccines. Talk to your OB/GYN about malaria—it can pass from mother to fetus. Pregnant woman may get a more serious case of malaria. Some prophylactic drugs are okay.

You're going to be tired. Travel with a little kid (or kids) is fatiguing anyway, and you're adding the normal fatigue of pregnancy. Be nice to yourself. Your best option is short travel times, parking yourself in a great location, and leisurely having fun.

Don't flip out, yet! A missed menstrual period on the road doesn't necessarily mean pregnancy. Many women's cycles become irregular under the conditions of travel and stress. If you regularly become irregular, take a couple of early pregnancy detection sticks with you. They may not be available in all countries.

Q

QUARRELS and Fights in Public

Q is for Quarreling. Fighting in public, screaming at your kid or your partner, *losing* it. Nobody is perfect. There are times when you will air your dirty diapers in public. You will make a fool of yourself. You're human. When you travel, you'll get deeply in touch with that fact.

R

"The RUNS" on the Road

R is for "The Runs" and how to avoid and treat diarrhea on the road. Stomach upsets are the most common traveler complaint (30 to 50 percent of travelers on a two-week trip experience symptoms). The main danger of simple diarrhea (I'm not talking major amoebas, here) is dehydration, especially for babies and little kids. Weak tea with a little sugar, soda water with sugar, or "flat" diluted soft drinks help rehydrate a child. In a tropical climate with a reputation for the runs, carry an oral rehydration mixture. Rehydration powder (also known as ORS) is available at the drugstore and consists of electrolytes that you mix with water. You can make your own by mixing 1 quart of water with ½ teaspoon salt and 3 tablespoons of sugar. (Read W, and make sure the water is safe!)

Pepto-Bismol is usually safe for all ages—though talk to your pediatrician for dosages, counterindications, and limitations (yes, there are some). Never use it for a child with the flu.

Lomotil, Imodium, and other drugs that "stop up" the action are not good choices for children.

Seek medical advice for any stomach upset that lasts more than a couple days. You may need treatment for diarrhea with blood and mucus, if it is accompanied by fever and lethargy or vomiting, or if there is extreme discomfort and bloating.

S

Sea SICKNESS, Car SICKNESS

S is for Motion Sickness. A lot of kids get nauseated in cars or on boats. Winding, bumpy roads; heat; and gas and diesel fumes can upset the stomach of a child sensitive to motion sickness. It's not only kids—adults get motion sickness, too.

How I remember those long drives on California's Highway 1, clutching the side of the car and my stomach as my parents remarked on the beauty of the Pacific Ocean. As an adult, I realize we were rarely on the road for more than an hour at a time, but it seemed endless. I also get seasick in a bizarre form. I'm fine on the water, but once back on dry land, I can't shake the odd, rocking feeling—as though I'm on a boat. This awful sensation lasts for the same amount of time I am on the water—an hour boat ride, an hour rocking sensation; three days on a boat, three days on land, rocking. (I'm getting queasy.)

Avoiding and Dealing with Car and Sea Sickness

Keep the air fresh. Crack the window, and no smoking in the car. (You should *never* smoke in the car with a kid!) Sometimes diesel fumes can bring on illness, so don't open the window if the air is fumy. Air conditioning can sometimes help.

Have your child look out the car window, preferably the front (kids can get sick by looking through the side windows). You can keep them focused by playing "I Spy" games and preventing them from focusing on close stuff like books or coloring. If the kid is really queasy, pull over. (I used to advise that you put the kid in the front seat. I don't any more, ever since I did my research. Kids should not ride in the front seat especially a front seat with an airbag. Better nausea than death, that's what *I* say.)

Avoid carbonated drinks and milk, which can be hard to digest, and too much cotton candy at the zoo.

Long car trips on winding roads are a good time to remember that your child's sense of time is very different from yours. An hour for a two-year-old is a far larger percentage of his life than yours.

Babies and small kids often fall asleep in rough weather on boats—this is their way of dealing with sea sickness.

Ginger is a natural remedy for motion sickness (just as it is for pregnancy nausea!)—it's available in powdered form in health food stores, as delicious chew candy in Asian markets around the world. Or brew up some gingerroot tea with honey (for the child older than one year) and bring it—warm but not too hot—in a thermos.

Try anti-nausea wrist bands, available in boating shops and catalogs, outdoor equipment stores, and maternity shops (they are also useful for morning sickness). They may be too big for a small child's wrist. You can also ask your pediatrician about medication for motion sickness.

Nibbling on saltines and sipping *small* sips of water can help.

Have the child focus on the horizon.

T

TANTRUMS

T is for Tantrums, Terrible Troublemakers, and Toddler Torture. Kids have their own agenda, and it may not include getting to the dry cleaner before it closes, or making the last train back to Berlin. On the road, normal stresses may seem more intense to a kid, leading to more tantrums just when you *least* have the time.

Babies and little kids hate to be misunderstood, and, especially at the ages when their internal development is greater than their ability to verbalize, frustration runs high. Understanding this—and taking time to really understand what a child wants, can avoid or deflect many stormy moments.

Kids have different tantrums styles. Some fling themselves down, beating their heads, screaming and flailing like windmills. Others are like Annie's cousin Wren, who slowly and dramatically lowered herself to the floor, wriggled around to make sure she was comfortable and, only then, let it fly.

Many tantrums happen because a kid is pushed. Slow down, and let Baby help determine the pace.

Real tantrums are huge explosions of energy and frustration caused by strong desire, minimal skills, and weak internal controls (sounds like the definition of a toddler to me!). Whatever else, kids this age should never be punished if they fall apart like this. A tantrum is terrifying for a child—keep her safe until the storm is over. Most tantrums end with sobbing and sleep. When the beast awakes, she's usually filled with charm and ease.

Supermarket Tantrums

Supermarkets can be disastrous. They are overstimulating. The child is confined and not allowed to run. The humiliation potential is high—and parents are often tense. Kids *want* what they see and can't understand why they can't have it. The best solution is prevention, often including small food bribes (we talked about this in Chapter 6), but what happens when the two-year-old tornado hits, screams, and falls on the floor?

You can ignore the stares of fellow shoppers, try to calm the child, or leave your cart in the middle of an aisle and haul the child outside. This is *not* about punishment—changing the physical place changes the emotional space. Let the child cry it out. Then return with your sniffling and subdued little offspring, find the cart, and make it snappy before the time bomb goes off again.

Ten minutes to let a child "get it out of her system" is a long time in a busy day. But this is part of taking your child with you—sometimes you have to operate on Toddler Time—if you slow your pace in general, your child will generally be more serene.

TEMPERAMENT

T is also for Temperament. Your child's and your own. Temperament is the way a person approaches the world; it's his adaptability and emotional style, and a lot of it is inborn. Think about you and your brother—same family, same upbringing, different as steak and tofu. Some people are generally relaxed and optimistic, others tend towards intense or sensitive, and all of us have both "easy" and "challenging" traits. When you plan your travels (even if they're just to the bank and post office), consider your child's temperamental style, and your own. Psychologists use nine temperamental characteristics to analyze a person's emotional style and to assess how well they adapt to situations. There's no correct way to be, and each set of characteristics runs on a continuum.

Adaptability: "We're going where? Cool!" or "THIS WASN'T ON THE ITINERARY!!!!"

Energy level: "First the Louvre and we'll stop for croissants at the bakery and lingerie at Printemps then head to the Moulin Rouge and..." or "Whew. Got here.

What's on French TV? Say, do you think the fondue place on the corner does take out?"

First reaction: "Look Ma, Albanian kids! I'm gonna go play with them, okay?" or "Let me peep out from behind your leg for a while, okay?"

Intensity: "I weep for the birds, the sky! The beauty of life, death, the universe..."or "Hey dude, whatever."

Mood: Cheery or gloomy, Pollyanna or Eeyore.

Perceptiveness: "Mom, you cleared your throat twice in the last hour. Is it sore?" or "Is something different in here? Oh, you got a new house!"

Persistence: "Didn't get it that time. Better try again!" or "Yeah, I took a sulpture class last Saturday. No, I'm not going back. I'll probably never be Rodin."

Physical sensitivity: "...so the crack on the wall is from an earthquake last night? Didn't notice." or "Are you *sure* the thread count on these sheets is 300? They feel more like 250."

Regularity: "We had rice *last* week." or "Where are my cornflakes?"

U
UNWANTED Attention

U is for Unwanted Attention. As the stranger in town, your child may get more than his share, especially if the "town" is across the world and he is the one blond child in a throng of brunettes, the one child of color in a crowd of Caucasians. People may stare, or try to touch his hair and skin. Little children may find this intensely uncomfortable. (You probably would, too!) Be the child's ally. Don't force him to socialize before he's ready. Let him cling to you, or remove him from reach. He'll soon feel more comfortable—and become more outgoing—if you allow him to take it at his own pace.

V
Lost VISAS, Passports, and other Missing Papers

V is for Visa. No, not the credit card, I'm talking about

your permission slip to get across the border to Burundi. Say you wash your hands in the airport bathroom, put your purse above the sink—and leave without it. No papers. No money. No tickets.

Before you leave, make two copies of each of your important documents. Store one set with a friend at home, pack the other set in your luggage—away from the originals.

If it happens, calm down. Most of these things can be replaced, with varying time and hassle. Remember your core values—you've got the most precious thing in the world with you—your family.

Get on the horn and start honking. Try the passport office, the consulate or embassy, and the airline. Things get lost—all these offices have procedures for taking care of the situation. Once a visa has already been approved—as yours was—it should take far less time to get it replaced. Worst-case scenario is a brief delay, and a headache.

W

WAVING Your Baby

W is for "When In Doubt, Wave Your Baby." Your child is your ally. An adult in trouble is just another person— a parent with a young child in trouble brings out the humanity in all of humanity. Wiggle the baby in the air, and the World Will Work With you.

WATER Safety

W also is for Water Safety. Water is vital to health, and it is easy to get dehydrated on the road. In many places, the water can be dangerous—it may carry amoebas, bacteria, or parasites that can make you a *very* unhappy traveler. The rule if you're served water from a mysterious source: when in doubt, dump it out. And don't eat the ice. If the drinking water is "risky," you have a number of options:

Bottled water is available in many countries, and usually inexpensive. Make sure the top is *factory sealed* (we've heard horror stories about shopkeepers refilling old bottles).

Water vigorously boiled for at least three minutes (up to ten minutes at higher elevations) is safe to drink.

Brush teeth with bottled, boiled, or purified water. Yes, even if your child spits it out!

A number of available microporous water filters remove bacteria and parasites. Some also eliminate viruses with iodine.

In an area where you are unable to boil your water (like the Himalayas), you can purify water by adding eight drops of a two-percent iodine solution to a quart of water. Wait twenty minutes. Some camping and outdoor-supply stores sell iodine treatment kits. We used this method in Nepal. "Iodinized" water has a slight taste (you might add powdered fruit juice for kids), but it's safe.

On an extended journey or living overseas, bring fluoride pills for your child. Most countries' water is not treated.

X

Over-X-CITEMENT and X-OTIC Locales

X is for eXcitement, and over-stimulation. One reason to travel is to gain new stimuli, but you can overdo it. Some kids are extra sensitive to excitement—but all kids can be over-excited. Here's the equation: Over-excited child = hassled parent. Know your child, know yourself, know your limits, and slow down!

X is also for eXotic. Living in California, the beaches of relatively nearby Mexico provide the occasional inexpensive tropical vacation, but Bali, on the other side of the world, seems impossibly exotic, frightening, and almost as foreign as Mars. Little do we understand (until we're slurping smoothies and fending off blanket vendors on Kuta beach) that Bali has become Australia's Mexico, riddled with surfers and hardly free from Western influences. The world has been televised.

Few places are untamed. Yes, adventure still awaits, but you can go almost everywhere—"exotic" or not—with your kids and still find the comforts of home.

Y

In the Event of YELLOW Fever, Cholera, or Revolution

Y is for Yellow Fever. Yikes! Preventive vaccinations of yellow fever and cholera are not recommended for little babies, but more than that, they aren't always effective anyway. Bail out. Safety is your first and primary concern. Yes, a revolution or a plague is interesting, but is it more interesting than watching your child grow up? Take advantage of the "children first" emergency evacuations, and get your child to safer, higher ground.

Z

Time ZONES and Jet Lag

Z is for Time Zone, and the disorientation it can cause. Changing time zones requires a period of readjustment. Allow time for body-recovery, but change the clock immediately, and break on through to the other side. The faster you adjust your schedule, the faster your body will adjust.

Time zones are often talked about in conjunction with jet lag. A lot of jet lag is caused by dehydration—which is avoidable. Drink those fluids! (Nag, nag, nag.)

Doing the Time Zone Shuffle will throw off feeding schedules and meal times. Make sure food is available. If you're a nursing mother, give in to the forces of nature and nurse on demand for a few days, until a new schedule is established.

Be prepared for wild bouncing at midnight, and glazed eyes at noon. Scolding and discipline will have little effect—your child's whole *system* is off-kilter. It will pass.

Some kids have increased incidents of night terrors after shifting many time zones.

Most people find it easier to go West than East. (Everybody I know, except for me and my dad.)

Get outside. The natural light will help speed your adjustment.

Children usually have an easier time than parents. (Don't they always?) Maybe because they get to *nap*, while you get to tote baggage, carry their sleeping bodies, and unpack. Life, she is not always fair. You'll have fun *anyway*, and if you're lucky you'll have somebody to care for you in your dotage.

If you're crossing many time zones, consider sedation. (Hey! Ask your pediatrician!) This is not *just* for your travel sanity—if your child is well rested, her body will more easily make the time shift.

Let 'em nap when they need to, but save the bedtime rituals for the All New! All Improved! bedtime.

APPENDIX

Recommended Reading

Travel with Children

Adventuring with Children, Nan Jeffrey (Avalon Books)

Going Abroad, Eva Newman (Marlor Press)

The Family Travel Guide: An Inspiring Collection of Family-Friendly Vacations, Ed. Carole Terwilliger Meyers (Carousel Press)

Travel with Children, 3RD. edition, Maureen Wheeler (Lonely Planet Travel Guides)

Trouble-Free Travel with Children, Vicky Lansky (Book Peddlers)

Tropical Family Vacations, Laura Sutherland (St. Martin's Griffin)

Safety, First Aid and Health

Baby Proofing Basics, Vicky Lansky (Book Peddlers)

Clean and Green: The Complete Guide to Non-Toxic and Environmentally Safe Housekeeping, by Annie Berthold-Bond (Ceres Press)

Overcoming Jet Lag, Dr. Charles F. Ehret and Lynne Waller Scanlon (Berkeley Pub. Group)

First Aid for Children Fast, Johns Hopkins Children's Center

Staying Healthy in Asia, Africa, and Latin America, Dirk G. Schroeder (Avalon Travel Publishing)

Where There Is No Doctor, David Warner, with Carol Thuman and Jane Maxwell (Hesparian Foundation, PO Box 1692, Palo Alto, CA 94302)

Wilderness Medicine: Beyond First Aid, William W. Forgey, M.D. (Globe Pequot Press)

Resources

Family Travel Resources

Rascals in Paradise

(415) 921-7000 and (800) U-RASCAL

www.rascalsinparadise.com

A travel agency dealing with both resort vacations and "move around" vacations only for families traveling with kids age 0 on up . Ninety-five percent of their services are international. They'll get you a flight, book you into a resort or rental, and arrange for cars and drivers.

Backroads

(800) 462-2848

www.backroads.com

This active travel company provides family biking, hiking, and horseback trips all over the world. Some might be a little *intense* for the little ones. They'll help you select an appropriate one! (It's an excellent website, too.)

On-Line Travel Information

www.carousel-press.com

This travel publisher's website provides general travel and family oriented travel information. Sign up there for your free e-mail newsletter here.

www.familytraveltimes.com

An on-line subscription newsletter giving the insight scoop on resorts, motels, and attractions.

www.fodors.com

Maps and info and mini-guides, oh my!

Arthur Frommer's Budget Travel Online— www.frommers.com

Famed travel publisher Arthur Frommer offers info., advice, and a searchable database for hotels and entertainment. You can even design your own guidebook (based on *your* itinerary) and have it sent to you, print-on-demand.

Rec. Travel Library—www.travel-library.com

Personal travelogues, trip reports, and worldwide tourist information. More than you ever needed to know, but fun to browse through.

www.travelwithkids.about.com

Feature articles, links, deals, and a free newsletter, all about traveling with children.

On-Line Travel Booking Sites

From cheap and quick to full service, these URLs give you a good place to start:

Concierge.com—www.concierge.com

Expedia.com—www.expedia.com

Internet Travel Network—www.itn.net

Travelocity.com—www.travelocity.com

Lodging Resources

IntervacU.S.

   (415) 435-3497

www.intervacus.com

Intervac has been helping people arrange national and international home swaps since 1953. They put your house's listings and pictures in "The Book" and/or on the web; you get to search for homes away from home.

www.homeexchange.com

Homes from Anquilla to Zambia. Some are also for rent. Happy browsing!

VillaNet

(800) 488-7368

www.rentavilla.com

Ready for that manor house in Portugal or farm house in Provence? This rental agency (one of many) manages reasonably priced and exorbitantly priced properties in France, Italy, and Portugal. (How about a French chateau near Cannes that sleeps 24 for a mere $12,800 a week?)

Hostelling International—American Youth Hostels
(202) 783-6161
www.hiayh.org

Hostel rates range from $10 -$30 a person per night (plus membership fee). Family membership is $35 annually and includes membership in Hostelling International®, access to almost 4,500 hostels in 70 countries, a directory of U.S. and Canadian hostels, and assorted discounts on restaurants, rentals, equipment, admissions, and other services.

Vacation Values
(800) We-Book-U
www.vacationcondos.com

Vacation Values provides rental information and reservation services at a wholesale rate for condominiums and villas in the U.S., Caribbean, Hawaii, and Mexico. You can check out the properties and prices, and book on-line (somebody will call to verify) or book through the 800 number.

Child Care Resources
Child Care Aware
(800) 424-2246
www.childcareaware.org

Child Care Aware is a national initiative designed to improve the quality of child care and increase the availability of quality child care in local communities. Along with training of child care providers, Child Care Aware helps parents identify quality child care environments, and helps parents locate quality child care in their community. Call for help locating your local child care resource and referral agency. Their free brochure includes an excellent checklist for measuring the quality of a child care home or center.

Internal Revenue Service

(800) 829-1040

www.irs.gov

Wait on hold here for information on paying taxes on your nanny. Or wade through the website—only slightly less snarly than waiting on hold.

Disability Resources

Through the Looking Glass

2198 Sixth Street, Suite 100, Berkeley, CA 94710-2204

(800) 644-2666

www.lookingglass.org

Through the Looking Glass is a national clearinghouse for parents who have disabilities. Publishers of *Adaptive Baby Care Equipment: Guidelines, Prototypes, and Resources* ($15 for consumers, $35 for professionals. All of their services are free.

Society for the Accessible Travel and Hospitality

347 5th Ave, Suite 610, New York, NY 10016

(212) 447-SATH

SATH is a non-profit organization dedicated to barrier-free access for travelers. They publish *Open World Magazine*.

Equipment

Columbia Medical Manufacturing

(800) 454-6612

www.columbiamedical.com

Car seats, seat extenders, and buckle guards for kids with physical or neurological disabilities.

Baby's Away

(800) 571-0077

www.babysaway.com

Baby's Away rents babies equipment—cribs, strollers, toys, rocking chairs, gates, potty seats, VCRs with children's tapes, you name it—in 30 "destination resort" locations. Branches are run by parents and grandparents working out of their homes.

Baby Travel Solutions
(888) 989-0302

www.babytravelsolutions.com

Baby Travel Solutions will deliver formula, diapers, wipes, snacks, and so on to any destination in the U.S.—for a fee.

National Highway Traffic Safety Administration Auto Safety Hotline
(800) 424-9393

www.nhtsa.dot.gov

Provides information on car seat safety and recalls. Also provides the free pamphlet: *A Safer Car for Child Passengers.*

Tushies Diapers
(800) 344-6379

Even a lot of the diaper companies are offering Tushies as an alternative—gel-free, perfume-free, dye free, they are a lot healthier (if pricier) than the normal disposable.

Train Travel

Amtrak
(800) 872-7245

www.amtrak.com

The website is fairly all-service; it takes reservations, gives route information, and provides special Internet promotional fares.

Rail Europe
(800) 4EURAIL

www.raileurope.com

Booking information for the Eurailpass, the Europass, the Eurail Selectpass and the Eurail ticket (and descriptions or the differences between these four things).

British Rail
(888) BRITRAIL

www.britrail.com

Train info, BritRain passes, newsletters, promotions. For when you want to chug-a-chug-a around the British isle.

Overseas Travel Resources

U.S. Passport Agency Information

http://travel.state.gov/passport_services.html

1-900-225-5674 – fee-financed passport information. If you have access to a computer, you're bettah awf.

U.S. State Department Information Services

www.travel.state.gov

The U.S. State Department runs a detailed web site with travel warnings and advisories around the world, information about emergencies regarding U.S. citizens, and details on every country's tourism status, visa requirements for U.S. Citizens, and the locations of its embassy or consulate in the United States.

U.S. State Department 24 Hour Emergency Hotline

(202) 647-5225

If you are traveling internationally and are in need of urgent help or urgently need to contact somebody who is traveling.

International Association for Medical Assistance to Travellers

417 Center Street, Lewiston, NY, 14092

(716) 754-4883

www.iamat.org

IAMAT provides a world directory of English and French-speaking doctors (trained in Europe or North America) in 125 countries and territories. Membership is free (donations encouraged).

The Center for Disease Control and Prevention

1600 Clifton Rd. NE, Atlanta, GA 30333 USA

(800) 311-3435 – general number

(888) 232-3228 – International travel information

www.cdc.gov

The CDC is the main authority, guys, for *any* traveler health-related issues: immunizations, travel advisories, and detailed information on food and water safety.

Other Resources

La Leche League

(800) LA LECHE

www.lalecheleague.org

La Leche League offers breastfeeding information and support. Call for a referral to a local La Leche League representative, or search the web site for a local group near you.

Community Supported Agriculture

www.nal.usda.gov/afsic/csa

Get information on CSAs and find a Community Supported Agriculture farm near you.

Medic Alert Foundation

(800) ID ALERT

www.medicalert.com

If you or your child has a chronic medical condition, allergies, or is on medication, you might want to join Medic Alert. Membership benefits include an engraved Medic Alert bracelet, set-up and maintenance of a computerized medical file, and emergency response service. Initial membership costs $35, with $20 annual dues thereafter.

INDEX

ABOUT THE AUTHOR

Ericka Lutz is the author of six non-fiction books including *The Complete Idiot's Guide to Stepparenting* and *The Complete Idiot's Guide to a Well-Behaved Child*. Her fiction and personal essays have appeared in books, anthologies, and journals, and her articles, book reviews, and advice columns have appeared in magazines, newspapers, and on the Web.

Special interests include travel (she's adventured in over two dozen countries on three continents), gardening (last summer she landscaped her garden using the brute force of a spade and aching upper and lower body muscles), and hiking in the woods with her dog and her husband.

The child of a bohemian San Francisco family, Ericka majored in interdisciplinary studies in creative arts at San Francisco State University. She's worked as a picture framer, writing consultant, bookseller, trail builder, performance artist, university lecturer, technical writer, and, of course, waitress. Ericka has been married for twelve years to communication expert and writer William Sonnenschein. They have one nine-year-old daughter, Annie. She contends she's still cool, though her daughter Annie is beginning to express doubts.